Awakening to the Dance:

A Journey to Wholeness

by

Georganne Spruce

Awakening to the Dance: A Journey to Wholeness

Copyright© 2012 Georganne Spruce

All rights reserved
No part of this publication can be reproduced or transmitted in any form or by any means, electronic, mechanical, without the permission from the author.

Library of Congress Control Number: 2012906425

ISBN-13: 978-0615606842
ISBN-10: 0615606849

Cover Design by Leslie Shaw

Author's Blog: www.awakeningtothedance.com

Dedication

For Polly and Bob Corder, my maternal grandparents, whose love was boundless, and to all the women and men everywhere who have the courage to be who they truly are.

Author's note

Memory is often unreliable, even when the description of an event is written down soon after it occurs. It is colored by personality, emotions, and belief systems. From the 1960s until today, I kept journals in which I recorded my feelings and the events of my life. They are the basis for most of this book. The names of the characters in this story and some details of their appearance and lives have been changed for privacy reasons. In different ways, each one was an important teacher in my life. Regardless of the circumstances, I am grateful for the lessons I learned from them as I traveled through this amazing dance of life.

Table of Contents

Prologue	1
Compromised	3
I Am I and You Are You	10
Integrating Mind and Body, Art and Life	21
Embracing the Darkness	29
Releasing the Old	38
Opening New Doors	47
To Be Free or Not to Be Free	59
Endings and Beginnings	68
A Balancing Act	80
Magician's Assistant	93
Releasing the Fear	103
Master Numbers	114
Time to Love	122
Turning Over New Leaves	137
Co-Creating with the Divine	150
Navigating the Inner Landscape	159
Butterflies	169
Hurricane Season	181
Paths to Healing	189
Land of Enchantment	200
Dust Devils	209
New Horizons	218
Breaking the Block	228
Letting Go into the Flow	244
The End Is the Beginning	256
Embracing the Light	272
Epilogue	279
Acknowledgment	281
About the Author	283

Prologue

Everyone is searching. We want a better life, more love, and inner peace. We want living to be less difficult. We want good relationships, respectful children, loving parents, and appreciative employers. We're tired of stumbling, failing, grieving, and picking ourselves up and trying again. We keep thinking there has to be an easier way. We want to live our dreams and fulfill our deepest desires. We want to know who we really are and what our purpose is in life.

In the 1950s, Dag Hammarskjold, then secretary-general of the United Nations, wrote in his journal, "The longest journey is the journey inward," acknowledging that this journey to find ourselves is spiritual and eternal, for we are eternal, chasing our desires through lifetime after lifetime, moment after moment. Finally, in desperation, at some final moment of reckoning, there are no more places to which to escape, and the only door that opens, opens inward. We are at once confronted with who we really are and who we are not. When we have the courage, we step through this door into the unknown and are transformed forever into a new and amazing life. I know because I am living that life.

As I write this, I look out the window on a perfect New Mexico day. The sky is intensely blue with white cream puff clouds drifting through it. The light is brilliant here and despite the heat, a cooling breeze blows. I am still amazed that I live in this sacred and magical land—a land of seekers and wisdom so ancient we cannot know when it began. The area is abundant with art, spiritual practices, and alternative healing. My worries about having the money I need to live on while I write have been resolved. I have friends who are loving, share my interests, and were supportive when my mother recently made her transition into the next life. I am healthier than I have ever been despite the fact that I'm well into middle age. I feel peaceful most of the time and my life is guided by Spirit and intuition. My spirituality is, for the most part, integrated into my daily life. I like who I am. Most miraculously of all, I am actually doing what I have wanted to do all my life. I am writing a book, and I see my life opening out before me.

Georganne Spruce, August 14, 2003

Compromised

I sat cross-legged on the floor between the stacks of the Memphis State University library, sobbing and shaking with relief as the tears streamed down my face, spotting the pages of the book on my lap. "Oh, my God," I thought, "I'm not insane. There are other women who think like me." Trying to wipe away the tears with one hand so I could see, I continued reading Betty Friedan's *The Feminine Mystique*. My attention was drawn to the chapters, "The Happy Housewife Heroine," "The Mistaken Choice," "The Forfeited Self." Chapter 1 was titled "The Problem That Has No Name" and described the yearning of wives and mothers who were asking, "Is this all?" A calmness fell over me. I was no longer ashamed of my deepest secret—one I never shared with even my closest girlfriends. I had no interest in being a mother.

For the last few years, I had felt depressed and resentful much of the time. A deep anger that I couldn't release had solidified into a hard knot under my right shoulder blade. I knew its source was the outrage I felt because everything I'd ever wanted to do with my life, even dress designing, was reserved for men. I was supposed to be a nurse, teacher, or secretary. I wanted to explore caves. "Nope, too dangerous," the critic in my head announced. A doctor. "Sure, but no man wants to marry a woman doctor." A writer. "Women writers are always old maids. Besides, no one makes money doing that." The voice was sarcastic that time.

I felt at the mercy of a world that didn't value my talents, and I finally realized that it really didn't matter to anyone whom I became unless I was a wife or mother, and if I weren't that, I was of no consequence. Okay, then, if that was the choice I had, I'd have a career and to hell with babies and husbands. My mother gave up her love of music, her friends, everything she cared about to be a wife. Living her martyred life through me, she was the unhappiest person I knew. I refused to live her life.

At a very early age, I dreamed of a career. I had fallen in love with musicals, watching Ann Miller dance down a staircase in top hat and tails. I begged for dancing lessons, but my parents had no money for them, and my mother insisted the doctor would never allow it because I had a heart murmur from the rheumatic fever I'd contracted at four years of age. I was heartbroken. How could I possibly be an actress if I couldn't dance?

At thirteen, I won a prize at a local shop for a shirtwaist dress design, but when I told my mother I wanted to become a designer, she replied, "That's a very tough field, you know. It's very competitive."

"What do you mean?" I felt my heart sink.

"A lot of people want to be designers, but only a few make it. You have to deal with cutthroat competition. I don't think you'd like that."

"Oh."

A knot formed in my stomach because competition certainly wasn't something I liked. Although I had outgrown the heart murmur when I was twelve, the only physical activity I did well was swimming. I was a disaster at every sport I attempted and was always the last person chosen for any team. I didn't know what competition in dress designing really meant, but the word *competition* was enough to stop me in my tracks.

Not long after that, I was inspired as I read about Albert Schweitzer's work with the lepers in Africa and decided to devote my life to helping others by being a doctor. My parents had always told me I could be anything I wanted to be and assured me they would find a way for me to pursue this ambition. However, when I almost failed high school chemistry, no one suggested a tutor. When my ex-Marine physics teacher said I didn't have the math background I needed for that class, although I had the same preparation the boys had, I dropped the class. By that time, I was dating and realized that people thought a woman becoming a doctor was weird, so I let it go.

Throughout high school, at my mother's urging, I had become involved with speech and drama activities. My mother, an extrovert and ex-homecoming queen, worried that I was too introverted and shy. I loved the camaraderie of working on a production with others, had sung in church from the time I was a child, and studied modern dance in gym classes. In my senior year, despite the family's move to Memphis and my attending a new high school, I won a Best Actress award for a role in a musical and an excellent rating for an original oratory I wrote and presented at the Southern Speech Convention. Although performing made me nervous, I felt successful and competent enough to pursue my childhood ambition of being an actress. I decided to major in drama in college.

My parents were less than enthusiastic, and my mother insisted that I get a teaching certificate so that I would have something to fall back on in case something happened to the husband I would, of course, have. I didn't have the courage to go to New York or Hollywood by myself, but I knew that if I went to Northwestern University, which had an excellent drama program, the professors there would teach me what to do in order to have a career in theater. It was my ticket out of a limited life.

"Mom," I said one afternoon, casually leaning against the kitchen cabinet where she was chopping onions and celery for a roast. "I've been doing some reading about colleges, and Northwestern has one of the best drama departments in the country."

"Is that around here?"

"No, it's in Chicago."

She stopped chopping, turned around and looked at me like I was crazy. "I thought this was settled. You're going to school here, at Memphis State. We can't afford to pay tuition and room and board some place."

"But I can work and get a scholarship and grants."

"You can't work and go to school. It's too hard. You'll make yourself sick."

"No, I won't. Mother, I'm well now. The heart murmur is gone. All through high school, I've stayed up late for rehearsals and gotten school work done. I haven't gotten sick, and I always make good grades."

"Forget this. You're father's not going to let you get a job."

"Why?"

"Because if his daughter has to work, it'll look like he can't take care of his family. Don't you ever mention this to him?"

"That's crazy!"

"That's enough. We've been through this. Even if you get a scholarship, we can't afford to send you away."

"But why can't we check into it and see?"

"Why are you doing this to me?" she demanded with her hands on her hips.

"Why am I ...?" I was astonished by this sudden reversal.

"Why are you so ungrateful? Your father works so hard to provide us with what we need. He can't do anymore for you and neither can I."

"But can't I just ..."

"That's enough!" she shouted. "Who do you think you are? You think you're too good for Memphis State? Well, it's a perfectly good school. It has a good drama department. I don't care if you like it or not, it's where you're going!"

"Mother, please…"

She turned her back and burst out crying, "If you loved me, you wouldn't treat me this way."

I dashed from the room crying, feeling angry and confused. I wasn't trying to hurt anyone. Was I an ungrateful daughter? Until then, I felt my parents had supported me, always pointing out that I was bright and talented and capable of doing whatever I chose to do in life. Suddenly, with the prospect of college in the immediate future, they seemed to be asking me to settle for less, to close off possibilities, to limit my horizons. Had they lied about supporting me to become a doctor? That was more costly than Northwestern. Was this just a game they played? Had they told me I was bright just to make me feel good?

Five years later, my mother, who had taught school before she married, returned to full-time teaching so that my brother could attend American University in Washington, DC. I realized, with a shock, that my parents lived by a double standard. Only a boy's education was important enough for my father to allow my mother to work and break the pattern of their traditional marriage.

I was very angry at my parents for undervaluing me, but I felt guilty at the same time. My brother deserved the best. When he was two and I was seven, he'd contracted all three types of polio. He was in an iron lung for thirteen weeks and expired three times. Surprisingly, he survived with a normal mind, but one side of his face and throat were left paralyzed and his face distorted by the paralysis. Throughout his childhood, we all lived with the constant fear that he would put something in his mouth like popcorn, which he couldn't swallow, and choke to death. There was so much he needed—braces, surgery, speech therapy. I never envied him a thing, but I had needs too, and as a girl, I was taught to always put others first.

By 1964, when I discovered *The Feminine Mystique,* I was a junior at Memphis State University, loved doing theater, studying modern dance and being part of a creative group of friends. Through the modern dance classes, I strengthened and healed my weak body; as a dancer, my skinny profile was beautiful.

Dance, theater, music, and literature fed my soul. Most of the people around me smoked marijuana, but when a guy offered to share his weed with me, I just laughed and said, "I don't need drugs. I'm already high." And it was true. I had always been a religious child, but I was deeply affected by my brother's surviving polio. After that, I was never afraid of death again. I knew that miracles existed, that death was not final, and that God answered our prayers. *Life* grew out of the darkness. But as I grew older, it seemed to me that God wasn't listening, and all I heard from the Methodist minister at our church was how sinful we all were. Because I thought most of the people I knew were decent and honest, I concluded that the church was no longer a place for me because its message was untruthful.

Participating in dance and theater was a deeply spiritual experience. I transcended the mundane and was connected to the inspirational joy of creativity that had originated with the theater's sacred origins in the worship of Dionysus, the god of wine, who inspired men to create. Each role I studied was a trip into the collective unconscious as well as a trip into the psychology of the character. Being unafraid of death allowed me to venture into deep places in the psyche where others feared to go, and through creating theater and dance, I could help others understand their darkness as well as their light. Being touched by beauty and understanding each other at a deeper level would bring out the best in people and, I hoped, change the world.

In the spring of 1964, my sophomore year, the boy who had been my steady since high school bought a red sports car, and all the girls in our neighborhood, who used to think he was just a Yankee nerd from New York, started chasing him. We had planned to marry and grow old together, but he broke up with me and soon became engaged to a girl who was studying to be a hairdresser. I felt betrayed.

By 1965, dance had become my first love. A close girlfriend and I planned to go to New York and study modern dance with Erick Hawkins, a dancer whose performance we had seen at a dance conference. However, my friend became engaged, and the money she had saved for New York bought her crystal and china. I felt betrayed.

Okay. I finally got the message. It was loud and clear. I couldn't fight the whole world anymore and I had to face reality. I didn't have the courage to go to New York by myself. Maybe it would be fun being a drama and dance teacher after all. That way, I could at least have a husband and still pursue my love of dance.

I met Gary, who was in the Army, on a blind date arranged by a friend a few months after my high school boyfriend and I broke up. He was built sturdily and had a blond crew cut and contrasting dark eyes that charmed me. I fell in love with him quickly. Unlike most of the young men I knew, he seemed like a grown man of the world, stable and solid, willing to work hard to make something of his life. I knew I would be safe in the world with him and that I could depend on him. My family welcomed him, and he easily embraced them, for he'd never had a stable home life. His father had left when his mother became pregnant with him, and she had died when he was a boy. After that, his step-grandmother and stepfather reared him. But what impressed me the most was that he never seemed to mind waiting for me backstage in the Green Room with the other actors while I rehearsed for a play or worked backstage. He got to know my drama friends, and everyone liked him because he was a sweet, friendly guy.

We dated for six months and on New Year's 1965, as we rode home from a party in the backseat of a friend's car, Gary put his arm around me and pulled me closer. I could feel the curve of muscles beneath his suit as he kissed me gently on the lips, whispering, "I love you." Pulling a small black box from his pocket, he opened it and said, "This was my mother's engagement ring, and I want you to have it. Will you marry me?"

It was a tiny ring with a bare chip of a diamond, but it had been his mother's, and I was filled with love as he offered it to me. We had talked about marriage and what we each wanted to do with our lives, so the proposal wasn't a surprise. He understood that I wanted to be a dancer and accepted it. All my friends were getting married. I needed someone to love and someone who would love me too. I didn't want to be alone.

"Of course I will," I said, kissing him. "But how will I ever stand your being in Vietnam for a year? It scares me."

"I'll just be on an airbase working on jets. It's no big deal. We'll just have to write lots of letters and make plans."

I held out my hand, he slipped the ring on it, then enveloped me in an embrace.

I Am I and You Are You

After reading *The Feminine Mystique*, I had decided I was going to be a survivor and not succumb to society's definitions of womanhood. I wanted a career, and fortunately Gary didn't want children, but in 1966, as I faced graduation, I felt confused and disoriented. Fear gnawed at me constantly—and guilt—overwhelming guilt.

"Hey, George," my best friend Tommy yelled across the stage one night just as we finished a rehearsal, "we're going to get a beer. You want to go?"

"Sure, but I've got a couple more costumes to put up," I said walking toward him, ignoring the silly nickname he used to irritate me.

"Okay, I'll wait for you," he said meeting me with a hug.

My heart was pounding and I knew I shouldn't be feeling what I was. Our friendship was becoming something deeper, and I was still engaged to Gary. Tommy was also a drama student, and we shared the same friends and were totally involved in theater. He was an incredible actor with a quick wit that entertained us all. Finally, I had to admit I was in love with him, directly contradicting my own values and violating my commitment to Gary.

It wasn't that I had stopped loving Gary; it was that I was no longer sure who he was. When I tried to picture my life with Gary, the picture in my mind was blank. I could share what mattered most to me with Tommy, but Gary was in Vietnam and I'd made a commitment to him. How could I be in love with two men? I had to choose one of them, and I didn't know how to make the right decision because I didn't want to hurt anyone.

One weekend when I was home, I talked to my mother about my confusion and the depression into which I had plunged. "I can't sleep or concentrate. I cry all the time. I'm so depressed I feel like I can't go on. I don't know what to do. I have to see a psychiatrist, please," I begged.

She looked at me with disgust, "We can't afford a psychiatrist and you don't need one. Pull yourself together." I burst into sobs, feeling totally lost.

All of my fears were magnified by the reality that I would soon be on my own and was sure I couldn't take care of myself after growing up so sheltered. I cried every night after being with Tommy, wishing I could share with Gary what I shared with Tommy. I knew I had to be honest with Gary and dreaded hurting him. Finally, I wrote the letter telling him I no longer wanted to be engaged.

It wasn't the first time that I had felt this depressing, paralyzing fear. I was an introvert, and although I had acted, danced and sung for years, I still couldn't think straight and felt as if I were going to throw up prior to every performance. Despite that, I never allowed myself to give into the fear because if I did, I'd never be able to do anything. The only way I knew to manage fear was to force my way through it.

Unable to afford professional help with my problems, I had to pull myself together. As soon as I graduated, my parents planned to move to a little town in North Carolina where my father had a new job. All my girlfriends were leaving Memphis. I was terrified of the idea of staying there by myself, but I didn't want to go with my parents, and Tommy's plans after graduation were unclear. When Tommy and I had started seeing each other, he broke up with Louise, his girlfriend of several years, but now he felt conflicted, and we decided to spend some time away from each other in order to sort out our feelings.

Three months before Gary returned from Vietnam, Tommy's mother called.

"How are you?" I asked cheerfully, briefly noting that she sounded more austere than usual.

"Not well, I'm afraid. I have bad news, dear. Tommy has suffered a nervous breakdown. We've had to hospitalize him."

"What?" I said. "This couldn't possibly be true," I thought.

"I can't go into the details now, but he won't be able to return to acting."

"What? Can I see him?"

"No, his doctor is very clear. He isn't to ever act again. He becomes confused about who he is. His doctor insists that he must also cut off all contact with his friends in the theater. He has his music. He'll devote himself to that."

"But surely I can see him when he gets well?"

"No, I'm sorry. That won't be possible. I have to go now. Please, for his sake, leave him alone."

"But I… love… him." I began to cry, but she quietly hung up the phone.

I was numb with grief; I didn't know what to do. Could this be true? It was too bizarre. It had only been two weeks since we had seen each other. I called his other friends, but no one knew any more than I. I called his mother again, but she refused to take my call.

A few weeks later, Tommy called. I was frantic. "Tommy, how are you? Is this true?"

"Yes," he said sadly. His voice died away as he spoke.

"How are you?" I asked anxiously.

"I'm better—on lots of medication and still resting often."

"What about us, Tommy? You're my best friend. I love you."

He was very quiet for a moment, then he spoke hesitantly, "I'm seeing Louise again."

"Why?"

"I still care about her. I can't continue our friendship—or anything else related to theater. I have to go."

"I still love you," I said through my tears, but he didn't respond. He hung up.

After graduation, I moved with my parents to North Carolina, and Gary and I become engaged again. He still loved me and forgave me. When he returned from Vietnam in June, he stayed with us, and being with him again reminded me of why I loved him. He was always kind to me, and I felt safe with him because he was a survivor. I was grateful to find a man who didn't want to have children and who accepted my ambition to be a dancer. Most men wanted traditional wives. I convinced myself that the differences in our education and background weren't important.

After a simple marriage ceremony, we moved to a steel town, McKeesport, Pennsylvania, where Gary went to technical school and worked part-time, and I taught in a junior high school. Our life seemed to be working, but since his return from Vietnam, his hands shook all the time even though he had never been in combat. He never talked about the war with anyone except his Army buddies.

"What's the matter?" I asked one evening when Gary was quietly sitting in front of the television not really watching it.

"Nothing."

"Your mind seems to be a hundred miles away."

"I got a lot on my mind."

"Are you thinking about Vietnam?"

"It doesn't matter."

"It does matter, Gary, because I care about you." I sat on the couch beside him and touched his arm gently. "I want to understand what happened to you there… and why your hands shake."

He continued staring ahead as he spoke hesitantly. "At night we took turns doing guard duty around the perimeter of the base. We'd take a thermos of coffee and crawl into the foxhole and wait." He was quiet a long time, then continued. "Sometimes the gukes sent kids in with grenades…"

"My god! Did you ever have to…"

"Forget it!"

"But won't talking about your feelings help?"

He looked at me like I was crazy, "People aren't supposed to talk about their feelings."

"Where'd you get that idea?"

"Men aren't supposed to talk about their feelings. Just let it be."

"But…"

"Geez. Can't you just let me relax?"

I sighed as tears came to my eyes. Why wouldn't he trust me? I went into the other room to grade papers, leaving him to watch television and smoke, wondering if this man would ever really let me know him.

I taught one class of ninth-grade English and Health and Physical Education to seventh, eighth, and ninth graders. It was sheer chaos trying to plan for so many different classes at once. I spent every moment grading papers and doing lesson plans. With no sports skills at all, I was fortunate that every day after school, the girl's coach taught me what I had to teach the next day to my classes. For the first time, I learned to dribble a basketball.

Drama was everywhere, but I wasn't teaching it. Racial tensions in the school were high, and students often threw bottles at teachers' cars when they left in the afternoon. A black student once slapped a teacher and knocked her down. Worse still, because I was from the South, people assumed I was a racist.

One day before gym class, I walked into the locker room to urge the girls in my class to hurry and get dressed for gym. One black student, who often didn't dress out, still hadn't done so.

"Justine, you have two minutes to get in those gym clothes and get out on the floor," I said.

"Fuck off, bitch," she countered, her head cocked at me.

"What did you say?" I demanded.

"You deaf or somethin'? I said fuck off!"

"Get your purse, we're going upstairs."

In the principal's office, she played it cool and lied, saying that I had misunderstood what she said. The principal was desperate to find a way out without a confrontation.

"Justine, we'll talk about this more tomorrow. Bring your mother with you in the morning."

"I don't know if she can make it," she said as she sauntered out the door.

I turned to him. "What are you going to do?"

"I'll decide after I talk more with the girl tomorrow."

"Don't you believe me? Why would I make up something like that?"

"I didn't say you did."

"You didn't support me either."

"We'll talk more in the morning. Now you need to get back to your class."

I shouldn't have worried. The next day when we met with Justine and her mother, and the principal told her to sit down, Justine said, "Fuck you, man, I ain't gonna take this sittin' down. You honky, you think you can tell me what to do. You…"

He interrupted. "You're suspended, young lady."

No one had ever talked directly to me using language like that, and this wasn't the last time it happened. During the year, the stress began to erode my health. I didn't know how to deal with being cursed out and threatened. If this was what I had to endure to be a teacher, I wasn't sure I could do it. I started having severe digestive problems that included frequent stomach pains and diarrhea. The next year, I was granted a transfer to the high school, but my stomach problems were so bad by November that I could hardly work. My doctor wasn't much help.

"The tests we took don't really show us what your problem is," he explained. "It's just stress. If you can't handle a career and being a wife, I suggest you quit working."

"I can't. My husband only has a part-time job and is in school. We can't live on what he makes." "Besides," I thought, "I can't let him down."

Gary assured me that we would survive financially, and I resigned and began to recover. We survived until spring when we decided to move to North Carolina to be close to my parents and where I found a new job. I taught English for the last three months of the school year and, in the summer, began work as the dance director of a fine arts project working with respectful students and parents who appreciated me. Gary found work in a nearby city and attended the community college. We enjoyed having time to spend with my parents, and it was the first time Gary had had a family, except for the Army.

As dance director, I taught modern dance, choreographed,

organized, and promoted the program. Having had minimal dance technique, I wasn't a great performer, but I was a natural teacher. I taught everyone—adults, teens, children, even the basketball team who laughed at the sissy dance stuff the first day of class and, on the second day, tried to hide their grimacing as their sore muscles rebelled. They discovered muscles they didn't know they had and treated me with new respect. I was also a creative resource for teachers, helping them research and create the whirling dervishes of Turkey or the story behind *Swan Lake*. I wrote press releases, gave speeches, and did radio and television interviews. I choreographed and directed the annual dance concert. Everyone in town knew about the project and strangers frequently spoke to me on the street. I was a local celebrity and I loved it.

Gary and I bought a used red Triumph and joined a road rally club. On Sunday afternoons, we raced through the mountains and plains of North Carolina, the wind blowing through our hair, the car hugging the curve of mountain roads as we laughed with exhilaration at this treasure hunt on wheels. Sometimes we discovered dilapidated barns covered with crawling vines, picturesque mountain streams and unusual scenery that captured Gary's photographic eye. Later, armed with his camera and often accompanied by our mutual friend Stuart, who was the drama director for the fine arts project and an amateur photographer, Gary led us to one of those places where I lazily wandered around the forest or fields picking wildflowers while they shot pictures until dusk.

Stuart was one of the reasons I loved the job so much. He was a talented coworker and dear friend. We shared a love of dance and theater, and I could talk to him about all the artsy things that didn't interest Gary. Without Stuart, I would have felt very isolated in such a small town, but I could have been happy doing that job forever. Gary, on the other hand, was known only as Georganne's husband, and he didn't love that. He began to spend more time after classes with the younger people at the community college. During the following summer, while I was attending a dance festival in the East, he had an affair with one of my former high school students, but I didn't learn about it until many years later.

One evening, Gary returned home from work frowning and irritable.

"I've fixed your favorite—macaroni and cheese," I greeted him with a smile.

"Great," he said, an edge of displeasure in his voice, and walked into the living room.

I followed him and tried to put my arms around him, but he pushed me away.

"What's wrong, Gary?"

He sat down, picked up the paper, looked at the front page, then closed it and put it down. "I don't want to be married," he blurted out.

I collapsed onto the couch near his chair. For a moment I couldn't breathe. My voice quivered. "Why?"

He didn't respond, but leaned forward and put his elbows on his knees. He opened his hands and looked at them as if the answer were written there.

Hardly able to speak, I asked, "Are you saying you want a divorce?"

"I don't know," he mumbled, "I just don't want to be married. I need some freedom."

"What kind of freedom?"

"I just don't want to have to answer to you anymore."

"What are you talking about—answer to me? I'm your wife. Why wouldn't you want me to know what you're doing?"

"I know, but I'm not happy."

"What can I do to make you happy?"

"You can't. It's just me, the way I was raised. I've always been alone and took care of myself."

"Gary, if you love me, please don't leave. I can't bear to lose you." I asked him fearfully, "Do you love me?"

"Yes," he insisted.

"There isn't anyone else?"

"No, honest, no, it's not that."

We continued talking for hours. In the end, he agreed to stay but never articulated a more specific reason for his unhappiness. He had suggested the unthinkable and I was shaken.

The joy I felt in creating dances and working with children whose imaginations were so ripe and exciting buoyed me up even when my marriage was rocky. I taught modern dance classes in the renovated elementary school that had become the fine arts center. Once again, the muse of dance played her melody and I was hypnotized. I loved this old building—the dark halls brightened by children's paintings, the cold iron pipes we used for a ballet bar, and the cracked, piecemeal mirrors in the dance studio. The joy I saw in the children's faces shattered the clouds and thunderstorms that appeared each afternoon in summer, and after the children were gone, their laughter lingered. I loved the children because they understood my dreams. If I could create beauty for them and see them dance the dances we both created, then it didn't matter so much if I were not the dancer. They reminded me that I must never stop creating beauty for others. Although others often judged this as superficial, it was what made my life vibrate with joy. This was God's gift to me and, through me, to the world.

And there were times when I felt that Gary and I were closer than ever. In one journal entry, I wrote, "I love Gary and marvel that I am sharing my life with such a wild and tender man. He's wise and innocent, harsh and practical and soft-hearted. He protects me and makes me face my fears." Meanwhile, in the world beyond us, Americans were fighting in Cambodia, and I lived in fear that my brother, now in college, would get his head bashed in participating in the protest marches in Washington, DC. Although I disapproved of war, I remained uninvolved politically, but when protesting students at Kent State University were murdered, I wore a black arm ban while teaching my classes at the high school the next day.

At the end of our second year in North Carolina, when it was time for Gary to attend a four-year college, we moved to Greensboro. While he worked on his bachelor's degree, I completed a master of fine arts in dance so that I could teach in college. Gary was still struggling to discover what he wanted to do. He took some art classes, and his sculpture was exceptional. For a while, we shared a mutual artistic interest, and it felt to me that we were closer, but eventually, despite his obvious talent, he decided art was too impractical to take seriously.

Our life together continued to be punctuated with moments of closeness and distance. There were nights when I was haunted by the fear that my pursuit of dance was selfish, that as a wife I had no right to be following my own path, no matter how much joy it brought me. Plunging deeper, I imagined that I was responsible for Gary's unhappiness and inability to find himself. I could hear the bricks of my walled world shudder, ready to tumble to the ground, on those dark nights. Somewhere I had to find the key that would allow me to understand my experience or I wouldn't last the night. Then, just before dawn, I would decide to go on, praying for help and forgiveness from a God I wasn't sure still existed.

Then, without warning, Gary was gone. Supervising the university dance studio one afternoon as part of my graduate assistantship, I was surprised to receive a message from my mother. She and my father insisted on taking me to dinner and afterward accompanied me home where I found the checkbook and a letter from Gary on the dining room table. He had called my mother that morning to tell her he was leaving.

"Oh, for God's sake. I thought we were through this. Where'd he go?" I asked, feeling the panic rising inside.

She walked over to me and put her arms around me. "He didn't say. Just that he needed to be alone. He said there's enough money in the bank to pay the bills."

"Wait, when did you talk to him?" I asked backing away.

"Early this morning. He didn't want you to be alone when you found his note."

"That's just great. Sometimes I think you're the only reason he married me. He'll talk to you but he sure as hell won't talk to me."

"Maybe you don't listen," she snapped.

"So now it's my fault! There is something badly wrong with you always taking his side. I've been here for him. I've loved him.

I've kept my marriage vows."

"All right," she replied sharply, "but I did tell him that he needed to grow up and accept his responsibilities as your husband."

"Really?"

Then I looked at the checkbook and panicked. "There's not enough money here for me to pay the bills that are due. What am I supposed to do?"

"Don't worry, we'll help," my father reassured me.

"No, I have to find him. I have to talk to him. He can't just walk away like this. I'm tired of understanding, of forgiving him because he can't make up his mind whether he wants to be married to me or what he wants to do with his life."

I was exhausted from this roller coaster marriage. My parents didn't have a perfect marriage, but they stayed together. Why didn't Gary take his vows as seriously as I did?

"I'd leave him alone, Anne," my father said, as if he'd already written Gary off.

"No. I won't let him walk away like that."

"Don't you want me to spend the night," my mother asked, offering me a hug.

"No, please."

"Are you all right?"

"I am, really. I just need time to think about this. I'll call you tomorrow."

As my parents were leaving, my mother pointed at a poster on the wall. "You need to get rid of that," she said. It read, "I am I and you are you, and when we meet, it's beautiful."

"That isn't working, is it?" she said as she closed the door.

Integrating Mind and Body, Art and Life

Not long after his disappearance, Gary returned, having spent a week at a female friend's house in Nashville. He insisted that she was only a friend and had simply offered him a place to get away and think. Despite his indecision and our conflicts, I still loved him. I couldn't imagine not having him to hold and to share my daily life. He was my husband and I was committed to making our marriage work, so I begged him to stay, and he did.

We had previously visited my brother in DC a couple of times and, energized by the opportunities of a large city, moved there in 1971. Gary became a police officer with one of the best suburban departments in the country, one that encouraged its officers to be educated and helped pay for their college courses. Like the Army, the camaraderie of cops became his other family.

I taught modern dance for an adult education program and English, speech, and drama at an innovative Catholic girls' school tolerant of my non-Catholic spirituality. I also took dance classes at local studios, especially at Jan Van Dyke's, where I studied Merce Cunningham's technique. In addition, Gary and I had great times socializing with my brother and his new wife.

One day, as I stood in front of a mirror in the studio dressing room, a smile spread across my face. I liked what I saw. How many years had it taken to bring about this change? Not only had dancing freed my soul, it had also healed my body and self-esteem. In the reflection, I saw a slender frame, a defined waist, and gentle curves created by strong muscles. My carriage was elegant. My previously rounded shoulders had been replaced by a wide, open chest and straight back. I had developed strength, agility, and endurance. This was a body that could hold me up, that I was proud was mine.

As I grew stronger, I felt more confident about living safely in Washington and traveling to the decaying Adams-Morgan area to take classes. Because of my strength, I was no longer afraid of being harmed physically but was cautious walking through the streets. I kept my eyes straight ahead and ignored the seductive calls of young Latino men as I inhaled the enticing odors of Cuban cooking from the nearby Omega Restaurant. I had no doubt that I reflected outwardly what I felt inwardly: I wasn't willing to be a victim.

What I felt more than physical strength was that I controlled my body, a body that previously had been ill so often that I could never depend on it. Before leaving North Carolina, a general practitioner had diagnosed my lifelong digestive problems as food intolerances, not just stress. By radically changing my diet, I had begun to heal and learned how to eat to stay healthy. This improved my emotional health as well.

In the summer of 1972, I studied with the New York dancers who were teaching at the Wolf Trap American University Academy for the Performing Arts. As always, dance continued to be my spiritual teacher. Art, whether it was theater, dance, music, or visual art, filled me in a way that religion never did. It connected with something deeper, richer, and beautifully ancient. The stronger I grew in dance, the more I became who I really was. My mind opened and my body opened. They were one. As I stretched the body, I stretched the mind. As I struggled to balance, I learned that to balance, I had to stretch muscles, not contract them. My mind had to be centered. If I moved joyfully, I was joyful. I was most alive when I danced.

The atmosphere at AU was competitive and that made me nervous, but Judith Dunn, a member of the experimental Judson Dance Theatre, was the quiet pool at the eye of the hurricane that expanded my consciousness. She dramatically shifted my perception when she said softly, "There are many ways of looking besides using the eyes. You look by listening to the sounds and silences. You look by sensing the body out of your eye range. You look by touching and feeling someone else's weight. You look with your nerve endings." As I practiced this, I felt like a child again, relearning what I knew naturally at birth.

Dance also expanded my mystical tendencies. Several years earlier, while working on my master's thesis one night, I had looked through a book of poetry written by the Arkansas poet Edsel Ford (not related to the Ford automakers) who was a friend of my family and like another uncle to me. He had nurtured my adolescent attempts at poetry, but by this time had been dead for several years from a brain tumor. His poetry about nature and my childhood spent close to nature had inspired my master's thesis dance, "Summer Run." That night, I felt that he was looking over my shoulder and guiding me to the image in the poetry I needed to complete a major section of the dance.

Liz Lerman, who had a studio where I also studied, told me that she had watched a repertory class learning one of Jose Limon's dances and felt that Limon was there. Through the teaching of his work and the receptive minds and bodies of the students, his spirit entered into a creative union with them and his presence filled the room. After having met Limon in 1968 when his company was in residence for the fine arts project in North Carolina, I never forgot his humility and warmth. That summer at AU, as his repertory class prepared to dance "Choreographic Offering," his homage to his mentor, Doris Humphrey, I felt his spirit and wanted to dance my part in such a way that those watching would experience my love for him.

I was learning that we all may travel different paths to arrive at the same place—yoga, meditation for some—nature, art, and dance for me. Jenny Scanlon of the Limon Company said, "There are no tight bodies—only uptight minds. Release the mind and you can eventually release the muscles." I knew this was true. My anger, inhibitions, and lack of confidence translated into physical restrictions in the body, which inhibited natural, flowing movement. Fear shook my legs and disrupted muscle memory, creating those frightening moments of not remembering. How could I learn to control this? How could I release the mental blocks in my mind?

That summer, one of the teachers told us a story. "The wild lion can travel at full running speed for only about a hundred yards before he becomes exhausted. As he lies sunning in total relaxation, all several hundred pounds of him, he sees an impala in the distance. He is hungry, but he waits. When the impala is within range, the lion closes his eyes a second—a blink—and goes from total relaxation to complete readiness to full-strength attack. All this happens in a blink, a split second, but during that second, he must come in contact with some deep, dark primitive root of his *lioness* from which the impulse comes."

Had we forgotten our roots, our source, our natural instincts? Perhaps it was just easier to walk in someone else's footsteps than to walk in our own, to put on the mask, the costume, and pretend we were who we wanted to be rather than becoming who we were, for becoming who we were required us to journey inward to that dark place we all feared.

The lighthouse at Cape Hatteras in North Carolina is a magnificent structure standing in defiance of the uncontrollable sea —as if saying, "Here I stand, my weathered stone and brick and iron will stand to do battle with you through all gales. We will fight together, and though you began with time, great sea, it will take you centuries to erode and destroy me, for man has built me for time—to give him safety, to give his ships light on their long journeys."

Walking the beach at night, I knew the water was out there, but in the darkness, sky and sea were one, broken occasionally by a flash of lightning from the storm that was brewing. Whitecaps appeared here and there, but, far out, I saw what appeared to be a long, slender white log floating on the moving darkness. Slowly it rolled to shore, seeming to stay the same size until it suddenly disappeared. Then, spewing, white spray exploded through a line of white caps. Curls of foam timed to detonate sequentially arrived at the shore in random tides, hissing and sucking the sand at my feet. The water receded as quickly as it came, and above the hiss of its leaving could be heard the breaking boom of waves like thunder far out to sea. The beach was quiet for a moment, but glistening underfoot were the jewels of polished shells and pebbles the tides left behind. In the dark, tiny crabs darted up the beach.

What was the matter with us? One minute Gary and I were a contented couple, loving the vacation and the ocean, and the next minute we were exchanging nasty words. He loudly snapped at me in public; something he had never done before. I found that I was impatient, restless, and critical of every move he made. At first, we seemed to be in accord about how we wanted to spend our time, but later we began pulling in opposite directions. I didn't understand it and I didn't know how to change it. One day I shopped and he went fishing. Maybe we just needed some time apart.

After Gary and I had moved to Washington, we bought a house in the suburbs fairly close to my work, but it was a forty-five minute drive into the city where I took modern dance, which made it more difficult to keep going to classes. I was thirty years old, and, in the dance world, thirty was middle age. I hadn't yet achieved the level of performing skill to which I aspired, found a full-time college teaching position, or presented my choreography in the city. I was torn between my dance career, teaching, and marriage, and often felt that doing them all well was a hopeless struggle. Depression returned on a regular basis. It took the joy out of life and left me feeling emotionally depleted. Every day, I felt I was holding my life in balance by an almost invisible thread.

At times, who I was seemed as mysterious to me as the mystery of who Gary was. What was behind the masks we wore? We put on our husband and wife masks and did the marriage dance, the balletic pas de deux—playing the prince and princess. We smiled, we touched each other affectionately in public. He brought me flowers when I performed and roses on Valentine's. We celebrated birthdays, promotions, and performances. But sometimes beneath his persona as a police officer, behind the uniform and the revolver, I saw moments I pretended not to see— moments of insecurity he pretended didn't exist, doubts—doubts about himself, our marriage, or me. And beneath my happy wife mask, I ached for him on the nights he worked from 11:00 pm to

7:00 am, but I never complained so that he wouldn't mind the nights I had to rehearse when he was home. I remembered the passion we used to have for each other, the way he looked at me as though he'd won the prize, as if no one in the world mattered but he and I.

Who was this man I married? I thought I knew, then who he was slipped away. His disdain for the intellectual dampened the relationship. A good book and a lively intellectual exchange invigorated me as much as dancing, and discussing theories and exploring ideas had always been at the center of my life, but he thought talk was a waste of time. Only doing mattered. I always thought that love was about loving the whole person, sharing all that one was. So what part of me was it that he loved? Clearly, it wasn't my mind. I wanted to be more than a receiver of gifts, a caretaker of possessions, or a companion to share half a life.

In the summer of 1974, I sat in a gym filled with modern dancers, all listening to a tiny woman dressed in black sitting on a stool. She was austere with sharp features, an elegant neck, and dark hair coiled tightly on her head. Anna Sokolow was small in size, but her presence was enormous.

The dance for which she was most famous was "Rooms." In it, we, the audience, saw into the rooms of people who inhabited a city apartment building, thereby becoming voyeurs to their despair, fear, and love. The movement was taut, frantic, and filled with the tension and longing of the city. Inspired by this dance, I had enrolled in her repertory and choreography classes.

Looking into Anna's eyes was like diving into the depths of the soul. Working with her as a dancer or a choreographer was intense: she demanded that we delve deeply into our psyches. This was painful for me because Gary and I were once again having difficulties, and I was depressed, realizing it was possible that our marriage might end. I didn't want my art to imitate the darkness in my life; I wanted to use dance to escape. But with Anna that was impossible.

She gave me a short solo in her new dance, one that would be performed later in the summer. I was a woman who lost her lover and frantically ran to the top of a tall building with the intent of throwing herself off the roof. The personal difficulties in my life were interfering with my sleep, and the dark sunken holes beneath my eyes gave me the perfectly depressed appearance for this role.

Martha Graham was right when she said, "Movement never lies." Anna spotted our lies in a second; nothing superficial was allowed; every moment had to be authentic. She advised us to listen to our inner voice and trust it would guide us, but it was hard to find time to get in touch with that voice in my over-committed life. Sitting alone at night in the dark, watching the smoke of my cigarette slowly dissipate into the air, I opened the interior gates I so desperately wanted to keep closed. The fear of rejection overwhelmed me. What if my work wasn't good enough?

Only in the cool, quiet darkness did I find the serenity to look at what I really believed and wanted. A hunger for integrity in my life gnawed at my heart—a desire to fly free of everyone's expectations and be who I really was. I wasn't as strong as Anna; I hadn't given myself totally to my art. I'd given away large portions of myself to my husband and my students, leaving less than what I needed for myself. Everyone needed so much from me. I suddenly understood why Stieglitz told Georgia O'Keefe she couldn't be both a mother and a painter.

To be authentic as an artist, I had to go to those places within that I preferred to avoid and be willing to expose for the audience what lay deep within the soul. It was this journey that allowed an artist to touch the great mysteries. This was the great and sacred purpose of art—to reveal the truth about ourselves to ourselves. And I was called, called to be a dancer.

It was finally August 8, 1974, at Wolf-Trap Farm Park's Filene Center, where the premiere of Elie Siegmeister's "Cycle of Cities" was to be performed by the National Symphony and danced by students of Anna Sokolow's repertory class. Not only was it my first performance on a major stage, but more significantly, it was the day Richard Nixon resigned as president. I was excited about the performance, awed by this strange synchronicity of events, and terrified that I would make a mistake.

A soft murmur, punctuated by an occasional staccato voice, flowed through the dressing rooms. The halls vibrated with the warming up of violins and basses. The day had flowed as if out of time—hours passed without my doing anything in particular except mentally preparing. Outside, the open air theater was clean and empty, awaiting the arrival of an audience and the magic their presence would bring to this ritual. The tall, pale, wooden beams framed the deep green of trees misty and muted from the day's rains. Only the high and low plinks made by the piano tuner echoed in this valley.

As we moved toward curtain time, the voices inside grew louder and the activity more frenetic. I felt as if I were standing on the inside of the mirror watching a silent transformation as I mentally prepared and applied make up. As we waited silently and reverently in the wings for our cue, time was suspended. At 9:00 pm, after the National Symphony played, the program would be interrupted with a speech by President Nixon. The suspense in the air was palpable. Would we hear words of resignation or more excuses for his greed for power? The theme for the summer seemed to be self-deception—his and mine. It was a strange night—a night to remember—beginnings and endings—the cycle of life—the cycle of cities and the people who inhabited them. It was time to step into the light.

Embracing the Darkness

Winding our way through the crowded streets of New York City, my friend from graduate school and I rushed past fresh fruit and vegetable markets to find the Nikolais-Louis Lab, where we were studying dance improvisation. The excited voices of shopkeepers and blaring horns of cabs invigorated me. Glancing up at the skyscrapers, towering like glass redwoods catching the brilliant light of morning in their windows, I was endlessly energized by the possibilities, diversity and sophistication of this city.

My dreams were coming true. In 1974, I had become a dancer with a modern dance company in a suburb of DC that performed choreography by Anna Sokolow, Bill Evans, and local choreographers. I'd been focused for so long on developing the strength and technical proficiency that performing required that I was stunned when I was actually chosen. All the work had paid off. I was able to dance and continue to teach at the high school. And now, a year later, I was actually studying in New York.

After graduate school in 1971, my friend had returned to New York to form her own company. We had stayed in touch, and I was thrilled when she invited me to stay with her while we studied with Murray Louis for a month. Gary had been very supportive of my going, and this was just the stimulation I needed.

I'd always been fascinated by the persistent high energy of Louis's company, a quality that set them apart. His improvisation classes challenged us to move and think in unique ways. The key to the company's dynamic presentation was passion. He said, "You have to keep the whole body burning so the motor can take fire." Too often, dancers were moving shapes without the whole body moving as one; an arm was bent or a foot flexed as if it were an entity separate from the rest of the body. To avoid this separation, Murray advised us to have a wide focus—to rid ourselves of the ego and show the movement itself. That gave the dance integrity. I knew what he meant intellectually, but letting go of the ego was very difficult. It was natural as a performer to be motivated by ego, of course, but one's real purpose as a dancer was to present the movement, not the self.

Long after leaving New York, I sensed that Louis's lessons had implications for more of my life than dancing. I loved improvisation, being in the moment and never knowing what would happen next, more than dancing a choreographed dance, but letting go like that and trusting life was also frightening.

In addition to dance, I was haunted by a performance I saw of Peter Schafer's *Equus* on Broadway. It was a profound story of Alan, a young man who blinded the horses he loved, and the child psychiatrist Dysart who treated him. Alan had constructed a mythology based on horses and his mother's religious fanaticism. To help Alan, Dysart had to take away his passionate worship of Equus, Alan's equine god. Reluctant to do this, Dysart said, "That boy has known a passion more ferocious than I have felt in any second of my life.... I envy it.... I shrank my own life." In the end, shaken by his own ability to return the boy to the normal world and its horrors, Dysart said, "I need—more desperately than my children need me—a way of seeing in the dark," for the voice of Equus never stopped calling to Dysart from the cave.

When the final curtain was lowered, the audience sat in silence. Then, almost in unison, we rose to our feet with a deafening roar of applause. I had no idea how long it went on, but afterward I sat in the theater until everyone else had left. So, this was what the Greeks experienced when they went to the theater, a catharsis that cleansed and purified the soul. By making this journey into the dark caverns of the psyche, they were able to learn from the experience and release the shadow. Without the rituals the Greeks used to release their darkness, we modern humans keep our shadows locked away until they explode in our faces in war, mental illness, or drug addiction. We have few rituals to heal ourselves. Like Dysart, most people shrink their lives to conform to society's image—like my mother. Although there were people who thought my life choices were crazy, I never lacked passion in my life and, in the end, I knew I would never regret my choices. I was not living my mother's life.

I was thrilled when Christmas arrived. My desk at school was full of cards and presents, lovely, sweet things students made, including a beautiful, tumbled agate a student chose for me because of the way it gleamed. So many cards said "Thank you." The school was alive with shrieks of "What will we give Eugene?" and "That's perfect for Mary," as the girls chose and wrapped gifts and goodies to take to the families they'd "adopted" for the holiday. I loved them for caring that each gift was just right for each person and for knowing that people in need were individuals with names, hopes, and dreams. As they trudged through the halls with their bags of packages, everyone was smiling and laughing with joy.

At home, Gary surprised me with a small eagle sculpture suspended on a wire rising from a marble base. It was inscribed with lines from the fall production I had directed, *Dark of the Moon*, a North Carolina folktale about Barbara Allen and the Witch Boy. I was touched that Gary was trying to bridge the gap between us and that this was his way of telling me he understood how important my work was to me. I, too, was trying to be more open to what he needed. Perhaps my giving more freely would bring us more contentment.

Staring into the fireplace one evening, I loved the smell of the fresh Christmas tree waiting to be decorated and the purring of the cat sleeping next to me. The warmth of my home wrapped around me, and I longed for the company of my husband who would soon be home. This felt like the peaceful Christmas of my dreams when I was loved for who I really was.

In April 1976, four months later, at two o'clock in the morning, I was exhausted from a marathon discussion, most of which I was having with myself. The memory of our perfect Christmas had faded quickly, and I found that Gary's attention and affection were only my illusions and his ploy to keep me from discovering his real agenda. In January, he had suggested that we start putting my paycheck in a savings account in my name, and I hadn't suspected a thing.

Sitting at the kitchen table, hunched over his coffee cup and pinching a cigarette between two fingers, Gary tried to retreat into silence.

Pacing the floor, far too much like an interrogating officer, I said, "I don't understand."

"I don't want to be married anymore."

"But why? I thought we were both happy with the changes we made at New Year's. I miss you not being here in the evenings, but it gives you more time with the detectives. I just use that time to try to get all my work done so when you are here, we can be together. I thought that was working pretty well. Aren't you getting to do what you want to do?"

"I guess" he yawned, scratching his head absentmindedly.

"So, you're happy at work?"

"Yeah."

"So, it's just me?" I slipped into the chair opposite him.

"No."

I hesitated as the tears started to well up in my eyes. "Is there… someone else?"

"No," he snapped, glaring at me.

"Are you sure?"

"Yes."

"I thought you wanted me to be able to do my work too."

"I don't care what you do."

In a flash, anger consumed me. "So when you said it was okay for me not to renew my teaching contract and spend next year teaching more dance classes, doing more choreography, and trying to build a career, you were just flat out lying to me?"

"I didn't say it was okay for you to do that."

"Yes, you did."

"No, when you asked me if it was all right, I said, 'Do what you want.'"

"I thought that meant you'd be here to support me while I did those things."

"I didn't say that. But even if I didn't want you to do it, you'd do it anyway. You never listen to what I say."

I sat in silence, realizing that nothing I did would make any difference. He continued smoking, looking at me with a smirk on his face. He looked proud of himself, but I couldn't fathom why.

"What do you want from me?" I cried in desperation.

"Nothing."

I was dumbfounded.

He put out his cigarette and pushed himself to standing. "Okay. I'm tired of you trying to control everything; everything has to be your way. I can't even eat what I want."

"What are you talking about? You're sixty pounds overweight. I'm trying to cook healthy food."

"It's my body."

I shook my head in disbelief. "What do you mean, you don't want anything from me?"

"I'm leaving. There's nothing you can do to stop me." He started to walk away, but I grabbed his arm.

"Gary, I love you; I made a commitment to you, but I can't live like this. I can't have my heart ripped out every time I turn around. Be sure you want this, because if you leave, this time it's really over." I was tired of trying to determine when he was telling me the truth, and I was tired of competing with the police force, which seemed to be the only thing he loved.

"I am sure," he said leaving the room.

He moved into his own apartment the next day, and when I went to withdraw money from our checking account, there was only thirty dollars left. After seeing my parents fight over money all my life, I had let him take care of all the finances. What a fool I'd been!

Financially, this was a disaster. I'd already resigned my teaching position, and the school had a contract in place with someone else. I had no job for the upcoming year, no insurance after the summer, and no home after August when he stopped paying the mortgage that I couldn't afford to pay. I couldn't get a credit card because our credit was in his name and belonged to him. I was numb. I trusted him. It became clear to me that he had been making plans to leave for some time. I suppose I should have felt grateful that he insisted in January that I put my income in a separate savings account. At least that would last a few months.

My mind was reeling with thoughts of all the things I didn't know about Gary. It was difficult to think straight because I was losing sleep from being awakened by phone calls in the middle of the night. The callers sounded like girls or young women, and they told me what a good time they were having with Gary. I was stunned by their cruelty. I called him. He insisted he knew nothing about it. We argued. Because I didn't believe him when he said there wasn't another woman, I was sure one of his girlfriends was doing this. Who else would?

Meanwhile, through the divorce, choreographing the annual school musical that the girls' school produced with a boy's school was a joyful distraction, but soon, that too, became a nightmare.

I finally found the principal, Sister O'Reilly, on the way into her office.

"Sister, may I speak with you?"

"Of course, what can I do for you?" she asked as she ushered me into the office.

"Sister, I have some serious problems with the musical." My voice was calm but I was mad enough to scream. I knew I couldn't be overtly emotional or she wouldn't hear me.

"Oh, my, what's the problem?"

"It's Mr. Sharpe. I think he's a good director, and St. Luke's chose a competent person, but he's interfering with my choreography, and I think he's trying to get rid of me."

"Why would he want to do that?"

"Because he wants his friend to do the choreography."

"Well, he was told in the beginning that he couldn't do that because the choreography is part of your contract. He's required to work with you."

"He knows that, but he doesn't care. He thinks that if he discredits me, you'll have to hire his friend. So, every time I choreograph a piece, he reworks it and tells the brothers that he has to rework everything I do. I even met with them last week and told them what was going on, and they reprimanded me for not cooperating with him. They accused me of not doing my job."

"Yes, well, they talked to me about that, but I know you well enough to know it isn't true. You work hard at everything you do. I just ignored them."

"Thank you." I paused a moment, then continued. "But I'm afraid there's more."

"Oh, dear." She sat back further in her chair as if she wanted to escape.

"Mr. Sharpe bragged to me the other day that he likes it when the girls get a crush on him because he can get them to do anything."

"I'm sure he didn't mean anything by that."

I shook my head in disbelief. I realized then that I had to tell her the one thing that would cause her to close down the show. I was still trying to decide if I believed it myself, but my source was a very reliable person.

"Sister, that's not the worst of it. An adult I trust who was involved with a high school workshop last summer has assured me that Sharpe is the man who had an affair with one of the students in that program—a student in our production.

She suddenly sat forward like a warrior mounting his horse. "I don't want to hear any more. That's enough." She gestured at me as if trying to brush me out the door. I protested, but she wasn't listening. "I'll get back to you. Keep this to yourself."

It had become apparent to me that I was just another pawn in the game the two schools played with each other, one that the nuns and brothers had probably played for years. They had a secret meeting to which I wasn't invited, but Sister O'Reilly told me the next day that Mr. Sharpe had submitted his resignation, and that we would be unable to go on with the show. She had serious doubts about the girls' school continuing the partnership with the boys' school. I had to tell the students that we were shutting down the show because Sharpe had resigned. They were broken-hearted and didn't understand why we couldn't find another director. Of course, I wasn't allowed to tell them anything else and could only say that sometimes we had to accept that things didn't work out the way we wanted them to.

The next day, another teacher came to me and said that one of the girls told her that the young women calling me in the middle of the night were some of my students. Sharpe had put them up to it.

When school was out for summer recess, I often climbed out of bed only to feed Ichebon, my cat, or when I was called to do a temporary office job that I then performed as if I were a robot. The emotional pain was intolerable. I tossed all night, restless from disturbing dreams, and as I awoke, I immediately wanted to disappear into sleep again. It was so much safer than waking life.

Gary found some excuse to visit every so often, and because he was the only fragment of my former life, I was appalled to find that when he hinted he wanted to stay, I wanted him to. Fortunately, for us both, he didn't stay. He said he was lonely, so perhaps there wasn't another woman, although he admitted that he had had several affairs while we were married. At least I was clear that if I took him back, I'd be someone less than who I was because I'd begun to understand how much of myself I would have to give up in order for this marriage to work. And it was too much.

The dissolution of the marriage was bad enough, but every school to which I applied had received 200 applications for every open position. Worse still, my mother chose to side with Gary.

In the middle of an increasingly bizarre telephone conversation with her, I blurted out, "You're blaming me?"

"I'm not saying he's blameless. But your career was more important to you than he was."

"Wait a minute. You're *my* mother. What's wrong with you?"

"Nothing's wrong with me, young lady. You need to get your priorities straight."

"Really? He's the one who left. He's the one who had several affairs. All I ever did was to try to do what I loved. I let him do what he wanted to do even though I was horrified that he brought his service revolver home and kept it in the chest of drawers. I hate guns. I hate uniforms, but I loved him so I lived with it. I never tried to get him to do anything else. I did everything I could."

"Well, I don't think he knew what he was getting himself into."

"I told him I had to be a dancer and what that would entail the night he asked me to marry him."

"I'm sure he didn't think you'd actually do it."

"Obviously, but you didn't think I could do it either, did you?" I felt a deep sadness and tears welling up. Her inability to accept who I was cut deeply.

"I thought you had better sense," she snarled.

"Go to hell."

I was dismal for days and felt abandoned by nearly everyone. I picked myself apart, seeing all the ways I'd been too self-absorbed and proud. I made excuses, blamed others, and felt cheated because my life hadn't turned out the way I planned. Only my grandmother understood my pain, for my grandfather had been dead for many years, and they had loved each other deeply. When I told her that the hardest thing to get used to was sleeping alone, she said in her soft, sweet voice, "Oh, darling, I know, I know."

Releasing the Old

While the country was celebrating the bicentennial, unfurling red, white, and blue banners on government buildings and creating a more spectacular fireworks display for the Fourth of July, I began to embrace my independence and see some light beyond the darkness. Overwhelmed by a tedious and unsuccessful job search, I often procrastinated to avoid more rejection. I had to learn to prioritize, let the trivial things flow by, and find a way to locate my center in the chaos. Deep inside, I knew I was on the right path with my life as some mysterious power shaped and guided it. I didn't know where it was taking me, but I knew I must follow.

Seeing a dance concert always stimulated my own creative ideas, so it was a relief after a long dry spell to receive a clear vision of a dance I wanted to create. In only a few moments, the outline for this dance came to me, flowing as if out of time like a dream. As it turned out, it was about much more than a piece of choreography.

The stage was dark. Figures scurried and stopped, were frantic and suspicious. Couples met tensely. Then, in dim light, one couple began a sensuous pas de deux. Lights faded to another couple waltzing, a gentle and formal courtship dance. Throughout the dark, dancers in simple native dress scurried through the other's scenes. Whenever they appeared, they were accompanied by drums. Some girls danced like children, encircling the couple doing the pas de deux and gradually enclosing them in a tight circle as the light focused on them. The woman in the couple became frightened and ran out of the circle to the front of the stage and crouched there. The man tossed the girls playfully here and there. The native sounds and dancers returned, then left, and finally the men and girls ran off stage.

Lying across the front of the stage were many kinds of masks. The woman who was crouching there moved, staying low and on her knees, moving from one side of the stage to the other. She finally stopped, picked up a mask, turned her back to the audience, put on the mask, walked to upstage center and turned to face the audience. She danced, then another girl came in. She gave the girl the mask and went to get another. This process continued until all the masks were on those standing in the semicircle. The woman looked around, then ran around the semicircle to look at what she thought were her faces. She crouched and the other women walked in a circle around her, then slowly moved backwards, off stage.

The man came in again, picked the woman up, and they tangoed. The dance changed into a waltz, and he held her face in place with both his hands as they danced, she looking around and he turning her head back to face him. He started to pull her away and the native dancers returned. He then backed off stage as the woman pulled away from him and fell to the floor. Lying crouched on the floor, the woman beat rhythmically against it. She began a ritualistic dance, gradually joining in the native rhythms, as if going back to her roots, creating her own dance, and working forward through pieces of styles she had danced before. Other dancers joined the dance and she accepted them. The dancers with the masks entered, and as they did, one by one, she took their masks off and danced with each dancer in turn. After each dance, she threw that mask away and that dancer exited dancing. Finally, she realized she was alone and suddenly stopped dancing, aware that the dance was now hers. Dancing to express all that she was, she began hesitantly, but ended whole and confident. She completed the dance and the native music came back. She listened, then turned and walked toward it.

When the ideas stopped flowing, I realized that this dance was a message about accepting all the parts of me and integrating them into wholeness. But how did I go about this? The dance reflected perfectly what I needed to do. Alwin Nikolais was right. "Art is not a statement of our problems, but a resolution of our problems."

I auditioned with the director of a theater company, and, although there weren't any current openings, getting the audition was a great ego boost. She came in with dark glasses, a headache, and a cup of coffee. "Not good signs," I thought. To my surprise, she was delighted by the two monologues I did from *Madwoman of Chaillot*, the play I had directed last year.

"I have to tell you," she admitted, "I really dreaded auditioning a dancer, but I enjoyed your work. I thought it was honest and you did what you said you would do in terms of the character's intentions in the scenes."

"Thank you," I said, relieved, but trying not to anticipate too much.

"I also was impressed with your appearance. You look a lot like Audrey Hepburn and you have the same vocal range she has. How long have you been away from acting?"

"About ten years."

"Well, I'm very surprised someone who's been away from acting for that long would do so well. I think you have potential, and you're young enough to get back into it. We'll have to talk about some things I think you need to do to revive some of your skills."

I left the theater thrilled by these new possibilities, but the company wouldn't have an opening for months, and I faced another dilemma. In order to dance and work with the theater company, I needed a part-time job, but financially I needed full-time work. I didn't know how to make this decision. In addition, there were no openings for teachers. Why was this all such a struggle? Was there a lesson I was supposed to learn that I hadn't learned? I alternated between hopelessness and faith.

Over time, I met women to whom I could relate, regardless of their marital status. Like me, they didn't see themselves as extensions of the men in their lives. They didn't give themselves over to men to be remade in a custom image, but they were not the strident feminists whose hatred of men kept me from exploring consciousness-raising groups.

It was not unusual for Gary and me to begin a telephone conversation about business and end up discussing our relationship. One day, he complained that when we were married, he was surprised that I had become so involved with dance.

"Well, it's not like I didn't warn you," I pointed out.

"You didn't warn me. I thought we were going to have a normal marriage."

"You mean you thought one of us actually knew what that was?"

Despite the fact we were on the telephone, I could sense the frown accompanying his "Um."

"Don't you remember the night you asked me to marry you? I told you I loved you and wanted to marry you, but that I had to become a dancer, that I wouldn't make much money, and that I'd be rehearsing and performing a lot at night. I told you that if you couldn't accept that, we shouldn't marry."

He said nothing.

"Do you remember that?"

"No."

"You're kidding. That's the single most important thing I ever said to you. How could you not remember!"

"Well, I don't."

"What did you think all this dancing was about anyway?"

"I just thought you'd get tired of it—outgrow it."

My mouth opened, but I couldn't speak. He thought it was a hobby, something childish. I wanted to strangle him, but I could only twist the phone cord.

"Outgrow it?"

"Yeah. I mean, I thought you were just having fun. Dance is so abstract, like those art classes I took. They were fun, but you can't do anything practical with them."

"Don't you get it? That's who I am, a dancer. It's what I want. That's why it should have mattered to you. I can teach it, for God's sake, if that's what you mean. I do actually make some money from doing that."

He snorted, "Oh, yeah that's right. I forgot."

"Don't be sarcastic."

"Look, all you needed was dance. You sure as hell didn't need me!"

"That's not true. I needed you to love me. Why do you say that?"

"You always knew what you wanted, so you didn't need me."

"Of course I needed you. I needed your love and your help to do what I wanted to do, so I could be happy."

"Yeah, that was clear. I wasn't enough to make you happy."

"It wasn't a contest between you and dance."

"That's not how it seemed."

I sat, silenced by all the things we didn't understand about each other. I didn't understand why knowing what I wanted from life meant that I didn't love and need him. When he finally saw who I really was, he didn't want to be with me. That hurt me deeply. Would other men feel threatened in this way? I felt the fear in the pit of my stomach.

"Gary, tell me the truth. Did you really love me once?"

"Yeah, I worshipped you."

"Worshipped?"

"When we were first married, I wanted to please you and do for you because I worshipped you. I'd cut off all ties with my family, you know, because my stepfather couldn't be trusted, and I needed to be able to depend on you."

"Why did that change?"

Like dammed waters being released, the words came spilling out as if he could no longer hold them back. "In college I was with these younger people, and I started to feel that maybe marriage wasn't what I needed. I felt like I had to punch a time clock, that I had to be with you all the time."

"That's not fair—I wasn't demanding—I thought you wanted to spend time with me because I wanted to be with you."

"Well, I felt like I'd given up my life. Something was missing. Eventually, I started resenting the things I did for you. I had to give up the things I liked, and it really hurt."

"Why didn't you tell me this before?"

"Because it would cause trouble if I told you how I felt. You were always trying to change me, so I just decided, I wasn't going to change."

"Even if it killed you."

"You don't understand how hurt I get. I didn't bring it up because I didn't want to be hurt anymore."

"But, don't you see, if you'd been able to talk about it, maybe we could have changed things. I have never, ever wanted to hurt you, but I couldn't read your mind. I'm sorry, but I couldn't."

"It wouldn't have mattered. I can't be with someone as strong-willed as you are. I'm just now beginning to feel I have my own identity back."

"I don't know what to say." What I had feared all along was true. To make him feel secure, I would have had to shrink my life and, as a woman, that's what I was expected to do. A tremendous sadness washed over me.

Dance brought me happiness that tempered even the worst moments in the divorce. As my guide, it provided me with experiences that were metaphors for how to change my life and integrate the fragments. I was very grateful for a scholarship from the Wolf Trap American University Academy that summer. For ten years, I'd tried to find a way to study with Erick Hawkins, and it was no accident I realized the dream during that particular summer of chaos.

I had first seen Hawkins in 1965. Several of us who danced together in college drove to Hammond, Louisiana, to see him perform and to attend a workshop. Louisiana was a romantic and exotic setting. We had never seen sprawling, ancient oaks hung with Spanish moss and ornate marble graves stretching for miles beneath them. Our hotel, like the set for a Tennessee Williams play, was white stucco with wide arches and a red-tiled roof. Inside, the rooms were papered with tiny roses on a gray background and lit with fluted antique sconces. Dark wooden blinds shaded the windows, and dominating the center of the room was an iron bed covered with a white chenille bedspread. Woven into it was a design of tiny, raised rose buds and trailing vines.

By the time we left for the Hawkins performance, my romantic sensibilities were fully awakened, and the moment he stepped onto the stage, I fell in love. At fifty-six years of age, he had the sculpted body of a Greek hero and a head of thick, flowing, blond hair. His movements and choreography were like haiku. In one duet, "Love Shouts Itself Transparent," he stood on one foot, the other one bent and crossed behind him so that the bottom of that foot was turned upward. His partner, bending her knees to lower her body, curved toward him and gently touched her cheek to the palm of his upraised foot. It was the most tender, private gesture I had ever seen two dancers perform, and in that moment I knew I had to dance such poetry.

Eleven years later, as I stood in his class, I tried not to force my body, but instead to allow my arms to tassel gently out from the spine. Hawkins' approach to movement was so different from other dancers that trying to do it was like learning to walk again. At Harvard, he had studied Eastern religions and incorporated their principles into his teaching of modern dance technique. Because of this influence, he brought calmness and sanity to dance, shining a light on its dark side, the ways we dancers abused our bodies for our art.

Near the end of the summer session, I was walking across campus with a friend totally engrossed in our conversation about Hawkins' classes. Suddenly my sandaled foot slipped off the sidewalk and turned, throwing me onto the grass. A searing pain shot through my foot. I could hardly stand, but leaning on my friend, we walked to the infirmary for an ice pack. That afternoon, she took me to the doctor.

When I saw Dr. Pardue, he wasn't very positive. "You have to give these feet time to heal. Even the one you didn't injure today isn't in good shape. The tendonitis you had last month still hasn't healed and you shouldn't dance on it."

"Doctor, I have to perform next week. I have to. The company is short three people already and it's a paid performance. What about those shots I read Joe Namath and other football players get when they injure their knees?"

"Those are cortisone. That's not a good solution. They'll stop the pain, but the healing will take twice as long, and there's always the chance you'll further injure yourself by dancing on the injury. You need to stay off the foot."

"Please. Please. I don't care about the risks. Give me the cortisone."

He shook his head, looked doubtful for a moment, but in the end he gave me what I wanted.

During rehearsals for the company's next performance, my feet were numb. I couldn't feel the floor; my grounding was gone, and I could hardly balance. I was very disoriented and panicked. Somehow, I managed to complete the performances, but as I sat recuperating, I realized I had committed a terrible act of aggression against my own body. I'd somehow crossed a line I'd never crossed before and was willing to abuse myself in order to not disappoint others. I couldn't stop thinking about the reverence with which Hawkins treated the body even in training. This was clearly a signal that something was very wrong with my thinking.

Because Hawkins showed me a gentle way to be, what I did in the studio as well as in my life changed. My movement became more efficient and less tense. I used less energy and moved in a more integrated way, mind and body moving as one, like a moving meditation. By using less tension, I didn't feel crippled at the end of a day of rehearsals or classes.

Working in this new way also transformed my thinking. Like most dancers and athletes, I'd always bought into the idea that experiencing and bearing pain was inevitable. Dancers didn't complain. They did what was necessary to keep performing, and I'd always seen this as a heroic choice. But Hawkins explained the error in this point of view. He said that in Western thinking, we believed we must conquer the environment and our bodies and force them to do what we wished. In contrast, Eastern thinking emphasized acceptance, detachment, and going with the flow of things. In his essay, "The Body Is a Clear Place," Hawkins pointed out that, in Western thinking, "The error consists in believing that because it is possible it is desirable." Because of this perspective, we placed no limits on the amount of injury we were willing to sustain. But most important in relation to technique was the fact that Western dancing, particularly ballet, was based on the belief that the body was supported by the muscles of the lower back, which is not the case. Conversely, Hawkins' own movement, like Martha Graham's, was initiated from the spine and pelvis, the actual center of the body.

That summer, Erick Hawkins was my spiritual teacher. One day, he said that in Zen one said, "Thank you" when things were at their worst. The idea was profound—that we should be thankful for all experiences because we could learn from them and become more aware. Although I learned to have more respect for myself after the injury, I wasn't yet able to see what positive things I had learned from my divorce. So I thanked Erick Hawkins for opening my heart and showing me how to have compassion and respect for myself as well as for others. I could even say, "Thank you for the chaos of my life," having faith that someday I would know what good sprang from it.

Opening New Doors

In the fall, a mortgage company hired me, but at $2,000 less than what I had made teaching. My friends and parents told me that I should be excited, but all I felt was relief that I could stop looking for a job and not worry about money every moment. Despite the relief, I still felt as if my spirit were trapped in someone else's body and that my life had started moving in a new direction that made no sense to me.

Those first holidays without Gary were traumatic, but after joining my family for Thanksgiving in Mobile at my aunt's and uncle's house, I bathed in their good wishes and laughed at my uncle's stories.

Christmas was another matter. Unable to afford to buy gifts, I decided to give everyone an inexpensively bound book of my poetry. Although they were gracious, no one asked me to read from it, nor did they ask questions about it later. I felt invisible and lost as to how to relate to them as a single person and had mistakenly hoped the poetry would stimulate personal, meaningful conversation.

My brother, who had been divorced shortly before my separation, was remarried during the holidays. I sobbed throughout the ceremony, hoping that people would think I was overcome with joy. I felt so many things that day: relief that he had survived the pain and divorce of his first marriage and was able to make another commitment, joy that he found another woman to love, sadness and loneliness because I had lost the man I loved, and fear that I would never find someone to love who I really was.

After Gary and I separated, I began seeing a therapist to help overcome my fears. When I told him about giving the family a book of my poetry, he suggested I read *After Great Pain: The Inner Life of Emily Dickinson*. It was a disturbing book and confronted me with how little I understood other people and life. It compelled me to look more closely at my relationship with my mother, and I saw that I couldn't relate to her as a feminine role model because she competed with me for my friends' attention and for Gary's loyalty. I still felt angry about this, and it was almost impossible for the two of us to have a civil conversation.

In addition, Mother's contradictions made it difficult to understand who she was. She saw herself as a tomboy, yet she wanted me to be a southern lady. She thought married women who flirted were cheap, but she "let slip" suggestive comments in mixed company. She always liked people, never met a stranger, and wasn't a snob. At the same time, she often felt that people didn't like her because she didn't have money or a fine house. My mother, an extrovert, always needed to be with people to be happy, so I became determined to learn to be happy alone and not to depend on others for entertainment. Because I wasn't extroverted, she thought there was something wrong with me. Unfortunately, I had internalized that idea and needed to release it.

After the holidays, my therapist asked me what I thought of the Dickinson book.

"It disturbed me, but I empathize with her. I feel like a recluse sometimes, and I'm repressed in some ways. Do you think I'm like her?" I asked.

"I don't see that at all."

I continued, becoming increasing agitated. "Sometimes I'm afraid that getting 'well' will destroy my creativity. It's changing something in me, and I don't feel I need to create so much. I feel like I'm losing my creative edge."

"How is it doing that?"

"Because it's the inner turmoil that makes me want to create. If I get well, I'll have no reason to create!"

"What if being healthy makes you more creative?"

I only shrugged, but as I thought about this, I was unable to imagine how that could be so.

At our next session, my therapist said he was surprised at my anger. "I had hoped that sharing Dickinson's story would encourage you to publish your poetry. In fact, I don't see you as being like Dickinson in the ways that you do."

"I'm sorry. I guess I'm just scared," I admitted. "Maybe I'm wrong in assuming that the conflict I feel right now has to do with living a normal life versus the artistic life or sanity and insanity. I guess I'm just frightened by so many changes."

We ended up having a positive, warm conversation that made me feel much better, but I felt pulled in two directions and often wanted to retreat back into my childish, dependent ways. When I felt healthy, however, I was empowered by my independence and comfortable being closer to other people.

On some days, I embraced life and was in the midst of loving it, accepting its pain of discovery and its great joy and liking who I was. On one amazing morning, I was crazy with excitement when I learned that Liz Lerman had chosen me for a solo in a dance she was choreographing for the company. When I saw the choreography and costumes, I thought surely she had visited my dreams. The synchronicity was uncanny.

In a recent dream, a young, blonde-haired woman in a red dress led me into an elegant room of gold, antiques, and rich draperies—the richness of life. The woman who appeared in the dream this time was actually a friend, another dancer in the company. In Liz's dance, Liz chose this same dancer, dressed in white organdy, to offer my character a rose, the symbol of delicate, traditional femininity. My character, wearing a red dress, accepted the rose but then became aware that it wasn't enough. As the other women continued to accept the roses offered to them, I kept falling away and was desperate to escape. The name of the dance was "Here Come the Prison Ships." Dancing this role was like dancing inside my psyche.

This wasn't my first visit from a blonde-haired woman in a red dress. The earliest dream seemed the most significant, a clear message from my subconscious right after the divorce began. I stood in a huge plaza with a large pool in the middle. On the far side of the pool was a several-story building that was a home for older people. Near me was a green ladder that curved over the pool and merged into an upper story of the building.

When I arrived at the base of the arch, a blonde-haired girl and a young man stood there. We all broke the bread she had baked, taking part in a ritual of communion. The man left. I knew I had to go across the arch but was afraid. The girl represented some part of me so I had to follow her, but I had to make the crossing on my own. The beginning was straight like a ladder and easy to climb, but as the ladder curved into an arch, I became frightened and had to crawl across on all fours.

It seemed to me that this blonde-haired woman in the red dress was my passion and that the dream was telling me to follow my passion, but move on. It suggested that if I followed the higher road, I would reach old age or a level of security that the building represented. Climbing the green ladder was a sacred act, part of my spiritual journey, a path through life leading me to a higher consciousness. Because the arch led over the water, which symbolized emotion, it was also telling me to move beyond just reacting out of emotion, which I did all the time, and it created problems in my relationships. I believed the dream was a sign I was healing, and the message in the dream was exactly what I needed to know at that time.

I was surprised one morning when Gary called me at work. "Can you talk a minute?"

"I guess so. It's not very busy this morning. What's up?"

"Well, the divorce will be final in a couple of weeks."

"Yes, I'm aware of that."

He cleared his throat. "I need to tell you something."

"Okay."

"I'm getting married two weeks after that."

I was flabbergasted. "I thought you were the guy who found marriage too confining?"

"Well, it's lonely when you're alone."

"Oh, so you finally figured that out. Who is the lucky lady?"

"She's someone I met through work so she understands what a cop's life is like."

"Really? And does she happen to work with the detectives you had to spend all your time with while we were married?"

"No," he said firmly, "I didn't start seeing her until after we broke up."

"So where are you going to live?" I was already thinking about how furious it would make me to see them together.

"We're not sure yet. I'll stay with her at first until we find a house. Her father's going to help us buy one."

I couldn't help noticing the lightness in his voice when he spoke of her. I wondered if he would give her the family ring I wore. Would he give her children?

"So you hit the jackpot. If she didn't have money, would you still be marrying her?"

"I love her," he snapped. "It has nothing to do with money. That's a shitty thing to say."

"Well, you were very disappointed when you discovered my parents couldn't help us buy a house."

"I should have known you would act this way. You know, I just want to say one more thing."

"You don't have to say anything else. You've done all the damage you need to do today."

"I'm starting a new life and you need to let go of this and start a new life for yourself."

"Oh, I have a new life, Gary, I'm no longer doing the work I love, I've had to make all new friends, I live in a dumpy little apartment, and I spend a lot of time alone with my cat. You've given me a wonderful new life."

"I don't want to see you anymore, ever. I don't ever want you to call me or get in touch with me again."

For a moment I was stunned. "We lived together for ten years, and you don't even want to know what happens to me?"

But something snapped in me. Whatever love I had felt for him died in that moment. "Don't worry. I promise I will never, ever contact you again. Goodbye." I hung up the phone. My hand was shaking. Slowly a calm came over me. Something good would come out of this. When the divorce was final, I'd have my maiden name back. I had never wanted his name anyway. Finally, I had myself back.

Slowly but surely, my health improved. For much of the past year, I had suffered with colitis and my doctor was alarmed because the medication wasn't working well. I was frightened about what would happen if we couldn't get it under control, but finally it healed.

I was unprepared for the intolerable feelings of inadequacy that Gary's marrying so soon caused me. I was on the verge of being out of control every day, fighting back the primal scream that kept rising to the surface, and struggling not to drown in the despair of my own failure. During a therapy session soon after Gary's announcement, my sadness and anger erupted into uncontrollable tears. Floodgates opened and barriers and defenses fell away. This vulnerability frightened me, like opening a wound under a scab and having it bleed profusely just when you think it has healed. Finally the outburst passed, and I felt calm and relieved I was still in one piece.

I had started dating an interesting man, but the experience was frustrating. Because of his erratic work schedule, he often canceled or came over at inconvenient times and used the stress of his work to excuse his emotional distance. I was feeling more confident and when I took a look at myself in this relationship, I wasn't pleased. I got upset when things didn't go my way and felt rejected when he was too busy to see me. Sometimes I resorted to making him feel guilty when I should have been understanding. I finally realized that I didn't know how to handle these conflicts because they made me feel insecure, and I was afraid he would leave me.

Things finally came to a head, and he made it clear that he didn't love me and had no intention of falling in love with anyone. Because emotional intimacy was the main thing I wanted, it was obvious I wouldn't have my needs met, and we parted amicably.

At the next therapy session, I opened up more. "It's depressing and discouraging that every time I move forward a little, I then take a step backwards. I can't seem to continue to progress in anything I do."

"What are you afraid of?" he asked.

"I don't know. Sometimes I'm as afraid of succeeding as I am of failing, so I don't complete things."

"You seem reluctant to change," he said. I frowned at him. "You jump from interest to interest and place to place, but always at the point you are about to become truly involved, you move on. It's the deep change you fear."

"I don't understand that. I don't think I jump from one thing to another. I'm just trying to figure out what to do."

He didn't respond to this. I hated it when he just sat there and said nothing.

"Do you mean relationships? I'm trying, but this last guy wasn't right for me."

"It's not just about relationships. You won't feel satisfied or contented until you can give yourself in a truly involved way. What do you think stops you?"

Tears welled up in my eyes and I could feel the energy of the fear flow through my body.

"I'm afraid I'll be hurt again. I'm afraid I won't make it."

Still, there were moments when I felt I was really growing, inching up like the green corn in the garden, and my inner world expanded to reach the outer. In those moments, I envisioned a group of people sitting in a circle around me, watching and waiting silently. I stood in the center, projecting expanding feelings to them telepathically. They knew and I knew that I would speak to them in time and that then we would leave the circle and quietly walk out into the world. Perhaps these were the various parts of my psyche wishing to be integrated. Perhaps they were spirit guides.

In a dream, I was walking down a dimly lit street in a safe neighborhood and felt that someone was following me. I wasn't afraid but was concerned that I should be prepared to face this person in the right manner if he appeared. I looked behind me but saw no one. I felt more confident, yet was cautious of the shadow that I felt flickered from street to street behind me. I almost anticipated the meeting and felt some curiosity and a little fear. Was this my own shadow that I had yet to recognize? Was this the fear that blocked me?

My range of friends increased and brought such joy into my life. Despite my contempt for organized religion, I attended a singles' class on Sundays at the National Methodist Church because I liked the people in it. One of the women, Lorraine, invited me to her home. The afternoon was glorious, just like the times I used to have with friends, drinking good wine, sharing feelings and philosophies. The apartment was bright and elegant, filled with fresh yellow daisies, good food, music, poetry, and the laughter of men and women. The men truly seemed to enjoy being with intelligent women, and I felt an easy camaraderie even with the new people I met. I left feeling joyful again.

Life was full of little miracles. One Friday night I went to Twyla Tharp's concert bemoaning another weekend when I didn't have a date. I thought, "How nice it would be to be taken to dinner and the concert." When I arrived at the theater, I was surprised that the concert was sold out, so I waited to see whether someone would return or not pick up a ticket. Further down the ticket line I saw a tall, slender, attractive man with shining black hair, dark eyes, and a coffee-colored complexion. As the line moved closer, we recognized each other. Phillip had taken a modern dance class I taught and offered me the extra ticket his friend had decided not to use. He was pretty sophisticated about dance so we enjoyed discussing what we saw. Afterward, we ate at a charming French restaurant in Georgetown where he semi-successfully persuaded me to try marinated sheep brains. His taste in food was definitely more continental than mine, but that wasn't surprising because he was born in India and educated by Jesuits, which I supposed also accounted for his sexy British accent. I was delighted that he wanted to see me again. My fantasy evening had actually materialized!

Life continued to shower me with miracles. Two weeks after meeting Phillip, I met another man who was also very nice. We spent the day riding on his motorcycle through Rock Creek Park, watching the pandas at the zoo, and learning all about elephants from his friend who worked with them. I was relaxed and pleased to be with someone who was such a warm, decent human being, and I admired him in particular because, despite the legal difficulties, he had fought and won custody of his two young children. His courage inspired me.

Life was full of surprises—like those exhilarating rides at the fair that circle the platform, then suddenly with a huge jerk reverse and whirl off in the opposite direction. My supervisor at the mortgage company called me into his office to tell me I was doing a terrific job, but that he needed me to resign because the other two secretaries had threatened to quit if he didn't get rid of me.

"They're jealous, aren't they?" I asked.

"Connie didn't like it when I let you take loan applications and you'd only been here a couple of months."

"But she takes most of them anyway. Why… oh, I see. You let me take that filmmaker's app."

"Yes. And she thinks you're unfriendly."

"You know, I have tried so hard to get along with those two women, but we have nothing in common. All they know are husbands and children. We have totally different lives, but that's okay with me. Why can't they accept it?"

"I know you've tried. This is unfortunate."

"But I don't understand. So what if they're jealous. That's their problem."

"No," he said firmly, "It's my problem. I have an office to run and I can't do it without Connie. She's the only loan processor I have, and she's good. I can't afford to lose her."

"But these women are blackmailing you, and Vicky is a mess. All she has to do is answer a two-line phone, and she has to take tranquillizers in order to get to work at all. I can't believe you're firing me and keeping her."

"Well, you're looking for a teaching job anyway."

"Except there are no teaching jobs."

I couldn't comprehend this. These women spoke terrible English, never dressed professionally, and told him what they'd do and wouldn't do. And he asked me to leave.

The ride whirled again. The universe didn't seem to be on my side. The next thing I knew, the director of the dance company fired me. I was stunned. I had made the mistake of suggesting that we use a professional photographer for the new brochure rather than her husband. In the picture she had chosen for the front page, I had been a second late on a jump and was the only person with slightly bent knees. It made the company look bad, made me look incompetent, and made no sense to even use such a bad picture. This wasn't the first time she and I had clashed. Any suggestion I made that would improve the company made her angry. She insisted on calling us professional, but wouldn't do what was necessary for us to really be professional. Why couldn't I get along with people? I really did try. Maybe I was too honest about things, but didn't I have a right to my opinion? I didn't see the point in doing something badly when a little more effort would produce a better result.

On top of all this, the man I was dating, the one with the motorcycle, started seeing his old girlfriend again. How disappointing! He was someone who had created a different lifestyle for himself that inspired me. I had thought he was a supportive friend. I hoped he would help me find the right lifestyle. What were these losses about? Fortunately, I was still dating Phillip with whom I had more in common, but it was unnerving that things could change so drastically and rapidly. When good things happened, I was almost afraid to enjoy them for fear they might suddenly disappear.

And, just as suddenly, a new opportunity appeared. It was November 1978. Waiting at a small airport in Nebraska to be picked up for an interview at the state college, I was amazed by what a mystery life was. A dancer friend in New York had sent me the notice about a position to develop a dance minor program. I thought I was unlikely to get a position like that in Washington, DC, so I applied. Although I was often in the top five candidates for local positions, I always lost to someone with a more prestigious degree or from a major New York dance company.

Like Oklahoma, where we lived during my teens, the land in

Nebraska was flat and rolling, punctuated by an oak standing alone in miles of space. The towns, flat and small, were full of functional, white frame houses like the ones I had lived in as a child, and the name of each town was printed on the silo of the inevitable grain mill. It was quiet and peaceful there. The drama professor who picked me up at the airport was from Arkansas, and we enjoyed sharing memories of a similar background. Prompting me about personalities, he suggested what questions I should press to get answered. From what he said, I would be doing some real pioneering and that excited me.

I spent the day interviewing and the evening socializing. The last night was comfortable, sitting in front of the fireplace in large leather chairs at a restaurant, waiting for our steaks, sipping drinks, and talking. The art professor, the romantic of the group, smoked his pipe and clearly hadn't resolved the problem of his singleness in a small, midwestern town, yet he found the solitude was good for doing his artwork. The director of theater, who would be my boss, was from Arkansas and a very funny man who reminded me of my uncles. The drama professor who had picked me up at the airport was clearly the resident rebel.

Being in the academic world felt right, but I was surprised that so few women, especially single women, were visible. Still, I was comfortable with the men and in some ways could relate better to them than I did to most women. Neal, the art professor, and I went dancing after dinner at a place that played country and western music, and I discovered with a little coaching I could follow quite satisfactorily although I'd never danced to this music before. Neal obviously had his own version of country and western dancing anyway, as well as a sense of humor I found contagious. We laughed and drank and talked until it was much too late. Years later he would tell me that he knew that night, if I were to accept the job, he would be in trouble.

Back at home, from my living room window, I could see a large oak still holding on to its golden leaves. Its radiance filled the park full of barren trees, a memory I would take to Nebraska with me. Despite friends' warning me that the salary was too low, I decided to take the position and immediately began to create new courses. Having lost my job and being fired from the dance company made it easier to leave. My only regret was leaving Phillip, whom I'd been dating for about six weeks. Our relationship was growing and we had much in common, but the reality was that I needed to know I could support myself doing what I loved more than I needed a relationship with a man right then. We said good-bye at his apartment over a delicious Indian meal he cooked from secret family recipes. I knew I would miss him and hoped I wasn't making a mistake. A great adventure lay ahead.

To Be Free or Not to Be Free

The Nebraska snow lay wide and deep, falling almost every day. After a January in which the temperature never rose above freezing, the months afterward felt no warmer. It was a constant battle with ice, cold, aching joints and frustration. Administrative processes were tediously slow and students were often late for class, yet their enthusiasm for dance made me smile and touched my heart every day. My choreography for *Kismet* was successful, and, having failed at my marriage, I desperately needed to feel I was successful at this job.

Donna, the wife of a faculty member, whose exuberance, lack of inhibitions, and directness were refreshing, became a close friend. I wanted to be as free as she was, but having to meet so many new people made me nervous. I sometimes felt socially withdrawn, even to the extent that I didn't attend the faculty art show because I was so attracted to Neal, the art professor I had met when I interviewed. I was afraid of loving again and was wary of him. I heard that he was living with a woman, and I was suspicious of his friendliness because I couldn't ascertain whether it was professional or personal.

I weathered the storm by keeping warm and full, cooking delicious meals as a distraction from thinking about my loneliness too much. I read Anne Sexton's poetry and was inspired by it but knew that I could never come near her clarity and brilliance of imagery. My efforts at writing poetry were rudimentary compared with hers, but my other creative work went well. For the spring concert, I was choreographing a suite of dances called "Louisiana" to Randy Newman's music. It was light and a bit satirical because I wasn't in the mood for dark themes. Even without a lover, I felt more alive than before my divorce.

Neal and I traveled together with other faculty to study dance programs in the region. At one city museum, as we stood in front of a large El Greco, Neal's passion and enthusiasm spilled out as he enthusiastically pointed out all the details he loved about the painting. During private moments, he laughed and talked about his personal fears and weaknesses, and I admired his openness. I loved the way he noticed the beautiful lines and textures in things, the curve of someone's shoulder or the way he reverently touched a building like my father or belly-laughed like my grandfather. I loved his crazy hats, and the way he walked in long easy strides like a person at home in his body. Although his light brown hair was thin and graying, he projected the energy of a man much younger, who indulged in the pleasures of life. Before long, we felt we had known each other forever. Despite our attraction, he was obviously in crisis and needed to resolve his problems with women and his isolation in this small town he called "the box."

At spring break, knowing we needed time away from the school and the watchful eyes of our colleagues, Neal and I rendezvoused in Denver. Driving through the night across the plains was mystical, aware that Neal was on another road heading away from his parents' home in Colorado toward our destination. Knowing he was among the lights, I watched the vast darkness pass by and the white line on the road unwound endlessly as his words echoed in my ears. He'd left the woman with whom he was living and wanted to see me, but not exclusively. He said he hadn't expected to meet anyone like me and was confused about what he wanted in a relationship. I needed to give him the freedom to sort things out, but I wasn't happy about his seeing other women.

After dinner that evening in the hotel, I became ill, probably from drinking too many margaritas made from a mix containing additives to which I was allergic. Neal followed quickly as I dashed for the bathroom and began vomiting into the toilet. Calmly, he held my head and applied a cold wet washcloth to my head. Lying on the bed, I kept saying, "I'm so sorry; I've ruined the evening."

"It's okay," he insisted, "I've had kids and an ex-wife who threw up when she had migraines. It's not a problem." I half-heartedly smiled. Only my mother had taken such good care of me when I was ill.

By the next afternoon, I felt better, and we relished the freedom of anonymously exploring the city, especially the art museum with its collection of South American art and Molly Brown's house.

Throughout the winter, we engaged in long and stimulating conversations on politics, history, sex, literature, architecture, art, dance, family, and dreams. As our friendship deepened, the barriers to my openness began to fall away as I shared my deepest thoughts. Finally, he said he loved me, but he had to find himself again. The more we talked, the more I saw that Neal's journey was a dark one, winding like a maze. Was I a fool to believe that, despite that darkness, he might be the man I'd always wanted? Our artistic connection gave us a spiritual connection I had not had in my marriage, and I longed for that.

Spring arrived quickly, but with snow still on the ground. My first school year in Nebraska was ending. The first dance concert for the new program was sold out, and I was gratified to see the community support it. What a wonderful celebration! I felt others respected me for the quality work I did, and I was proud of the way I solved difficult choreographic problems, using inexperienced dancers and creating movement so that the dancers looked more skilled than they were. This challenge stretched me as an artist and improved my way of working with people. Sharing this with Neal, who appreciated the artistic struggles, brought us closer. He even designed the set for one suite of dances, "Louisiana." The spring was all a spring should be—the beginning of a new life, a celebration with friends, and falling in love.

In May snow was still on the ground, but overnight summer winds blew in. In the heat of June, Neal left for California for over two months. Two months—exactly how long we had been seeing each other. Perhaps the separation would be good.

Before he left, I asked, "Why don't you want to be with me this summer? We'd have the time to really know each other?"

He was adamant. "I'm not clear about why I'm choosing to be with you. Going away is the only way I can know if I'm dependent on you or freely choosing you." I felt he was sincere because he'd already begun to work on his fears, but his unpredictability undermined my trust in him.

Perhaps it wasn't that he meant to be irresponsible as much as he was confused about what he wanted. Weeks had gone by when we laughed and were together in a tender, deep, and spiritual way. I had never before experienced such a baring of souls in one relationship. When we made love, he acted as if his only desire was to satisfy me, and I often cried because I could never have imagined such generosity from a man. As a result, my confidence as a woman soared. This felt like a love for all times.

Just as quickly though, the sparkle in his eyes turned to pain, and I was terrified that he would leave. He needed solitude and any attempt I made to communicate was an intrusion. He had fears of being trapped by a woman, and he already had children and didn't want more. It was a shock to me to discover for the first time I considered having children. Could I give that up? He either wanted to keep the relationship at a distance or develop it toward marriage.

In the quiet of the summer without Neal, I moved into my dormant stage—resting, recuperating from the tremendous expenditure of energy during the school year. I floated through the days, reclaiming my energy and realigning my mind for the next round of creativity. Whenever I drank tea, I remembered all the conversations Neal and I had shared over it. Or if I saw tulips, I thought of the ones he had brought me. No one had ever given me tulips. The silence was full of him. I missed him, yet I wasn't miserable. I loved him, but I didn't feel emotionally dependent. In this relationship, I was loved for who I was.

Swimming in the pool at the sand pits, Donna and I discussed feminist literature. We sunbathed and drank tea in her backyard with her children running in circles around us. This friendship nurtured me in a world unhealthy for women. I longed to choreograph pieces about women—perhaps one titled "My Grandmother's Songs." I brainstormed with Donna about creating a touring company of students to perform in the schools and the choreography I hoped to create the next year. Neal had already agreed to design sets for me.

Those were the summer days of sweet hay when magical things happened, when I found the perfect house to share with Jamie, a community arts organizer, who was my friend, when music and sun resonated with my being, when my heart beat with excitement and I was content. My new home was delightful with its authentic 1920s sculptured carpet and wallpaper. In the living room and dining room where people could mingle, the conversation of friends flowed like the breeze through Nottingham lace curtains. I could love here and cook, write, dance, and laugh. It was a house that welcomed me. And on the screened porch was a swing, like one from my childhood, where I could read and sip tea with Donna or Neal, where my roommate's birdcage and finches brightened the place, where my cat Ichebon dozed lazily, his black fur shining in the sun.

In the quiet of an early Sunday morning, I reread the letter from Neal that had arrived the day before. Embracing me with his words, he said I was very dear to him and that he found pleasure in my mind, smile, laughter, and movement. How lucky I was to have found a fairly liberated man, but a part of me was afraid to surrender and love him completely because losing him would then be unbearable. The spiritual bond that our art created between us was deep, for sometimes he thought he was me—that was the only way he knew to describe it, as if we had developed from the same root. We hurt in similar ways, we grieved in similar ways, and we celebrated in similar ways. When we danced or made love, a sheer, pure pleasure flowed through us. We could appreciate silence, share it, and not feel ill at ease. Even with hundreds of miles between us, I felt his touch.

In July 1978, I returned to Washington, DC, for a visit with friends and to participate in the ERA March with Donna and Jamie. Waves of women dressed in white filled the streets accompanied by a few men. The energy of 100,000 women was powerful and empowering, and I regretted that I hadn't participated in the peace protests during the late 1960s and early 1970s when I felt so estranged from politics. After the deaths of my heroes, the Kennedys and Martin Luther King, I had given up. But the highlight of the day was hearing Betty Friedan speak and seeing the human being behind the words that had saved my life.

Neal called one evening, sounding confident and self-contained. I was shocked by my rising fear because I knew that his belief in his own strength could only create a more positive relationship. For the first time, I almost felt intimidated by his strength and at the same time hoped it would free him from his fears of being trapped. We were moving toward a serious commitment: he wanted me to meet his children and his parents and travel together in August. I wanted this, but I was also afraid I wasn't strong and well enough to handle this correctly. Did I really deserve the good things happening to me?

Glad to leave the heat and pollution of Washington, I headed to New York and stayed with an old friend from Washington who had become a dance writer and editor. I delighted in hearing the latest dance gossip and felt she lived a magical life when she told me she had to transport John Cages' cacti from his apartment to the theater for a performance in which he plucked the cacti thorns like an instrument and amplified the sound.

I became enamored with a poster I bought of Georgia O'Keefe's, "Cow's Skull and Calico Roses." Haunted by the Southwest and its open spaces (which I'd never actually seen), I envisioned a dance. The purity, cleanliness, and calmness of white struck me. A ritual was involved, an awakening, a mystery—something deep, solemn, breathtaking, something profound. In the middle of the dirtiness, derelicts, fighting, violence, the city blurred—a soft pink or golden light emerged, opened out and pushed the walls of the city away—cleared the path for the skull with roses. Was the figure wearing the skull mask the moon goddess or the Mother God? She was primitive, lyrical, and light—she was in white with roses in her hair, but she was strong. Perhaps this was the primitive "white" ballet born of the open spaces of the west—a tribute to solitude. Perhaps it was tied to the ghost-dancer's religion. I didn't know, but my research and intuition would lead me where I needed to go when I started choreographing.

When Neal and I returned to Nebraska, we established a daily routine. After his run every morning, he stopped at my house for coffee, and we talked about the important issues in our relationship. His children were staying with him, so our private time was precious. One conversation as we sat at the kitchen table was particularly unsettling because it made me wonder whether there was any way for me to stay close to him and not get hurt. I knew I had to make a decision and made my feelings clear to him.

"I just can't make a commitment to you unless we have an exclusive relationship," I said.

"I can't give you that now. I'm confused about what I want, and I need to see other women," he countered.

"Why?"

"To only see you makes me feel trapped. I need to be free."

"I don't understand. What am I doing that makes you feel trapped?"

"It's not you. It's just me—just the way I am. Why can't we just be friends?"

"I don't know. How do I stop feeling what I feel? I've been hurt before by being close to someone who was involved with other women. I don't know how to do this without getting hurt."

"I'm sorry. I don't want to hurt you. Look, I'm afraid if I'm in a relationship with you that you'll want kids. I've already done that. I like the idea of giving you kids, but I don't want more kids."

"I know, but I really don't think I have to have them. When I have dance and I have you, I feel like I have everything I need."

He smiled and reached across the table to squeeze my hand. I returned the smile and said, "It's been nice meeting your kids, but it does make me aware of how difficult it is to be a parent. I don't think I'd be good at it."

He laughed and shook his head. "You haven't seen the half of it."

Despite what I said to him, this fire raging in me to be a mother seemed inescapable at times. No one was more surprised by its unexpected arrival than me. I wanted to ignore these maternal instincts because I meant what I said about parenthood, and I wanted to continue working in dance, but I was afraid I'd regret it later. As usual, we resolved nothing, but each conversation led us closer to understanding each other.

The trip to see Neal's parents was wonderful, but I had difficulty stomaching the critical remarks his children made to him, especially about money. They thought he never had enough. It must have hurt him, but he laughed it off. I was much more flexible on this trip than I usually had been, and Neal started making some adjustments too. He became considerate about calling me in advance when plans changed instead of just showing up with different plans and expecting me to accept them. This used to drive me crazy. But I still found it hard to let go of "the dream." I plunged into a depression when his need to withdraw surfaced, and, when he moved closer, I convinced myself that all I had to do was enjoy him in the moment. We both agreed that to love irrevocably meant that we did not have to give up what we wanted to do with our lives. I was strong enough for this; in fact, I had done so with Gary, but Neal didn't feel strong enough to risk it. He was still afraid he would lose himself in me.

I loved the sunny, crisp days of October, filled with fun and peace. My friend Carolyn, who was also Donna's friend, knew many Chicanos through her work at the university and invited Neal and me to a dance at their community center. As we entered, my spirits were lifted immediately by the cheerful sound of accordions and trumpets and the shuffling of dancing feet as grandmothers, fathers, and children danced with each other. It reminded me of my childhood when the whole family square-danced together. Carolyn's Chicano friends gathered round to welcome us and made sure all evening that we had plenty to eat and drink. Donna insisted I try the menudo. When I said it was delicious, the whole table started laughing. They knew I didn't know that it was made from a cow's stomach and that I would never have eaten it if I'd known.

Sharing Neal's enthusiasm for dancing always felt like a celebration of life, and in this joyful atmosphere, I could relax and exuberantly be who I was. Most of my colleagues, who seemed so open when I arrived, were like many people with Germanic and Scandinavian backgrounds; they kept their feelings hidden and also this side of town, the part on the wrong side of the railroad tracks.

Feeling much older than our years, Neal and I sat on the porch in the fading sunlight of a fall afternoon, earnestly talking of bearing children and not bearing children. It was one of the most poignant afternoons of my life.

I cried as he confided, "There's a part of me that wants nothing more than to plant my seed in your belly and see you happy and glowing with my child. I love you so much, I want to give you everything you want ... but I can't."

He held me tighter, kissing my tears and wiping my hair out of my face.

"Neal, I don't want to want children. I've done everything I can not to want them. Maybe it's all just hormones. Maybe six months from now, I'll come to my senses, but I also want some stability. I want marriage, a husband, a home, and children."

"I understand. I do. I really do. You should have those things."

"And you should have the life you want, whatever you decide that is."

We sat without speaking for a while, then I whispered, "I wish so much that I could be who you need me to be."

"No, don't wish that," he said lifting my chin so he could see my face. "Don't ever change who you are. I'll always be your friend, always."

I felt my life was shattering, but it was only my illusions. I had shared more with this man in one year than I had ever shared in ten years of marriage. I sobbed, and the tears ran down his cheeks as we both felt wounded by our failure to be what the other one needed. This beautiful free spirit—what would he want tomorrow—where would he go? The path we had chosen was honesty, and there was no turning back.

Endings and Beginnings

Learning again how to be alone, I stayed at home and filled the house with warm food baking and calming music. Watching television, I was amazed by the chaos in the world. My own inner chaos had been the focus for so long that I'd begun to feel the world outside, beyond these plains, no longer touched my life. Fortunate to have this isolated time to look deeply at myself, I tried to discover who I really was without Neal. One night I dreamed that behind my house was a rather wild garden. I walked up a rock path and around a pond where an old man was working. I found a bird nearby and brought it back to one of the rooms in my house, but it got loose. I hurried from room to room, struggling to catch it, and when I did, I put it in the freezer. I realized it would freeze, but the old man who seemed to be in control of the bird thought that was what I should do so that the bird would be safe.

So I put my passions on ice, afraid to feel so much again. Unfortunately that didn't protect me from being hurt, and my intuition that I couldn't trust Neal proved accurate. Despite the love he professed for me, he was involved with other women. I was tired of being cast in the role of parent or prison keeper, roles I adamantly refused to accept, which made him angry. It was impossible to even be his friend, and I refused to believe my desire for a healthy monogamous relationship was a sign I was too puritanical. There was no inherent virtue in loving a man who screwed around.

The next time he tried to justify his behavior, I said, "But, Neal, you aren't healing the real problem."

"Well, I don't feel trapped," he retorted.

"But isn't the real problem that you're unable to feel healthy and free in a monogamous relationship? You use sex with more than one woman to escape dealing with *why* you feel trapped."

"Um… I see your point. Berger told me sex was too important to me and that I needed to get into therapy."

"He's a psychiatrist and friend—will you listen to him?"
"I don't know."

I had hoped Neal and I could remain friends and continue to experience what was good between us, but what followed were many exhausting, confusing, and awful days. We were people with dark sides. He was often defensive, and I was often suspicious and demanding despite the fact that we had broken up. He started the process of leaving, going to a new life in Seattle. I was still building my life here. Why couldn't I just let him go? There was a bitter demon in me carved from all my failures and disappointments that refused to accept another failure. Having lost all faith and trust, I barely remembered what was once so good for us, and without that dream, I no longer felt pleasure being with him.

At Christmas I visited my family, all of whom had moved to New Orleans. The Louisiana bayou was gray with a misty rain that was only a hint of winter. It was jarring to go from snowy plains and icy streets to this warm land where breezes were balmy even in December. In this city, the romantic and exotic were entwined with daily life, blending reality and dreams, creating a longing that was never satisfied. It was tropical and ancient here, a mixture of dark secret rituals and modern progress. Flowing rivers and still swamp waters suggested many paths flowed to the sea, many choices that could be made in life, many adventures to be risked. I felt calm there most often when I was alone. Like Neal, it seemed to me that my family lived in "the box," complaining and conflicted, and I could feel that who I was becoming was taking me away from them.

In the spring, when some scheduling problems arose with the dance program, Neal helped resolve them, which brought us together again. Talking about our relationship, he once again reiterated that he never expected to meet someone like me, and that I had shaken his ideas about what his life could be. He seemed quieter and calmer, but just as I began to wonder if he was changing, he visited a woman who was a friend of mine while I was on a trip to New York and made a pass at her.

That spring I choreographed the dance based on Georgia O'Keefe's "Cow's Skull and Roses," a ritualistic interplay of dark and light. The dichotomy of life and death in the painting's imagery suggested other dichotomies. I admired O'Keefe for her refusal to buy into the limited role of a woman as we were defined in her time. For example, the integration of the archetypes of the whore and virgin were necessary for a woman to be a whole person, but it was a dichotomy that had imprisoned and split women for centuries. When I was growing up, to appear sexual meant that you were a slut and no nice boy would ever marry you. We all wore girdles, even if we had no hips, because if our behinds shook, it was a sure sign we were sexual. Then, on our wedding nights, we were supposed to suddenly become sexual beings, passionate to please our man, and overnight forget that our sexuality was sinful. These contradictions had marred our lives.

The primary dichotomy for the dance that emerged from the painting was life and death, represented by light and dark. Perhaps we had to know death so that we could live life, and that was how we became free. The miracle of my brother surviving polio had freed me from the fear of death and that liberated me in some way. Drawn to the Native American culture of the Southwest, I began to look for rituals to incorporate in the piece that could tell the story of moving from the dark into the light.

Despite our conflicts, neither Neal nor I had truly let go. One night, driving around in his pickup, we talked about how our different values made it impossible for us to have a serious relationship.

"I have to make a decision about you," he said. "This is driving me crazy."

"Well, what do you want from me?"

His eyes suddenly glazed over and he turned away from me, resting his head on the steering wheel.

"Are you all right?" He looked like someone about to go into a diabetic coma.

He looked at me again for a moment. "Every time you ask me

what I want from you, I short-circuit."

Was he afraid he would get what he wanted or afraid that he wouldn't?

"Neal, you'll be moving soon to Seattle. I know you feel like you're shut up in a box here and need to get away, but we need to find some resolution."

"But you're still coming to study with Bill Evans this summer?"

"Yes, but…"

"Look, all I know is that I want to build what's positive between us."

"So do I." But my fears about him were overwhelming me. I needed to start seriously thinking about a life without him.

It was April 1 and what was probably the last snow of the season lay like cotton candy on the bare, dark branches of trees and melted on streets and sidewalks. I loved going to sleep with the snow falling outside, burrowing into my warm cocoon of quilts. Neal was showing more consistency. He was kind, confident, and feeling less threatened. Or was I just seeing the chameleon he sometimes became to keep peace?

Collaborating on a concert with Neal, other artists, and tech people was creatively energizing. Our concepts for costumes, set, and lights came together quickly for "Skulls and Roses," now renamed "Rites of Passage," but the jazz piece I'd been choreographing for two weeks was missing a dynamic concept that would give it life.

Then, one morning, I awoke at five o'clock laughing at a dream about a group of wandering minstrels and actors led by an eccentric man who looked like Neal named Dr. Pepper. This group had great fun wandering the countryside and reminded me of Neal and his artsy friends from California. The next morning when I played an album of 1930s and 1940s music, I knew the dance had to be a comic jazz piece titled "Dr. Pepper and His Traveling Companions."

The concert was a success, and with it over I wandered around the house and enjoyed the expansiveness of afternoons with no plans. But outside it was February when it should have been May, when the fragrance of spring flowers should be wafting through an open window. What was I doing in this Godforsaken land? It was too much. My joints ached from the cold every day throughout winter—I'd almost forgotten what it felt like not to have this pain.

Simone de Beauvoir said that the independent woman had to find a man she saw as her equal (and who really was) and who didn't see himself as superior to her. Then it was possible to love freely. I knew she was right. As Neal prepared to leave for Seattle, I understood he had to find his place in a larger world, something I had already done before coming to Nebraska, and I hoped that it would give him the confidence and inner strength he needed. As he climbed into his car and drove away, I knew our story was not over. I still loved him despite how ridiculous that made me.

Soon afterward, I had a disturbing dream. In it, I was a pregnant princess in hiding. Just as I told a woman I was about to give birth, I felt a slight pressure and the baby popped out, bloody with no umbilical cord. The people who were after me were near, but somehow the baby was safely hidden. I was taken captive and so was the prince. He was a beautiful young man, and I knew his fate was tragic, but I felt detached and calm because the baby was safe. Our captors brought this awful plastic cage that smelled like feces and looked like an animal's travel cage. The prince was locked in it and thrown into the sea. I screamed, and for a moment his fate and our separation seemed too horrible for me to bear. I was sure that this was going to happen to me too. One of the captors then brought another smaller cage that just went around the head. I expected him to put it on me, but he put it on himself, padlocked it, and it immediately filled with water. My captor and I stood stunned, then I realized that he was about to drown. I also realized that he expected me to save him, so I quickly undid the lock. Somehow this set me free too. So, then, the prince I imagined Neal to be was dead and by freeing Neal my captor, or the part of myself that kept me tied to him, I had freed myself. But what had I given birth to?

* * *

When I went to Seattle in July 1979, the city was more beautiful than I ever imagined. Despite being a large city surrounded by water, it had the soul of a small town where everyone smiled in passing and spoke as if they knew you. I stayed in Neal's friend's apartment in a charming Victorian building with interesting nooks and crannies.

That first week of adjusting to Seattle and classes at Bill Evan's Seattle Summer Institute was relatively easy. In the cold mornings, I piled on the socks and warmers, then gradually shed them as technique class continued. Generally, I felt calm and positive about my dancing, pressured only by my own need to do the best I could. But on Friday, doing one of the beautiful spirals to the floor that I always associated with Bill's technique, I felt a pain in my left hip, heard a pop, and could not get up. The sports medicine specialist I saw that afternoon reminded me not to expect the kind of endurance from my thirty-four-year-old body that younger people could expect. I didn't want to hear that, but I had to admit the hip injury was a warning to slow down.

I knew I couldn't teach modern dance technique forever. The university's movement training in effort-shape, articulate body, or other movement forms would give me additional therapeutic skills I could use to make a living. When I told Neal what I was considering, he went into a tirade about how screwed up all institutions were and how could I possibly consider such an option as going to school for training. I was furious at his lack of support.

Living in the moment and being spontaneous were two things Neal did well, but sometimes his spontaneity was a problem for me. One day, having suddenly decided to visit the rainforest, he began packing the car. He wanted me to join him, but refused to take time for me to buy food to accommodate my food allergies. I had no intention of missing the rainforest, so I went with him anyway. As a result, the junk food which was the only food we found along the way gave me a stomach ache. His self-centeredness angered me.

Still, being in the rainforest was truly magical. The light shimmered and burst through the trees. Silences lingered, shadows sculpted the light, peace reigned, and the moss wrapped gently around tall trees that reached forever upward. Fallen nurse logs gave birth to new trees and nurtured them. Circling gnarled roots wrapped and flowed through and around other trees. The breeze blew strongly all day, but night was absolutely still. Luscious ferns and needles from spruce and hemlock blanketed the forest floor. The images that Merce Cunningham used in his dance titled "Rainforest," although created by chance, suddenly made sense to me, even the Mylar pillows bumping against the dancers' legs, reflecting light. I felt I had stepped into another time and dimension and this beauty filled me with joy.

In August, I drove back to Nebraska, savoring the lovely moments of the summer and feeling relaxed. Neal and I had found some balance in our friendship, but his rebelliousness still drove me crazy just as my acceptance of the value of institutions upset him. Driving home, I enjoyed the beautiful country I passed, especially in Montana, where the colors in the land were amazing —purple and red clay, green and pink pebbles. The sunset was a burning gold changing to lavender, then just before dark, the blue-black mountains seemed etched against a sky full of clouds. I'd seen much beautiful art over the years, but Nature still surpassed all of it.

At Thanksgiving, the family met at my grandmother's house, and she and my great aunt looked healthier and happier than when I last saw them. This was the place where I'd always been loved unconditionally, and I felt secure being surrounded by family and objects from my childhood—the ivory elephant that used to sit on Papa's desk and Mama's collection of china horses. Rooms, blocks, and houses looked smaller. The neighborhood was more run down and seemed closer to the railroad tracks.

I grew restless. My brother, happy to sit by the television listening to his baby daughter coo, embraced his role as a father. When my niece had been born in September, I was not prepared for this miracle. I was flooded with incredible feelings of love and was awed by the realization that she was blood kin. My niece was beautiful, delicate, and contented, and the thrashing of her strong legs promised an active childhood. I loved her deeply, but after seeing her, I did not feel overwhelmed by the feeling that, in not having children, I'd missed something I needed to make me whole. I felt no sadness, only joy, that she was here and pleased that my brother wanted her to have choices in life so she could find her own way.

The smell of talcum, the spotless rooms, the piles of food, the warm arms, the stories of children filled the days. My cousins came from this world and seemed content not to travel far. I realized that no one was really interested in dance although Mama said she'd like to see the ballet if she had a way to get there. I wished I lived closer so I could take her and drop by on Saturday afternoons for a visit. There was a price I'd paid for my independence, but, as much as I loved my niece, I was finally clear that I didn't want to have children. I had chosen a life far removed from my roots.

After Christmas, I went to Seattle. Neal and I, dancing our way into the New Year, attended a party given by his friends. On the way home, we started arguing. I thought he had been rude and insensitive to some other people by pompously derailing their conversation to the subject he wanted to discuss.

He stumbled into the kitchen and sat at the table, finishing off the last of the tequila. As I sat and let the relaxation from the wine flow through me, Neal's chatter about the party receded into the background and a vision began to form in my mind. At first the vision was blurred, but it gradually came into focus as a tiny elf about a foot tall. It was slender and graceful and flew out of my head to perch cross-legged on my left shoulder. Clearly the liquor was causing me to hallucinate, and I resisted looking at it, believing it was my demon and fearing its real identity.

"Neal," I said quietly. "Is there anything on my left shoulder?"

"No. Did you have a little too much to drink?" he said, laughing.

"Neal, I think my demon is sitting there."

"Really," he replied, leaning forward with intense interest, "And what does it look like?"

I allowed myself to look, and in my mind's eye, I saw a female Peter Pan with sandy blond hair, wearing a yellow green suit with a red feather in her cap. I burst out laughing because she was definitely not the horrible, dark creature I had expected.

"It's Peter Pan."

"Well, Georganne," he said laughing again and leaning back in his chair as if he were looking the creature over, "that is definitely the personification of your demon."

"Do you know what your demon looks like?"

"Oh, yes. Mine is a red sandstone gargoyle, an ugly medieval one, sitting down, with his head down and tucked into his chest." I guess I looked surprised and I didn't know what to say. "He's a dark one, that demon," he added. "At least yours is friendly." And he laughed again.

After returning to Nebraska, I dreamed I was in an old, large house where I lived with many women. We had to climb a huge staircase, but all the steps weren't there, and it was dangerous near the top because the steps that were there were very small and far apart and there was no railing.

Feeling a need to reconstruct my history as a woman, I had read about the old goddesses and images of ancient femininity. Unlike most people, Donna and Carolyn understood. A woman needed to understand her history to truly understand herself. We had an awesome task ahead of us, to reconstruct this, and as the dream suggested, not all the steps existed, so we had to build them. Traveling down this path, we had no railings to protect us or define our search. As Donna suggested, we had to mother each other, guide each other, and share what we found because there was no archetype now for the kind of women we wanted to be.

When spring break arrived, Donna, Carolyn, and I went on an odyssey through Colorado to celebrate our womanhood, especially exploring their heritage. It was a week-long slumber party, talking all day and night and sharing secrets. I met Donna's mother in Trinidad and Carolyn's brother in Ft. Collins. In Raton, we ate tamales so hot that tears ran down my cheeks, baptizing me as a real western woman. In Denver, we had dinner and stimulating conversation with two men Donna knew. I especially liked Michael's warm, quirky humor and was curious about his Zen practice. Unlike my stereotype of people who practice Zen, he exuded high energy. But, as always, the time with these women friends was a rowdy, belly-laughing good time that we didn't want to end.

Reading my students' choreographic journals at the end of the semester, I was thrilled to witness the creative working of their minds and how many openly shared their feelings. Thankfully, I had gotten through to a few remarkable students, so as a teacher I felt successful. Why wasn't that enough? I still longed to know if I was good enough to be a professional choreographer, but in this isolated place, there was no one to critique my work.

Teaching was always a sacred responsibility to me, for I knew what I did could change lives. One day after improvisation class, Jimmy, one of my most talented students, approached me quietly. "Can I talk to you?"

"Sure, but let's go sit on the stairs in the hall," I said, pointing to the basketball players who had noisily started shooting hoops in the gym where I taught classes.

Jimmy seemed distressed. He sat down slowly. "You know I've always loved to be physically active—I used to swim competitively, but nothing has ever made me feel the way dance does. I'm more alive than I've ever been. I love it, and when I do it, I don't want to stop." He hesitated, looking at me hopefully. "I wonder if I could do it professionally."

I laughed, "Jimmy, are you kidding? The first time I saw you jump, I was stunned. I kept thinking, 'This must have been what Mikhail Baryshnikov looked like before he was trained.' I've never seen anyone with so much natural talent."

"Really?" He was smiling broadly. "But I'm already in my

mid-twenties."

"It doesn't matter. Men often start later than women, and in modern dance, it shouldn't be a problem if you're willing to work hard."

His face clouded over and he rubbed his hands over his face. He looked down, hanging his head for a moment, and when he looked up again, I could see tears welling up in his eyes.

I reached out and gently touched his arm. "What's the matter?"

"In this part of the country, men don't dance. Not if they're straight, anyway. My family would never accept this or understand it."

"How can you be sure?"

"Oh, trust me, I know. They're upset that I'm taking classes. If I told them I was going to be a dancer, they'd disown me." By this time, tears were flowing down his cheeks. "I can't live without dance!"

I put my arms around him, and he put his head on my shoulder as he cried. I knew only too well the pain of not being understood by those we love.

"Jimmy, I saw a film about Paul Taylor once, and when someone asked him why he became a dancer, he said, 'Because I had to.' If you have to, you'll find a way. When you feel this passion, it's impossible to ever be fulfilled without your art. Don't short change yourself for anyone. Maybe someday your family will understand."

He stood up, wiping away the tears, but there was still fear in his eyes. He hugged me and thanked me and left the gym quietly by the side door. I prayed that this young man would find the courage to become who he really was. He was clearly a chosen one.

Always aware of the cycles of nature, I acknowledged the cycles of life as well. By summer, my life in Nebraska naturally came to an end. Jamie, my roommate was suddenly transferred to Omaha, Donna was leaving for Omaha where her husband would work on his PhD, and Carolyn was off to Texas where her husband was taking a sabbatical. Without their love, laughter and outrageousness, I would wither and die here. Like Neal, I couldn't live in "the box" any longer nor endure the physical pain the cold caused. So, after two and a half years, I decided to move to Denver without a job.

As the time to leave approached, Donna, Carolyn and I began withdrawing from one another. When we realized what we were each doing, we decided that we needed a ritual to complete this cycle of our lives. When the moon was full, we went to the sand pits where we used to swim. We brought with us tokens of the life we had shared: flowers, tea, rocks, shells, dryer lint, unfinished pot holders, orange water, herbs, a fan, and a feather. We played instruments, and Carolyn, with bells around her ankles, and I danced. Donna, with her curly, sandy hair, watched, looking like a wild lion with a morning trumpet rising like a horn from her head. In this sacred space, the moon goddess blessed us, shining clear and bright in the darkness. The water was cool and serene, and the sand was soft beneath our feet. Our burning candles were hidden from the road by a small dune, and while we were there for two hours, no one disturbed us. My friends were like two sides of myself: the daring beast and the mystic. Speaking, I honored them.

"Donna, the Leo, you give me strength to speak my own name, to believe in my beauty; you are laughter in my life; you are the fire of anger that sets me in motion; my defender, sister traveler, my comforter, my equal, my loving friend. You are the flower of celebration."

"Carolyn, the Sagittarian, you make the cycles of nature sing in my soul; you help me see the beauty, the humor in simple things; you are constancy, you are calm, you show me humility and forgiveness, my sister traveler, my equal, my loving friend. You are the simmering fire that warms the tea we drink together."

I would never forget the peace of that night when all good forces in the universe came together to protect us, when we brought the ancient into the present and transformed it with our love.

A Balancing Act

The first time I saw Michael, in Denver, having dinner with Donna, and another friend of her husband, I was mesmerized by him. His red hair, now almost completely silver, sparkled with the light, and the energy of his tall, strongly built body radiated like the heat of a bonfire. He was solid, fast, and sharp, his mind moving at the rate of light traveling through space. His belly laugh filled the room, expressing his amusement at another's joke or his own, and when he spoke, his liquid Mississippi accent belied the intelligence behind his mischievous smile. Armed with a PhD in literature, over the next few years he proved to the management community in Denver that he was an asset. With his intelligence and willingness to learn quickly, he became an excellent management consultant. As I watched his transformation over the next five years, he inspired and supported my ambition to become successful, but where he succeeded, I failed, and where I succeeded, he failed, so that despite our desires to cement a partnership, we were unable to do so. I needed him to go places in his psyche where he was not ready to go, and he needed me to pretend those places did not exist.

Despite our immediate attraction, Michael's welcome when I moved to Denver was rather ambiguous. I was supposed to stay with him for a few days, but he was uncomfortable, then decided he was fine with it. After this, though, Michael charmed me with his positive thinking and supportive attitude. He was open and willing to work things out when there were problems, and we touched on some difficult issues in past relationships fairly early. He tried to meet my needs for consistency, and I tried to meet his needs for work time, Zen, and mountain climbing. Feeling more secure, I was able to trust and love him more freely. When I felt suspicious about the time he spent with his friend Sarah, I knew it was a reflection of my own insecurities. Having been with two unfaithful men, I was prone to think it could happen again.

My intention in moving to Denver was to find a full-time college teaching position and build a career where I could be creative and financially secure. In the meantime, I found enough part-time work to survive and an inexpensive, but pleasant efficiency apartment in an old Victorian house in Capital Hill near Cheesman Park. I taught a modern class at a community center in Boulder, two modern classes at Colorado State Ballet, plus work at another studio. Wanting to broaden my skills and make myself more marketable, I considered wider applications for dance. It worked. Metropolitan State College asked me to develop a Movement for Musicians' course.

It often felt chaotic, trying to start a new relationship and to create a new lifestyle. Because I needed more balance and peace, Michael taught me zazen, the Buddhist sitting practice. It was simple, but definitely not easy. I sat cross-legged and simply breathed, focusing my attention on the exhale and doing nothing on the inhale. I was supposed to do this with my eyes open, but I often closed them in order to stay focused. My mind was full of monkey chatter, and I wasn't very patient, but every time I noticed my mind wandering, I brought my attention back to the breath. It was a challenge to sit for five minutes, but doing even that much helped to relieve stress and calm my mind.

I was attracted to the Buddhist concept of detachment, that we can relieve our suffering by detaching from our desires, letting go of our expectations of others and ourselves. However, I had no success with it in relation to Michael. Like Neal, when he felt threatened or dependent, he became domineering and I became angry and defensive. I couldn't accept his behavior simply as a choice he'd made. No doubt this reaction was why some men said I pushed them away. When I hadn't taken the time to take care of myself, I was more easily angered and his emotional needs seemed too much to handle.

Neal and I remained friends and talked from time to time. Despite our differences, I could count on him to accept my negative as well as my positive side, even my angry outbursts, and that felt like love. He had a great compassion for people, which I admired; therefore, I found Michael's constant judgment of me and others more disturbing, partly because I had a tendency to do the same thing. We were both perfectionists with less patience in our personal lives than we had in the workplace, but Michael's support for my career goals was invaluable.

My honeymoon with Denver lasted beyond all expectations. After the first of the year, I was offered a temporary position at the Naropa Institute in Boulder and an opportunity to teach an improvisation course at Colorado Women's College. The new job hunting techniques I learned from Michael were paying off, and they helped me explore a new life vision. How could I make a living doing some combination of movement or body-related work, teach dance, and eventually write about dance and the body?

Life was vibrant with contrasts. The atmosphere at Colorado Ballet was intensely competitive, steeped in hierarchy and tradition, but at the Naropa Institute, it was noncompetitive and fluid. Naropa, a school created by Tibetan Buddhists to bring together eastern and western psychology, was the perfect place for me as I studied Buddhism. I had always admired the avant-garde artistic work of the teachers there, such as Allen Ginsberg and Anne Waldman, for their experimentation and respect for spirituality. The gentle, nurturing attitude toward students and teachers and the respect for each person's spiritual journey contrasted sharply to the politically charged motivations of the people I'd worked with in Nebraska.

Until that year, Naropa's approach to dance had been dance therapy, but they realized that their students also needed the discipline of technique to complete their understanding, so I was hired to teach the first modern dance technique classes offered there. The position only lasted from January to March because the permanent teacher they had hired wasn't free to leave New York until spring.

I was nervous about teaching at Naropa because the head of the program, Barbara Dilley, had danced with Merce Cunningham, so I knew she'd readily spot my imperfections. At the same time, she also seemed like a gentle soul who would nurture me as a teacher.

Meditation made me more aware that this fear of not being good enough was my own egotism. I could change only if I were aware, but it continued to be more difficult for me to maintain a gentle spirit toward myself than toward others.

The night before I started teaching the improvisation class at Colorado Women's College, I was nervous and excited and finally fell asleep around midnight. Suddenly I was awakened by someone knocking on the door. For a moment, I thought I was dreaming, then I realized it was real and dragged myself out of bed. With the chain still on, I peeked through the crack. It was Michael.

"I need to talk to you," he demanded.

"It's one thirty in the morning."

"Can I come in or not?"

"I guess."

We sat down at the kitchen table and I could clearly see he was very angry. "What's wrong?"

"I don't ever want to see you again. You undermine me—you're very destructive."

"What are you talking about?" I rubbed my eyes thinking maybe this was just a bad dream.

"You don't think I can do all the things I want to do in my career, do you?"

"Of course I do."

"No, you don't. You talked to me like I was a child the other night. I told you about my dreams and you told me I had to choose, I had to set priorities."

"Wait a minute," I interrupted angrily. "You were the one who was worried about how to do it all. I suggested you do what you always tell me. Set priorities. Set up a timetable to get things done."

"Well, it hurts when you don't have more confidence in me."

"You're not listening. I think you're amazing. You do everything well!"

"I'm not doing them well right now. Everything's going wrong. I can't see you all the time. I have to concentrate on work."

"Oh, great! Here we go again." I jumped up and walked away

to the window so I wouldn't leap for his throat. "I'm tired of being your problem."

"I don't have the time to be with you. What do I have to say to make you understand that?" he said in a very parental tone as he got up and walked over to me. He hated it when I turned my back.

"Nothing. I get it." I said right to his face. "I know I've talked to you a lot lately because wonderful things are happening in my life, and I want to share my good news, but I guess you're the only one who gets to have good news."

"Maybe you talk about it too much."

"You're an ass."

"Do you think this is worth it?"

"That's not a good question to ask right now."

"Well, I've had it."

"So have I. I'm tired of being put in 'cold storage' whenever you're too busy. That's like saying I'm just a woman and ought to stay in my place—which is wherever and whenever you want it to be. Then when you want my attention, you're so sweet and charming, and I'm supposed to drop whatever I'm doing and be there for you."

"Like I said, 'I don't want to see you again.'" He headed for the door.

I sat down again, leaned back, and crossed my arms. "Bye."

He glared at me, then left, slamming the door behind him.

I crawled into bed exhausted, cried to release some tension, and slept a few hours until the sharp morning light woke me. I felt hung over from lack of sleep and just as the memory of last night's argument rose to my consciousness, the phone rang. I looked at the clock. It was seven-thirty. I couldn't imagine who was calling this early. I reluctantly answered it.

"Hi."

"Michael?"

"Sorry to call so early, but I wanted to talk to you before I left for work."

"Last night was enough. Please."

"I'm sorry about last night. I didn't mean what I said. I do want to be your friend. I'm under a lot of pressure and what you said before really hurt me."

"But I was trying to help, not hurt. Do you realize you were acting out everything you accused me of?"

He was quiet a moment. "I know."

"You do?"

"Yes. I need to go, but let's have dinner Friday. Okay?"

"I don't know."

"Please."

"I guess."

"I love you."

"Talk to you later."

Michael's unexpected anger and erratic behavior burned away my passion. He was supportive most of the time, but I didn't like being his target when he was upset. Whatever game he was playing, I refused to play it, but at least he could see what he was doing when he reflected on it. Maybe he would change.

It was often difficult to know during those years in Denver, what caused my recurring depression—lack of sleep, fatigue, or relationship difficulties. My meditation practice went well, especially after Ichebon, my black cat, stopped constantly meowing for attention and became quiet when I sat. The meditation helped me to look honestly at my real feelings. Despite our arguments, Michael and I remained close, but I always felt a bit leery. Was I just emotionally dependent on him or was this actually love? Perhaps I hung on to him because he was the only man I'd dated who wanted to marry and have children. My former certainty about not having children had disintegrated as my biological time clock ticked faster than ever. Michael had most of the qualities I wanted in a man: he was intelligent, funny, successful, responsible, and supportive of my work. But deep issues haunted him.

In November, Neal stopped by for a couple of days on his way to see his parents for Thanksgiving. Soon after that, a change came over Michael. He let some defenses drop and made a commitment to work things out. He commented that, when he was with me, Zen and I were one. That was very beautiful, and I had felt that peaceful connection at times too. We both needed to release our fears so they wouldn't cast a shadow between us. Like me, he functioned mainly with his head, which always reminded us of all the things that could go wrong, and it often blocked what was in our hearts.

But his intellectual, philosophical side was part of what I loved about Michael. There were times when having a conversation with him was like making love. Our conversations stretched and opened my mind. When he was coming from his intuition, he often understand what I was doing when I couldn't see it, and his stubbornness was often a fight to retain his independent spirit, a quality that made me trust him because he was true to himself. He was a good teacher in this respect.

On one of those magical Saturdays in early December when people were sunbathing in Cheesman Park and the intense sun warmed the cool air, Michael and I sat outside a café having lunch. He was asking questions about my relationship with Neal.

"He'll never be more than a friend because he won't be monogamous. That's what it comes down to," I reassured him.

"Really? I don't think it's that simple. You haven't resolved your relationship with him, so that keeps you from being able to commit to someone else."

"All right. Maybe it's unfair to say it's resolved, but he will never give me a monogamous relationship or a child, so what's the point? I want marriage."

"I still wonder how committed you could be to anyone else."

"Well, at the moment, it's really irrelevant, isn't it? No one else has asked me for a commitment."

"Um." He squirmed slightly in his chair.

"But why do you continue to see him?" he probed, sounding frustrated. "It makes it hard for me to trust you."

When I asked, "Why do you continue to see Sarah?" he didn't respond. "Michael, Neal accepts parts of me that others judge. Much of my own healing took place because Neal loves me for my eccentricities and emotional nature, which drive most men nuts, including you."

"Not me," he laughed, trying to look innocent. "Oh, well, who am I to think I know how to have a relationship. I had a marriage that was pretty hard to screw up, but I managed to do it anyway."

"Don't be so hard on yourself." I said, noticing how appealing he was when he laughed at himself.

"It's just that I don't trust myself not to screw it up again."

I sympathetically squeezed his hand and thought that maybe if I could give him the accepting love that Neal had given me, I could help him overcome his distrust of himself.

Finally, 1981 arrived. I still looked good at thirty-seven, but I was dragging around with low energy. I needed to stop smoking, pay more attention to eating good food, meditate regularly so I would sleep well, clarify and simplify my life, and choreograph again, but I couldn't bring myself to write down resolutions. How could I find the time to choreograph again? How could I pay dancers to perform when I could hardly support myself? Maybe I could afford that if I had a regular part-time job at one of the art schools. At least I'd be earning money in an art-friendly place.

Judy Chicago's latest artistic achievement, "Dinner Party," came to Denver. It was another powerful experience in recovering my history as a woman. On an enormous table, each place setting represented a woman in history, many of whom had been erased from the history books. With this beautifully controversial statement, Chicago gave them life again. It was a mammoth cooperative project using women's traditional arts: china painting, needlepoint, and embroidery. Chicago said, "A feminist is one who believes that the life experience of all persons is equally valuable and important." I liked that definition. Seeing this piece of art was an education because I'd never heard of many of the women represented, and I swelled with pride for all that women had done. I wanted every young woman to see this so she could reclaim her history.

Sometimes, in the 1980s I was amazed by how little had

changed in our society concerning women. I needed more than a survival income, so I took a career change workshop from Michael's friend Sarah, who was an excellent teacher. In class, a man commented that he believed the reading list of eight books was heavily weighted in favor of women. It included one book on money by a woman, *The Managerial Woman*. He considered *The Hazards of Being Male* femininely biased although he hadn't read it yet and it was written by a man. Another man referred to "being prepared" like a good boy scout. A woman asked if she had to be a boy scout.

A few nights later, while I was having dinner with Michael, the waitress asked him if he wanted the check, and I said, "I do." She put the check in front of him. Even after I put the money on the plate and put it beside me, she returned the change to him. I left the tip on the plate beside my plate, but she thanked him. I was invisible.

This reminded me how important women were to me—helping them, loving them, nurturing them to feel strong and proud as women. I missed the close women friends I had in Nebraska and had not yet met any women like them in Denver. But while I wanted to have positive, noncompetitive relationships with women, I was uncomfortable with Sarah. I liked her and admired her accomplishments, but I felt jealous because she and Michael seemed as emotionally intertwined as Neal and I had been. In this area of my life, Buddhist detachment was still a concept, not a reality. When I saw the way he looked at her, I knew she was the reason for his ambiguity with me.

I had never understood what people meant by a maternal instinct, but now I was overwhelmed by raging hormones that programmed me for procreation. However, I didn't want to bring a child into the world without two parents who had a solid relationship. A fog of depression frequently enveloped me, then, for no reason I could identify, lifted. My stamina in dance classes was decreasing, but I refused to accept this as a natural result of aging. I was thirty-seven and running out of time to have children and be a dancer, realities that haunted me constantly.

Outside, the winter snow, recently plowed to the sides of streets, grew gray and icy, another obstacle for pedestrians to navigate, and the obstacle between Michael and me became too great to surmount. When he broke up with me, I knew it was because he wanted one last chance with Sarah and was afraid her boyfriend would soon ask her to marry him. The dreary winter seemed to drag on forever.

In the spring, when my teaching at Naropa was over, I missed the peaceful, soothing energy there and the vibrant students. For the grading process, I was required to write an evaluation of the students' progress as well as assign letter grades. What a pleasure to be able to look at the whole person and evaluate, not just on technical achievement, but on overall growth as a human being.

When Neal heard Michael and I had broken up, he wanted us to be close again and begged me to come to Seattle. I went, hoping I could more accurately evaluate his intentions if I were with him. Arriving at the airport on a beautiful sunny summer day, he and two of his male friends met me, dressed in tuxedos, carrying roses and champagne to drink in their camouflaged kubawagon. People were staring as if trying to decide what celebrity had arrived. What fun! No one knew how to create romance and fun like Neal. Art and life were always one for him. After eating a lovely lunch at an outdoor café, we attended a Chopin piano concert performed by a friend of his. After the concert, the pianist and another friend of Neal's invited us to his house for drinks and dinner. I loved his friends; they were kind, creative, unique, and always made me feel welcome. Most of all, I was deeply touched that Neal had gone to so much trouble to celebrate my visit.

He seemed happy renovating old Victorian houses that drew on his artistic expression for completion and that provided him with shelter and income. He'd found an excellent lifestyle that looked very appealing, but I had to remember, fun and art were what he did well, not commitment. Despite Neal's dramatic welcome, nothing had changed. We enjoyed a delightful vacation, filled with much laughter, then I returned to Denver, and we continued our very separate lives.

Like Sisyphus repeatedly pushing the same rock up the mountain, I was in perpetual motion going from job interview to interview. Finally, I found a solution to my immediate financial needs, a part-time evening position at a commercial art school to assist the director of continuing education. She was a young vibrant woman, who actually hired me because I was overqualified. That was refreshing! At first I mainly answered phones and registered students, but other responsibilities were certain to develop over time because the program was new. I had doubts about staying in Denver, but I decided to see whether my business ideas would come to fruition. With the evening job, temporary office work two days a week, and teaching a class or two of dance, I could survive if I lived a simple life. After all, wasn't simplicity a virtue? But simplicity didn't make me feel secure.

Finding a dance position in a college continued to be a challenge. While I pursued that ambition, I took a business management course at Metropolitan State College and developed an idea for a business that would meet all my needs: dance exercise and body awareness classes offered as part of a corporate wellness program. At that time, corporations were very interested in wellness, so if I could use my dance skills in that environment, I would be well paid. The challenge would be learning to operate in the rational world of business. Despite our differences, Michael continued to offer help with my business ambitions and suggested I conduct information interviews with people who ran wellness programs to assess how to design a program.

When I forced my attention away from work, my reflections created space where I could see internal patterns I wanted to change. I was so easily hurt by others, and I realized I had internalized my mother's remarks when I was a child that when other people hurt me, it was because they were bad or mean people. She taught me nothing about understanding their behavior because she had no other coping skills. Naturally, I grew up thinking that all conflicts were personal and had no skills other than withdrawal or anger for dealing with being hurt. Now, I needed to learn more effective ways to deal with conflict.

I also limited myself, as did Neal, by always wanting to do things by myself to prove I was strong, but in the process, I rejected people who could help me learn what I needed to know. I also saw change as my enemy. It continued to be an emotional struggle even when I chose to change. I was stuck internally as well as in trying to set up new classes, market my wellness ideas to business, and find a college position. Nothing was moving and my limited finances restricted my life. I felt angry and depressed that I was unable to move forward.

One evening, sitting at Michael's dining table, I talked about my anger and discovered we had a similar issue. Now that we were only friends, we were able to be more open. He admitted, "When I'm compliant to keep peace, it creates anger that has to be expressed at another time. So later on, I explode for no apparent reason."

"Unfortunately, I can relate to that."

"Part of my problem is that it's very difficult to be a man right now."

"In what way?"

"Much of our anger comes from trying to appear more liberated than we are to impress women. We suppress our masculine side so that we don't appear too macho."

"This is going to sound weird, Michael, but I've faced a similar problem. When I was younger, I didn't like the choices I had as a woman, so I developed my masculine side more than the feminine side, but when I expressed it, I was rejected. I was supposed to be soft and nurturing. To keep peace, I ended up suppressing the masculine traits in order to appear more feminine, but was always angry about it. Now I'm afraid to assert myself."

"Because you weren't being who you really were."

"Exactly, so the anger came out at an inappropriate time." Our conversation was encouraging. I'd never thought about this before.

So this was what stopped me from being more assertive.

As another year in Denver came to a close, I lay alone in bed, Spanish guitar music from the radio filling the room with its passionate and delicately mystical quality. I was glad to be alone in my own space, feeling optimistic about the New Year. The part-time job at the art school provided me with the most secure base I'd had in a long time, and I enjoyed getting to know the artists who taught there. But none of the men I knew or dated were interested in a serious commitment. Was the universe telling me to forget about babies? Men, work, money, babies. How could I do this? Where was the balance in my life?

Magician's Assistant

Dance and reading about ancient femininity led me to search deeper into ritual and ceremonial magic. To my surprise, Sarah, who worked so successfully in the business world, also taught a class on ceremonial magic. It was a secular approach to Wiccan, Native American, and other traditions, and I took the course as a way of learning to see and acknowledge things that were unseen. At this point, she and I were both friends with Michael, but neither of us wanted a relationship with him. What she taught was good magic based on the rule of three—that whatever you put out into the world comes back to you threefold and based on the principle "As above, so below," acknowledging spiritual equivalents in the physical world. Having become more aware of the role of energy in the mind-body connection, I was eager to understand it through ritual.

When I found a willow wand to use in the rituals we performed, I became uncomfortable with the idea of using it. Puzzled by this, I mentioned it to Sarah who asked me questions related to past lives.

She paused, "I think you were a witch in a past life and hurt someone by mishandling your power."

"Really?" I was skeptical about the existence of past lives. "Well, regardless of the cause, I have plenty of power issues in my relationships, and I still have to solve those in this lifetime." She nodded in agreement.

During that time, most of my dreams were about journeys. One night, I was in a go-cart traveling up a hill when the pavement dropped off into gravel on the right side of the road. I thought the solid pavement was my lane, and as I moved up the hill, a line of cars suddenly appeared over the hill, came toward me, and ran me off the road. I stepped out of the vehicle, got back in, adjusted the seat belt, and started up the hill again. I awoke, surprisingly encouraged, knowing my unconscious was urging me not to give up. I was grateful for this encouragement because my self-esteem often faltered as I was exhausted, hustling to find one more class to make ends meet. Late periods and broken veins heralded the onset of middle age, and I panicked that it was coming much too soon.

A man in my modern dance class who was learning to be an astrologer asked to do my natal chart for practice. I agreed. I was open to receive any information that might help me understand my difficulties.

When he called to share the information, I listened intently.

"Now, understand, I'm just sharing with you what I see in the chart. None of this is a judgment of you."

"I understand. Go ahead."

He began, clearly nervous, but excited to be able to practice his skills. "One thing I see is that you feel weak because you can't create the things you want on the physical plane, but you go ahead and work anyway, trying to work things out through your emotions. You also use your analytical abilities to see the different aspects of a situation and deal with any erroneous ideas you have."

"Do you have a sense of what is at the root of my current problems?"

"Yes, and this is very significant. Your most basic conflict is between emotions and mind. The goal of your life is to express yourself in the world, which certainly supports your creative desires. Let's also look at your planetary balance. One planet is in an earth sign. It's about being grounded. One planet is in fire (action), four planets in air (intellect), and four planets in water (emotion). Do you have difficulty staying grounded?"

"Oh yes," I declared, amazed by how the balance of the planets supported the conflict between my emotions and intellect. So that was the challenge. How could I learn to balance my emotions? Meditation was only a beginning.

Working at the art school, I was often pleasantly distracted by Alan, a teacher I'd met there. He was slender like a runner with piercing blue eyes and dark hair that always fell across his forehead. Unique and honest with a certain delightful child-like quality, he was sensitive and caring but had difficulty revealing himself.

The first long evening we spent together was unlike anything I had ever experienced. At first, I thought I was experiencing sexual tension. It was there and we acknowledged it, but he centered and channeled positive energy, thereby centering me. There were moments when I opened to him completely, and the power of those moments was very intimate. Each touch awakened all my nerve endings. Something broke open inside both of us and our hearts expanded, releasing what he called our psychological garbage, and I felt I was being healed. Our energies merged, flowing together in a spiritual experience as powerful as making love although we were only holding hands.

Alan listened intently, perceived deeply, and remembered everything. Like other men I'd known, he had many women friends. However, I felt so loved by him, although he hadn't used those words, and I received so much from him that, if he had more to give others, I lost nothing by his giving it. He drew closer to me, not further away, so his involvement with others as friends wasn't a way of distancing himself from me, but of fully expressing who he was. He was also a man who wanted a family and was looking for a similar balance in life. I often thought of a line from Edsel Ford's poem, "Love is to come home dying from the world and find life there." That was how I felt when I was with Alan.

As we talked one night, he said, "I think you're like a magician's assistant and as you learn about the universe, you blossom and become who you really are."

I couldn't help smiling. "That's interesting."

"Yes?"

"I'm actually taking a class in ceremonial magic."

"Really?"

"Yes, and I love it. I mean, it's strange sometimes, and I don't know if I'm actually experiencing something or it's just in my mind. Do you know what I mean?"

"Yeah," he said quietly, patiently watching for me to go on.

I thought for a moment, then decided to take a chance.

"There's something I want to tell you that I've never told anyone."

"Okay." He smiled, happy I trusted him.

"As I drifted to sleep one night recently, I thought I saw a flash of a past life. I was dressed in long dark robes with a gold snake on my headpiece. I guess that's Egyptian. I held a wand in my hand and angrily pointed it toward someone, unleashing my full power. I'm afraid I harmed someone by doing that."

He looked at me very seriously. "Maybe I was that person. Maybe this time you won't hurt me."

I looked at him stunned and remembered the fear I'd experienced the first time I had to use a wand and Sarah's comment about abusing power in a past life.

He looked concerned and touched my face tenderly, "I'm not saying you're mean or anything."

"I know. It's just that… I thought it was you, too. I feel like I've known you before."

"That's very possible."

"Maybe we do have past lives, and the karma from those lives affects this life. Until now, I haven't been sure about reincarnation."

"I think we do live many lives."

I remembered that my horoscope recently said that the things I feared wouldn't come true. I hoped that meant I wouldn't misuse my power again.

Like me, Alan was struggling to make a living and was often depressed from unsuccessful interviews. Regardless of how he felt, he was kind to me. When I was sad or needed to cry, he took me in his arms and comforted me, but I began to notice a pattern that concerned me. Whenever I expressed an idea passionately or with anger, he seemed to withdraw even if the anger wasn't directed at him.

Despite all the positive things in the relationship, the issue of punctuality had been simmering below the surface for some time, and my patience was finally stretched beyond the limit on the afternoon we planned to go to the state fair. When I arrived at his house, he was in his puttering mode, folding towels and starting to put away the dishes stacked in the drainer. I said, "Alan, couldn't you leave this until later? I'd like to have some time alone with you before we meet Ron and Kathy."

"I'm almost through," he said smiling. But he wasn't; he spent another thirty minutes looking for a particular magazine, picking the lint off a sweater, trying to decide which shirt to wear. My frustration finally reached the breaking point.

My voice quivering, I said, "I don't understand. You said you wanted some time with me before we met your friends." It disturbed me that Alan was frozen into a pattern that he had to complete what he was doing before he could go on to the next thing, and because he moved so slowly, we never did anything on time.

I waited a moment, but he didn't respond. I turned sharply and walked out, slamming the door. I waited on the porch to cool off. It wasn't long before he was ready to leave, but he was quiet.

In the evening, his friend Paula, with whom he had once lived, joined us. Because she and I didn't know each other, and she wanted to talk to Alan about her problems while he was cooking supper, the situation was awkward. Neither of them included me in the conversation. He always cooked very slowly, and by 9:00 pm when we ate, my energy had bottomed out, and I felt very irritable.

After this conflicted day, Alan was a bit aloof, but not long after that Sarah and I ran into him with a woman friend as they were leaving Zach's Restaurant. His face lit up and he immediately took my hand and kissed me. Turning to his friend, he said cheerfully, "This is Georganne."

She reached out to shake my hand and said enthusiastically, "I'm so glad to meet you. I know you're really important to Alan. He talks about you all the time." Alan blushed slightly. I introduced Sarah and we all stood at the entrance talking for a few minutes. It was unusual for Alan to show me so much affection in public.

Soon, Alan was plunging into part-time work and setting deadlines to complete other responsibilities, and I was working to develop the corporate programs. I missed the sweetness and closeness of our first days together—living with the heart instead of the head, but we both needed to focus more on our work.

He then shocked me by saying that he no longer wanted to see only me, but was unable to explain why he felt this way. I cried for an entire day. Why wasn't I ever enough for a man? Exhausted, I went to sleep that night feeling cleansed by the tears as if a catharsis had taken place. The next morning I was rested and energized, but when Alan called and wanted to talk to me, I was too busy. The dance festival in Boulder and a major Dance Alliance meeting that weekend took all my time.

When Alan and I talked again about our issues, I realized that my passionate, expressive behavior stimulated his fear that some destructive event from his past would be repeated. A darkness seemed to hover around him, for even his house was shadowy. It was a quiet, comfortable retreat from life, but not a bright or warm place. Even during a party, with the house filled with people, Alan didn't allow himself to be spontaneous and let go. He was a perfectionist, and moving slowly lengthened the time it took to do things, so the mundane necessities conveniently filled all of his time; none was left in which to venture out into the world he feared. I let go of my illusions about our romance. As much as I loved him as a friend, I would never be able to live with him.

I was thankful that, despite our differences, Alan and I remained friends who could share food, nature, and simple things in life. But what weighed heavily on my heart was how bowed he grew from carrying the burden of his fear or guilt. I wanted to nurture him the way his mother should have done, but I was tired, so tired, of the men in my life needing so much emotionally from me.

Alan and I were at our best outdoors, and a few weeks later spent the weekend camping in the grasslands. Away from the city, I felt contented, centered, and renewed in a profound way. I suppose my intellectual side needed city life, but the spiritual side needed nature. The beauty of the grasslands was subtle, but the sunsets boldly filled the sky with pink, gold, and purple. The highlight of the weekend was a baby bird that watched us watching him until his mother distracted us with a broken wing act. On the Pawnee Buttes, we watched circling hawks as the peacefulness of nature permeated our time together.

A few weeks later, I made a brief trip to visit Donna in Nebraska. We talked well into the night about ritual and magic and how much we would like to live in a community together. After I returned, I dreamed that I lived in the mountains with women. I wore jeans, a flannel Native American shirt, large leather belt, and boots. Another woman and I were digging and lifted a large shovel of earth that was black, sandy, and full of varied colors, especially green and rose, and contained different textures of rock. I cleared away the dirt and realized that some of it was encased in rings, forming an open globe with rings that crossed and touched at the top and at the bottom and were held together by their own pressure. On the other side of where I found the encased dirt was an Indian painting of a white thunderbird and other smaller images.

In the dream, the scene then shifted to a meeting of women dressed like me sitting around a rough, wooden, rectangular table in a dark, sparsely furnished building. We were discussing modern dance as if we were participating in a seminar or planning a program. In the next scene, four or five of us were in a bedroom talking. I had taken off the pieces of Indian turquoise jewelry I had been wearing. As I started to speak, a white substance spotted with brown started flowing quickly out of my mouth. Observing myself, I could see this happening, but I couldn't feel it. Then, from a point in the room further away, I saw a red and white vapor roll out of my mouth and cover my face and head like a huge lion's mane.

We were all a little afraid, and someone suggested getting a doctor. I had difficulty talking but tried to communicate to them to call the doctor who had given me a certain piece of jewelry, a round pin with an image on it. He was the only one who would understand what was happening. I felt more awed than frightened because I knew this was a shamanic experience, and I felt a deep connection with Native American culture. Was this a healing or a sign I was a shaman? Wouldn't I have to heal myself before I could heal others?

I was determined to stay focused on developing the material for the corporate workshops I hoped to teach. When I met Cindy, a psychologist who had skills and contacts that I didn't, I knew she was the perfect business partner. Because I'd had no success booking classes for wellness programs, we decided to focus on selling to training programs. By this time, Michael was teaching corporate managers and was able to put us in touch with Judith Terrance, who did corporate creativity workshops on left brain/right brain thinking. I was intrigued by what I had read on this topic. When we met Judith, she said that I was too low key to sell a company and focused on Cindy, who was very outgoing but knew little about this area. By the end of the interview, Judith seemed very unclear about my role in the venture, and I felt rejected and nervous because I was unable to repair the poor impression I had made. At least she gave us the names of other people to contact.

But there was still another problem with the corporate courses. Michael called it "a withholding of energy." I was afraid; I still hadn't surrendered completely to the project and had to break through the barrier that I created. I was puzzled by how to remedy this, but I needed to do it soon. Cindy and I were almost through preparing the courses and would soon be ready to make appointments and begin selling.

When I was promoted to administrative assistant at the art school, I was given a raise and finally made more than an unemployment check. My expenses were always more than my income, yet I was never in debt, and when I absolutely had to charge an item, I paid off the debt quickly. I always prayed that I would have just enough money to pay my bills and I always did. However, I was becoming concerned about the economy. So many people were having difficulty financially, and several evening art students had been laid off their jobs because of it.

Not long after the interview with Judith Terrance, she invited Cindy and me to do a movement activity in a corporate creativity workshop she was presenting. We were thrilled and the people with whom we worked responded beautifully. Ms. Terrance was pleasantly surprised at the way I "came alive" during the workshop and gave us an invaluable reference that I hoped would open the door to other opportunities.

The ceremonial magic class continued to open my mind and made me more aware of the interaction of energies. Part of one exercise involved envisioning what we wanted. I had already become fairly adept at attracting a parking place in congested downtown Denver, and as a choreographer, I was used to envisioning dances in my head, but I became more aware of how I could create my own reality by visualization.

The exercises we did often shifted my perception in valuable ways. Recently, Sarah asked, "How do people's energies connect? Draw it." I drew lines emanating from a center outward and energy moving in a circle around it. Without commenting, she drew interlocking rings and two masses somewhat overlapping.

"Wow, those are very different."

"It's a matter of seeing us as separate or related," she clarified.

I shook my head in agreement. "This is the issue that keeps coming up for me. It's like the issue of seeing people's differences instead of their similarities, of dwelling on poverty instead of wealth. The same thing came up in my conversation with another friend the other day."

"When you dwell on the differences between people, rather than seeing the similarities, it separates you from others. It's the similarities that bring people together."

This insight was so obvious. Why hadn't I seen it earlier? What I focused on could determine how I experienced life.

I pondered this for a moment, then asked, "Could that be part of my problem in relationships? When I see the big picture, I see similarities, but I still become attached to the differences."

"Becoming attached to the differences causes us to have expectations. They're the problems."

"Of course! Without the expectations, I can accept others as they are; there would be less conflict." I sighed. "I'm such a novice at understanding life, much less magic."

Sarah smiled and looked me straight in the eye. "You're doing much better than you think you are. You could be a very fine practitioner if you wanted to be."

Releasing the Fear

As the fall of 1982 moved toward winter, my life lay in pieces like a shattered china bowl. Here and there a piece fit, but the shape of the whole eluded me. I felt that I was back where I started—confused and uncertain about my ability to work in the world and take care of myself. A successful outcome with the corporate work was doubtful, and my anger manifested as a mass of knots under my shoulder blade. One minute I wanted to explode but couldn't light the fuse, the next I curled into a ball and withdrew. I forced myself to meditate, knowing that even if I did it poorly, it was the only thing that would keep me balanced during the day.

Despite my depression, Thanksgiving was one of the nicest I could remember. Alan's house was warm, peaceful, and filled with his friends—a healing balm for my ache. Michael was there too, and I met friends of Alan's that I'd never met before who practiced transcendental meditation. I felt for the first time since I had come to Denver that I had a nice community of friends. Many people here were on a spiritual journey similar to mine, and each friend I made was a teacher whose experiences enlightened me.

As a feminist, my challenge was to reconcile the feeling that my life wasn't complete without a man. I knew that wanting a man to take care of me was a trap, but having a partner to share the intellectual and passionate aspects of life brought me joy. It was clear that Alan and I would never be more than friends. The intellectual, artistic, emotional, and physical connections with Neal made it difficult to walk away completely, but I doubted he'd ever make the commitment I needed. I had to be financially independent to be truly independent, and my failure to create prosperity and security overshadowed my strengths in other areas of life.

Michael and I had been doing well as friends, and I secretly harbored the hope we would become compatible enough to marry some day, but when he learned that Sarah's boyfriend had finally asked her to marry him, he rushed to ask her also. Poor desperate Michael. Sarah refused his offer. I was saddened, though, that I was still second choice.

At Christmas, Denver was paralyzed under several feet of snow—this was the blizzard of 1982—the answer to everyone's wish for snow and proof that mass consciousness has power. The airport was closed for three days and two thousand travelers were stranded for the holidays. I felt sorry for people who were trying to get to their families and thankful that I had headed out early to sunny New Orleans.

However, being with family so long required patience and an extra effort to stay centered. Because my parents had lived with my brother's family for several years, it was hard for me not to feel like an exile despite my choice not to live there. The family dynamics, with their constant negativism and criticism, were contrary to what I needed and eroded what cheer I'd been able to summon for the season. At least my brother was aware of how I felt and made a point to reaffirm that the family accepted me despite their lack of involvement in my life.

Because my mother rarely read books now and had no interest in outside activities, much of her talk was trivial. I missed the meaningful, substantial discussions we used to have. Although she had discouraged many of my interests, she had always encouraged my love of books. I hardly knew the woman she had become. My brother encouraged her to develop interests, but she chose caring for her grandchildren to be her whole life. It was a task that left her with too much time on her hands. I watched her in the kitchen, rearranging the blue and white canisters, refilling the napkin container, wandering from stove to sink pretending to work, like a ghost haunting her own life. I worried about her and fought back the tears when she expressed her love for me and her desire to help me even though it was difficult for her to understand the life I lived. After all our conflicts, at least we had found some peace with each other.

* * *

My depression lifted as I concentrated more on finding solutions to problems rather than allowing the negative energy from the problem to pull me down. I found more peace with life and developed a new female friend with whom I had more in common than Sarah. Janet took my noontime modern dance class, and afterward we had lunch. Our conversation flowed so easily that I knew we would quickly become close. She loved to hike, had been married to a very successful artist, and was concerned with spiritual matters.

About this same time, the apartment building where I lived was sold, and I had to find a new place within a month. I was very upset, but the universe was generous. I soon found a larger apartment for less rent, and it was still in the Capitol Hill area and near the park. It wasn't available for two months, but a friend of Sarah's had an extra room I rented for the interim. Life seemed full of positive changes. I found a better studio in which to teach classes and another part-time job typing motions and documents for Alan's lawyer friend. The extra money relieved some of my stress.

When it was time to move into my new apartment, Neal came to help. I was delighted to have a real bedroom and a tiny sunroom for my plants. I returned to meditating regularly and reading the Tarot for guidance. I bought a book on numerology and became fascinated with it. My search for spiritual understanding continued, for I knew it held the secret to a happy life. I continued to find creative ways to teach movement. This time it was a class, "Can You See, Can You Move," designed to help people who had difficulty learning in aerobics classes because they didn't know how to *see* and learn the movement.

My new friendship with Janet grew steadily, but a few months after it began, my relationship with Sarah became increasingly strange and uncomfortable. As a friend, she became unavailable and distant as I struggled with mood swings that almost undid me. When I tried to talk with her about her sudden change in behavior, she refused and said she didn't want to see me for a few months.

In a dream one night, I kept falling down and down through a murky blackness. I stopped at one level and a scenario was acted out, then I dropped through the darkness again. This happened several times. The last time I landed on solid ground still in the darkness and looked up from where I was lying to see a perky black pony with a light brown quilted blanket over his back. He was full of energy—young, vital, cute. Perhaps I was being reborn in some way from the darkness, and he was there to escort me to a new life, for horses were symbols of the soul's journey. Often they carried a person to the underworld where she learned about magical secrets or gained great wisdom. Hopefully, my periods of darkness were part of a path to a new life.

A visit from my Nebraska women friends uplifted me briefly, but as soon as they left I was again tormented by the idea that I was creating unnecessary entanglements in my life, repeating some pattern I couldn't break. People's unkindness triggered anger and anxiety from the past. My paranoia ran away with me, and I created negative images that then became true. On some level, I knew that some of the people and activities in my life weren't good for me, and I wondered if I were unconsciously creating these situations to break what I couldn't break consciously.

Because I couldn't handle my problems alone and had little confidence in talk therapy alone, I found a Lomi practitioner who did body work and talk therapy. During the first session, I discovered that I was locked into a pattern of behavior that had deadened much of my sensitivity, partly the result of my no longer dancing. With the Lomi work, my body came alive for the first time in a long time, and the energy flowed and pulsed. Even my fingers tingled—a peculiar sensation I'd never experienced.

After the body work, the therapist and I talked for the first time. I liked her peaceful energy and trusted her.

"Holding your breath is very common. It's how people separate themselves from their bodies and feelings."

"I haven't even noticed that I don't breathe much in my upper chest," I said rather shocked by how much I had shut down. "My face feels dead too."

"That's because your breath gets stuck in your upper chest and throat."

"This is ironic considering that I've done deep breathing in singing, acting, and dancing."

I must have looked discouraged because she continued with a lighter tone, "On the other hand, you have a strong base in your hips and legs. The part of your body that is most alive is the pelvis. That's a very positive aspect since it's your center, but you need to take walks, observe your body, and get in touch with it again."

These patterns related to the reactive emotional behavior I wanted to change. Staying grounded had always been a challenge. If I stayed grounded and sent my energy back down the body instead of letting it rise and get stuck in my chest or throat, then perhaps I would feel stronger.

Unfortunately, this work didn't create changes fast enough. When I talked with my doctor, he immediately recommended crisis therapy. I was stuck in this deep emotional pain, unable to focus or make good decisions about my future. I hated my weakness and indecision. When I tried to discipline my will power and work harder, I ended up repressing my feelings instead of dealing with them. I knew this hopelessness, this ongoing grayness was a disease of spirit. The crisis therapist was no help. Despite having good friends, I felt I had no one to lean on, no one to be my mirror, no one to take into consideration. I was worn out by relationship power struggles I had no idea how to win. The question, "What did I want?" made no sense. Getting what I wanted, love and financial security, seemed hopeless. The question became "What could I actually do?" There was a great sadness in my heart, for the passion and wonderful hope about life that I used to have no longer existed. The life I had expected to live was dead.

Despite such periods, I managed to go on. A shaft of sunlight through the window, the laughter of a friend, watching the squirrels race around the trees in the park—some small thing would make me smile, and I would begin to climb out of the despair again. One evening Janet invited me to join her at a friend's, and that evening was a healing retreat.

Shafts of early evening summer light slid through the high windows that surrounded the kitchen in her friend's spacious house. As Janet, a couple of her friends, and I watched and learned, Janet's friend Mona prepared a gourmet meal. Surrounded by the luxury of this home, I remembered how I truly loved beautiful and sensual things despite the frugal way I'd always had to live. Talking and eating together, surrounded by beautiful plants, china and candles, I thoroughly enjoyed the women's company and Mona's enthusiasm for cooking and sharing her talents. After supper, as we sipped champagne in the jacuzzi, I felt embraced by the comfort and warmth of a perfect evening and wondered if I would ever know this kind of comfort in my daily life.

At lunch one day, Janet and I were sharing our spiritual beliefs. I remarked that I had discovered bits and pieces that made sense to me, but I didn't know how it all fit together. The dogma of organized religion seemed unnecessary and seemed to exist only to control people. On the other hand, ceremonial magic was primarily too esoteric to provide the practical guidance I needed. Janet encouraged me to attend a lecture given by Gladys, her spiritual teacher.

The next week, Janet and I sat in the back of a metaphysical bookstore as the room quickly filled with people, many of whom, like Janet, returned periodically to absorb more of Gladys's teachings. I expected her to be dressed like a hippie and thus wasn't prepared for the formally attired, soft-spoken former accountant. Later, I learned that she sewed many of her clothes and was a devoted grandmother.

Gladys began with an explanation of the cycles of life, including reincarnation. I still wasn't sure whether I believed in past lives or even cared what they were. It was what she said about fear that captivated me and gave me hope. As she began explaining the process, I leaned forward and took copious notes.

"When we respond to a comment or situation with fear, it is because we feel inadequate or rejected. These psychological fears block the mind from being able to draw information from the unconscious part of the mind to solve the problem that caused the fear. Instead, the fear stimulates the mind to pull through information related to the fear, such as a bad experience we've had with the same issue in the past. When we are able to release the fear, the mind can pull through information from the unconscious and spiritual part of the mind to help us solve the actual problem. Eventually, this process retrains the mind to release fear the moment we feel it. Unless it is the innate fear that protects us from physical harm, it has no value. With fear out of the way, one can actually deal with the problem, but as long as the fear is there, a person is only coping with the fear, not solving the problem."

As I immediately began to practice this technique, I realized that the fear of inadequacy or rejection had always kept me from moving ahead in life. At first, the challenge was to remember to direct my mind to release the fear as soon as I felt it. When I remembered, the process was simple. All I had to do was to direct my mind to release the fear and let go of it. Letting go, however, was often difficult. I didn't always recognize that what I felt was fear, but returning to Gladys's lectures and discussing my experiences with Janet increased my awareness. I came to understand that any resistance, reluctance, or negative thought was about fear, and I didn't have to understand it; I needed only to release it.

As I practiced these teachings, I felt good again, finding it easier to reach out to others when they reached out to me without fearing their motivations. When I was around Sarah, I felt no fear. With enough part-time work, I stopped worrying about money. Many of the old notions about being rescued by a man, being protected, being given double messages, and being confused about who I was resurfaced, but by releasing the fear around these issues, I grasped connections or understood patterns that were unclear before.

However, the old bitterness and anger I felt toward my parents and Gary for trying to make me choose between love and career wasn't fully extinguished. That duality still haunted me, and I struggled to accept working for its own sake without expecting the work to be fulfilling. Other people seemed to accept this reality even if the work were a waste of their talents. Most people thought making money was enough. I suppose I valued it too little.

In addition, what to do about my friendship with Neal was still a dilemma. Every time he and I failed with another relationship, we gravitated back to each other, hoping we could reconcile our differences. Even as friends, though, the differences between us were vast. He and I used radically different approaches in life, and I hoped he would find peace as he continued to learn spiritually, but I needed someone who lived in flow with life, not one who chose to force his will on me and rejected everything that was organized or institutional. Although he insisted that he loved me and our intimacy and sharing was some of the most meaningful I had ever known, he could never tolerate the closeness for long. When he withdrew, I felt abandoned. Now, as I thought about those moments, I realized that I clung to Neal because I was afraid I'd never find another man who would accept my artistic and emotional nature. At least, he accepted that, but it shocked me to realize how much fear was mixed with my love for him. It was not fear that was easy to release.

On my thirty-ninth birthday, I felt calm, centered, and happy to be who I was. I had dinner with Gladys and several women from her class and enjoyed the companionship and stimulating conversation. Later, Alan stopped by with a gift—a tiny, beautiful crystal.

The path I'd chosen, practicing what Gladys taught, worked. The more I released the same fears, the less they reappeared. Even the most gripping ones began to lose some of their power. I felt positive and empowered by this practice. Finally, I began to acquire some control over my unruly emotions. I accepted just being, accepted the fact that I didn't want to exercise even though my body was getting soft, and accepted that it was all right not to have a man in my life. I began to understand the detachment the Buddhists talked about. It was wonderful making new, more spiritual friends, okay to be doing the work I was doing, and awfully nice to have more money. With all my belongings out of storage, my new larger apartment finally felt like a home.

I continued the Lomi work and found there were many sensitive, painful places on my body. When the therapist worked with my breath and chest, a deep, tender sadness surfaced. I floated out of my body and expanded my awareness but was very afraid of losing control and being unprotected. Hiding within was a way to avoid being hurt by people, but my focus became foggy. After a session, I could literally see the world more clearly.

I began to observe my own movement more and noticed tension in many of my activities. I used my arms as braces, straightening them like ramrods when I scrubbed or washed dishes, tensing, rotating, and locking the shoulders instead of using them freely as I did when I was dancing.

I shared these thoughts and observations with my Lomi practitioner. "You need to do the healing with yourself that you would like to do with others," she suggested, "especially working with the spine because it relates to feeling."

At the next session, she worked with my arms, trying to release the breath through them. Unable to do that, I felt fear move through my upper body, "I don't want you to touch my heart or chest."

"Why is that?"

Unable to stop the tears, I whispered, "I cry when someone touches my heart or when I start to let go and open up." I put my hand over my heart. "I want to protect my chest."

"Does this happen when a man touches you there?"

Feeling great anxiety, I admitted, "Sometimes I cry when I'm intimate with a man. I can't control it and they don't understand."

In addition to her lectures, Gladys saw people for individual counseling, and after the lectures, she allowed individuals to ask her one question. We sat at a small table in the front of the lecture room where a screen had been placed for privacy. I asked her what she could tell me about the next six months.

She began slowly. "It would be beneficial for you to accept

that you are more secure than you believe. Some of the past will not be repeated, and you must believe that is so. By allowing yourself to experience the strength of that belief, you will feel secure and able to make some changes that would be of value. Those changes will not be a burden, so you need to allow yourself the freedom to make the changes to correct the burdens that do exist."

After the next lecture, I knew I had to ask her about my dance career, but I was fearful of her answer. Sitting at the same tiny table, she became very quiet and ready to receive the information that came to her from a higher source.

"It would be beneficial to look at the reality of your activity and accept that it has limitations and restrictions that are eliminating some of the value for you. It would be difficult to change those at this point in time. You need to accept that they exist and that unless they could be changed, there will be a continuing elimination of the value you desire. As you accept that this is so, you will be able to allow yourself the freedom to search in other directions. That is your correction."

Giving me a regretful, sympathetic look, she said, "It just isn't in your area. I'm sorry about that."

I thanked her and hurried to my car, where I started sobbing. She had confirmed what I already knew, but it was a relief that it wasn't just my inability to make a career in dance work. The economy in Denver was based almost exclusively on the oil and gas industry, and it wasn't doing well. Institutions were beginning to drop programs and people had less money to spend. Accepting this reality was painful, but I wasn't alone; many other dancers were struggling to survive too. It was costly to rent space with sprung hardwood floors. They were the only floors safe for dancers, and the competition from aerobics classes, which were so popular, lured people away from modern dance. Many of those classes enrolled huge numbers of students, charging half of what I did, and they often exercised on concrete floors. Most people were unaware of the many injuries that would result from that.

My identity was so wrapped up with dance and being an artist that I wasn't sure who I was without it, so I concentrated on the other changes I knew I needed to make. I avoided confused or noisy people, especially the ones who felt such a need to defend, argue, or create struggles. People who didn't continually burden others with their anxieties were more attractive to me, but despite their warmth and laughter, I often felt their passion was missing. Always needing to express myself emotionally, I observed them with curiosity.

As I made these changes and released my fear in so many situations, my life became more peaceful, and I awoke almost every morning delighted to greet the day. Still, I missed the adrenaline rush of an adventure and the excitement of a performance. When I saw the movie *The Right Stuff*, I remembered what it was like to do something I'd never done before, "pushing the edges of the envelope back."

But the greatest change in my life came from the greatest gift in my life, Gladys, whose reading identified health problems my doctor had identified as psychological without bothering to run tests. Gladys discovered that my adrenals were very fatigued, my thyroid fluctuated, my pituitary wasn't functioning normally, and there was an imbalance in my pancreas and digestive system. She recommended a particular combination of glandulars, vitamins, and minerals to correct these problems and pointed out that my headaches, restlessness, and mood swings were hormonal. What a relief to know that these problems could be corrected and that my depression, to some extent, had physical roots.

Amazingly, as 1983 ended, my ability to release fear had changed my life. I felt wonder and joy in day-to-day life and had gained new emotional control and balance by also following Gladys' health advice. Although it had been mostly a celibate year, I had new friends and had grown closer to old ones of real value. I had ridden the black pony out of the darkness and found a new way to live.

Master Numbers

Like many esoteric subjects, numerology intrigued me. I bought a book on it but didn't take it seriously until I read about my life lesson number. According to that, my greatest challenge in life was to learn to balance my emotional and practical nature, confirming what my astrologer friend had said. Hearing the same message again made a deep impression on me because that conflict was the most challenging issue at the moment. For once, though, I made, not the emotional choice, but the practical choice to get a full-time job.

Soon after this search began, the head of student services at the art school offered me a position as an employment assistance counselor and raised the salary by $1,000. In addition, my supervisor tried to get my job made into a full-time position immediately and said that she'd fight for me all the way. It was all very heady and exciting. Because I enjoyed the environment of the art school so much, I was excited by the possibility of remaining there.

Within the week, the corporation decided not to increase my present job to full time, so I took the job in student services despite a friend's warning that Harold, the department head, could be difficult. I liked the idea of helping students find part-time and freelance jobs and developing new job sources for them. However, leaving my current manager was difficult because she was the best manager I'd ever had. She was a terrific, wonderfully positive human being, and we got along beautifully.

The transition to full-time work was stressful, and my nervous system was still very sensitive, primed to handle emergencies. However, I liked coming and going to work during the day when most people were also working. I was happier not pulling against the current, and I liked the security of knowing the bills would be paid, that I could travel, and have time for evening dance classes and Gladys' lectures.

***

I was in high spirits when Thanksgiving arrived. The family met in North Little Rock at my grandmother's house. She had recently fallen but miraculously didn't break any bones despite her fragile condition. Instead of focusing on the positive, my mother and great aunt kept replaying how terrible the fall was. Worst of all, they talked about my grandmother and her business as if she weren't in the room.

Steeped in bitterness from the past and geared to the fighting mode, my mother, with her fluctuating moods, was always on the defensive and created problems that didn't exist. Growing up, I had been close to her. She was my best friend, and we spent long hours talking about everything. My father was a distant undemonstrative man who showed her little attention, and despite her mood swings, she showered love on her children and desperately needed our love. She was often entertaining and funny, but as the years wore on, she grew bitter about life and adopted a martyr role.

Even at my grandmother's, my mother and father fought. It wore me out emotionally to hear their raised voices and hateful exchanges. I couldn't shut it out, and my stomach was upset and intestines ached as they had when I was young. I still longed to see my parents express their love to one another. I wondered if even Gladys could help me overcome my fears and avoid the same destructive patterns I saw in my parents' behavior. My attempts to share with my mother what I had learned about releasing fear went over her head.

Life was difficult for many people, but Gladys gave us hope when she insisted that, if we could survive this year 1984, life would improve. A biologist friend of hers told her if six percent of a diseased organ was healthy that was enough to revitalize the organ. Using that analogy, Gladys said that, by 1986, six percent of the population would evolve to a point where their higher consciousness could begin changing the world for the better. I hoped this transformation would affect my parents as well as me.

In May, I felt very optimistic when my manager Harold said he thought I was doing a fabulous job in the time I'd been there. Seeing that I needed more support, he requested a clerical helper who would handle errands and paperwork. I was relieved to find that he didn't expect the number of students hired to increase much for six months because I had no doubt I could increase the numbers by then. Accepting my life as it was, I let go of former expectations. I was dancing with life and, for the moment, it was a waltz.

As the weather warmed, an undercurrent of turbulence developed at the office with Harold watching one of the other employment assistance advisers like a hawk. I suspected that Harold would fire him soon. I'd had nightmares for two nights that included people from the office. One night I awoke about 1:00 am from a dream in which people were struggling and flailing their arms. I was hit in the mouth and my teeth were broken and my mouth was bleeding. As I walked away, my teeth started crumbling and falling out as blood gushed from my mouth. It seemed so real that, as I rose to consciousness, I put my hand to my mouth and was shocked to find my teeth were still there. My breathing was fast and my heart raced. It took at least a half an hour for me to relax and go back to sleep.

Although I felt the turbulence in the office, I knew nothing of the specifics and remained somewhat apart from the conflict, not letting it interfere with my work or upset me during the day. Others who were troubled came to me, so I listened and supported them. Those conflicts were my teachers, showing me how to read the truth in another's actions and how to make logical, commonsense decisions and be a peacemaker. The daily practice helped improve my ability to deal with conflict, and I learned not to make every issue personal. My foundation became more solid and I felt amazingly secure.

By this time, Michael had been gone for a year. Sarah and her husband had moved to the West Coast, and Michael moved there soon afterward, believing that there would be more opportunities for professional growth. I had recently asked the universe to fill my need for a possible mate who was loving and gentle, and Michael reappeared for a visit, wanting to renew our friendship. We spent pleasant time together and tried to revive the relationship over the next few months, but in the end, we found it impossible to meet each other's needs.

Gladys always cautioned that when we asked the universe to meet our needs, they might be filled in ways we hadn't envisioned, so we needed to remain open to all possibilities. I was rather spoiled in this respect since, recently at work, I had gotten exactly what I wanted. I learned that I might lose both students who called to obtain job leads, so I talked to the student I preferred for the job, and she accepted my offer. I decided I needed to get more training; soon afterward, the corporation created the student financial services training and included me.

According to numerology, this month was ruled by a master number, a time that presented more challenges and difficulties, but also a time when one could potentially accomplish more. As such, it was also a time that required me to exercise more emotional balance than usual.

At the office, I was very uncomfortable with what I defined as gender discrimination issues, so one day when I knew Harold was out of the building, I met with my former supervisor about them. She warned me, "Don't share your personal frustrations with Harold. Keep things on a very professional basis and expect him to bend the rules some on the discrimination issue."

I couldn't help looking surprised. "So, I'm not imagining this?"

She shrugged and smiled.

When I consulted Gladys, what she had to say was similar. "If you don't rock the boat at work, you'll continue learning skills that will perhaps prepare you for advancement."

"I really need more money. Should I ask for it?"

"No, this isn't the time to ask—just get a part-time job."

Soon the September start date was upon me, overwhelmingly intense for the first few weeks of the quarter because it was the largest enrollment of the year. I was just recovering from the intensity of it when my fortieth birthday arrived. I released my expectations for the day and tried to enjoy whatever unfolded. My coworkers gave me a wonderful card, yellow roses, and a champagne toast. Alan called to wish me a happy birthday, and my former boss brought a card to my office. In the evening, Janet and a couple of friends came by my apartment for a little party. I was thankful to have such caring and fun people in my life and was grateful for my family and new life—to think my life was half over! I wondered where it was heading. Would there ever be a loving partner and security?

I tried to have faith and find peace in practicing detachment. Living in the city, amid the cold, polluted air, and crowds, I longed instead to be among the pines and hear the ripples of a clear mountain stream, to breathe fresh air, and be alone with the spirits of nature. Perhaps I needed to be a monk and let the solitude attune my spirit to more peaceful things. My only resolution for 1985 was to continue doing the positive things I was doing.

In April, Alan and I finally found time to go the mountains to hike. On his dashboard was the statement, "Doubt is a belief in limitation."

On the way home, pointing to the statement, I said, "I think that's true."

"How does that work for you?"

"Well, after I first began this job and during the summer, I felt great faith in life and great hope. I felt freed by the job and the possibilities seemed limitless for positive change. I saw the potential, not the limitations, but then I began to focus on the money and believed that would be my reward for good service. When I found that wasn't true, I lost faith and saw only the limitations and now the limitations burden me. The job hasn't changed much, but my perception has, so maybe the actual circumstances have little to do with what I feel; it's my perception that creates the benefits or limitations."

Soon after the conversation with Alan, the secretary at work, who seemed less mature than her sixteen-year-old daughter, lashed out at me in anger when I reminded her of a deadline she seemed in danger of missing. Her laid-back attitude and preference for talking instead of typing was an ongoing problem.

"Look," I said, "If you miss the deadline, it reflects badly on me and you, and you often miss deadlines. This is your job."

She flipped her long dark hair and narrowed her eyes, glaring at me.

"Why are you so angry with me?" I asked.

"Because you're so perfect. You do everything right and your life is so together," she replied venomously, slapping her pen down on the desk.

"My life isn't perfect. I have difficulties, but I still come here and do my job. I don't take it out on you."

She exchanged a meaningful glance with the student workers sitting at desks nearby. So, I hadn't been paranoid in thinking that she and the student workers talked behind my back. She was a negative influence on them. I needed to trust my intuition more. Obviously, I needed to talk to the students. By remaining peaceful, sticking to my values, and believing in myself, I could positively influence the outcome of events. I remembered something that Neal once said. "We need to make something really beautiful out of the clay we have instead of wanting a different kind of clay." I knew Harold wouldn't fire the secretary so I had to win her over, somehow.

It felt as if the whole year was governed by the challenge of a master number. Generally work ran smoothly, but the same problems cropped up repeatedly. The students didn't do their work when I wasn't directly supervising them, and the secretary continued to be unpredictable and to ignore deadlines. I didn't realize how bad the stress was until I had an anxiety attack, which I hadn't had in months. Suddenly my mind shut down and my shoulder seized up. My chiropractor said the muscles felt like bone instead of muscle. I desperately needed a vacation but unfortunately couldn't take time off even to join Carolyn and Donna on a trip to Mexico.

In July, training Mary, the new employee who was supposed to be my assistant, was difficult because she wasn't focused and became defensive whenever I gave her constructive criticism. She wasn't the person I wanted, but Harold had pressured me to hire her, and I was afraid to go against his wishes. I thought she seemed very distracted. I needed her especially for the September start date when we had to find the largest number of student jobs. She had to go to court around that time, but she insisted she could set the date so she'd be available for the start. I was skeptical.

As we approached the September start date, I experienced a really positive time. Several old ideas became unstuck. My friendship with one of the women at work was growing—I was there when she needed me and that created a bond. Harold posted a memo announcing that students had earned $500,000 last year from jobs they received through us; it felt good to get some recognition. In addition, we were hiring another person to work the new evening shift instead of me. My discipline and patience had paid off.

The September start was excellent, and we had more students hired than ever before, even by Harold when he had my job. As I feared, Mary was in court the week I needed her and acted as if I were unreasonable to object to that. Then, when she returned, she accepted a job opening for the students that was unpaid and filled it without notifying me. Harold's rule was that we didn't accept job leads that didn't pay the students. What happened as a result of this was unthinkable.

I felt that this incident and her not working the start date were reasons for her to be reprimanded. When I tried to talk to Harold about this, he became very angry with me. He called her into the office and talked to her, but didn't support my position as her supervisor. Finally, he smiled and said, "Now, you girls need to get along." It was then that I realized that he wouldn't fire or reprimand her because he liked her flirtatious attention despite the fact that she lived with a man. I'd been warned about his temper, but I didn't think he would do anything to me if I spoke my mind because I'd done such a good job for him. It didn't occur to me until later that I may have done my job too well by exceeding his numbers.

Before I knew it, Harold started blaming me for all the problems in the office, even for the secretary that he hired who was so incompetent. Mary continued to violate his rules with impunity, and once again I tried to get him to take action or change the rules. He became very irritated with me for bothering him and he asked if I could work with Mary. I knew it was dangerous for me not to agree, but my mind was very clear, and unable to stop myself, I said, "No." He flushed bright red immediately, and I thought he was going to have a heart attack. "You're fired," he shouted, "be gone by the end of the day." Surely, he wasn't serious. After working so hard for him, he discarded me like a piece of trash. I left his office and went immediately to the director of the school, but she refused to talk to me.

I thought surely he would calm down and take me back, but two weeks later, when the director finally took my call, she supported him because he had accused me of insubordination. When I learned that he and she had originally opened the school together, I knew that was the end of it. However, the way he fired me violated company policy. If I protested and asked friends at the school to testify for me, he would find a way to hurt them. I couldn't ask them to jeopardize their jobs. I wrote letters to the members of the executive committee thanking them for the opportunity of working there and was grateful for the wonderful support of my friends and family. The shock of being fired from a job I did so well would haunt me for far too long and undermine my confidence, but in the weeks immediately following the event, I was surprised how little fear I felt.

Time to Love

When one door closed, miraculously another opened, and amazingly it was the door to Neal's heart. In a telephone conversation, I was shocked when he said to me, "Georganne, I was wrong. I do want a monogamous relationship. I do want us to be together more and would like for you to be in Seattle."

"I'd like that too. Unless we're together, we'll never know if our relationship can really work." A feeling of joy and hope filled me. Despite our differences, I knew he wouldn't expect me to be a traditional woman, and because of our art, we had a deeper connection than I'd ever had with a man. Perhaps we could take what was good between us and create a relationship that would benefit us both.

Still, I wondered why he had been afraid to express his feelings, and as he opened up, I found the courage to ask, "Why are you afraid of a relationship?"

It took him a moment to find the words. "Because I'd have to change my image of myself, and that scares me."

"What do you mean?"

He laughed, "I think I'm the lone cowboy riding the range who doesn't need a woman."

"Really?"

"I'm afraid so. I bought into the Western image of a man, and I've got to come to terms with it. It's hard to admit I need a woman, but I do need you."

"What is it about me that you need?"

He laughed shyly, a bit uncomfortable with answering my direct question. "Well, I like talking to you, making love—you are the most generous woman I've ever known when we make love, and I like your cooking too."

"My cooking! Really?" I couldn't help laughing because I was notoriously undomesticated although I did try to cook simple, healthy meals. "What a surprise."

"Well, surprises make it more interesting, don't they?"

"Yes, when they're good surprises like your wanting me to come to Seattle. You know, I will have to get a job there."

"That's good. Whatever you need to do. I'm behind you all the way. I want you to find whatever will make you feel secure."

"Neal, when it comes to work, I really worry that you won't approve of what I choose."

"No, the more successful and glamorous you are," he joked, "the more I'm attracted to you." He sighed deeply, "I really need you here." His voice was soft and sincere, embracing me in its warmth. I felt invigorated despite the cold and snow falling outside. He was my soul mate and I knew we were meant to be together.

I was excited, but also nervous and needed some reassurance. The next time I saw Gladys, I was almost afraid to ask, "Does Neal really mean it when he says he wants a committed, monogamous relationship with me or is he just creating illusions again?" I leaned forward, my elbows on the table.

"Allow yourself some freedom to accommodate the relationship and experience the value that is there. You're not making a decision and he isn't making a decision. Don't feel there's a commitment beyond the experience of establishing a relationship with the consideration that has not been a factor before."

Her words helped because I was so emotional that it was difficult to be objective. This was a way of thinking about the situation that made me comfortable. Perhaps with consideration and trust, we could build the respect again.

I wasn't successful finding work in Denver. Gladys said that the market would be stimulated in January, February, and March, and she encouraged me to job-hunt in Seattle and not go there cold turkey. She also suggested I go to school part time to develop more job skills, so I planned to take a computer course.

I asked again about Neal's commitment to our relationship. Gladys said, "He may have difficulty considering your choices as he makes his choices, but there has to be a period of adjustment. Don't expect too much too soon. Growth and support are what allow a relationship to grow, so you need to support each other's strengths and help each other be responsible in your own lives. Respect each other's needs to make different choices."

"Gladys, one thing that bothers me is Neal's image of himself as a man who doesn't need a woman."

"Well, it isn't really about his manhood. He's talking about a stereotype, but his feelings have no gender. The stereotype is that a man should be competitive, but some men would prefer not to compete like they think they're supposed to do. You have different ideas than the ones expressed in the environment where you grew up. That environment was wrong, but your feelings aren't wrong. You should applaud yourself that you are free of some of the stereotypes."

"It's just so confusing to know how I should be as a woman sometimes."

"If what you experience is different from the ideas you thought, the ideas were wrong. This is the best guide."

Taking a deep breath, I admitted, "I'm really afraid. I want to go to Seattle, but what do you really think about this?"

She paused to listen for guidance, then continued. "Overall, concerning the relationship with Neal, you will experience a degree of benefit so that you will not develop too great a burden. In going to Seattle, you need to perceive that you are investing in some beneficial things for your future. The only thing you need to spend money for right now is for new skills, not career counseling. In the relationship, you need to give the most attention to trust. You should maintain it through consideration and respect and giving each other freedom of choices. With those in place, you will develop a relationship that benefits you both without your fears being stimulated. If you decide to let go of the relationship, you will feel that is all right, and it won't be that painful for either of you, but with those things in place, most people decide to go on." She smiled and patted my hand. Her words gave me hope.

* * *

Nineteen eighty-six started out being a wonderful year, though Gladys warned it would be difficult. This year was the turning point when six percent of the population would reach a consciousness level where real change could occur. I was fearful and excited about my trip to Seattle as I finalized the plans. I wasn't waiting to find a job there, and even though I knew that it was a risk, I usually was stimulated by the risks I took and often grew from those new experiences.

I had a dream that I was outside a house with someone and started to cross an open space, looked up, and saw a big cat walking around the corner from behind the house. She was a medium brown Siamese as big as the house; we saw her from a mouse's eye view. We dashed inside, barely escaping from her sight. My mother was inside and said, "Thank goodness she's gone. You chased her away. She was howling one night when Uncle Henry and his girlfriend were here—I mean really howling." In the dream, I remembered that evening. I was inside and wasn't afraid of the cat. The size of the cat in this dream led me to believe that whatever it symbolized, perhaps intuition or feminine instinct, was important.

In Seattle, Neal shared an old Victorian house with two roommates. They had their own rooms and shared a bath and kitchen. On the top floor, he had a spacious living and sleeping room and a separate kitchen and private bath. It was cozy and warm with a wood burning stove and rocking chair.

Nearly every day was rainy, cold, and dreary, but at least I knew how beautiful the city was in summer. If the sun came out at all, it did so around noon and by 3:00 pm had started going down.

The first few days were a touchy time when I feared that being there was a mistake. Just before I left Denver, I was offered a job registering students for the classes at a computer store. I wondered now whether I should have taken it. Neal and I were naturally going through a few adjustments, but after four or five days we found more balance. I was grateful for his sensitivity about my feelings and was touched by his discipline, patience, and understanding. We gave each other some space during the day but were always together in the evening, and that time was sweet and healing.

After a week or so, I began to wonder what he'd told his friends and housemates about my being there. This time, I wasn't just visiting, but I had the impression he had explained very little. Without a job or definition for the relationship, I felt a bit unanchored. I started to look for work and took a computer class at the university. Trying to balance all of that with the relationship was stressful.

One evening after we settled into his space, I noticed Neal seemed very restless when I started talking about getting a job. Finally I asked, "What's going on with you?"

"I don't know what to tell you about a job. I'm feeling very tied down here in Seattle. I don't really want to be here."

"Now that I'm in Seattle, you don't want to be here?" I realized I was shouting.

"It's not that I don't want to be with you. We could go anywhere we choose, couldn't we?"

"I suppose," I looked at him puzzled. "What do you want to do?"

"I want to sell one of the houses so I can move anywhere."

I knew from the problems he was having with the houses that wasn't realistic. "Where do you want to go?"

"I don't know. I don't have a specific place in mind yet."

I could tell he was feeling trapped again and needed to hope moving was possible.

"If you knew that, you could begin building a base there and so could I, but since you don't, what the hell am I supposed to do. I need money. Should I look for something permanent or temporary?"

He threw up his hands. "I don't know." I looked at him and shook my head. Why did he always have to complicate everything? Sometimes I couldn't tell when he was talking hypothetically and when he was serious. Maybe this would pass.

After completing the computer courses, I found that I had too much time on my hands and begin looking further for a job. Rather quickly, I was interviewed for a position selling copy machines and thought I would be offered the job. I knew Neal was feeling pressured because of the work he was doing on his houses, but I needed to know where he thought our relationship was going because I might soon have to make a decision about the sales job. On Friday, he agreed to think about it. On Sunday night, I brought it up again when he was packing his tools for the next day.

"Neal, I need to talk to you." He looked up. "I asked you last week where you think our relationship is going and you haven't said anything. Are you avoiding this?"

"No, I just haven't thought about it. Look, ninety percent of the time I'm in my own head, and I can only give someone else ten percent."

"I think those percentages are little low for a relationship to work." Puzzled by his response, I asked, "What's your idea of a perfect relationship?"

"Well," He stopped fooling with tools and stood thinking for a moment.

"The Victorians had the right idea—the man was at sea most of the time and the woman took care of the home and kids."

I laughed, "Be serious."

He laughed, "I am."

"That's ridiculous!"

"No," he said becoming angry, "what's ridiculous is the amount of time and energy I spend on this relationship. You demand so much that I've been neglecting my parents and children."

I was taken aback but couldn't help laughing. "Is that a joke? You seem to have forgotten you weren't spending your time with me the last year. You were running around the country with your last girlfriend."

He said nothing and started digging through drawers.

"So where are we now?"

"Georganne, I can't make a commitment to marriage because I don't have the financial resources."

So that was it. I always knew when he came up with an extreme story, he was hiding his real feelings. I was touched that he wanted to be able to support me. "Neal, why do you think that? I don't need you to support me."

"I don't know. That's not clear to me."

We talked about alternatives, but I saw none and he had none to offer. Finally he offered, "I want to do all I can to help you."

"But as things are, you'll never be around, and as we know, a long-distance relationship is pretty limited interaction. That's not what I want."

Despite the underlying tension, the next week was a nice one: we had fun and laughed often. Then, one night as we sat reading, a telephone call interrupted the silence.

"Hey man, what's up? You did? Fantastic. Sure. Sure. You can count on me. Hold on a minute."

He put his hand over the phone and turned to me, "Joel's bought a twenty-six foot sloop that's moored in Bellingham, and he wants me to help sail it home."

"When?"

"This weekend."

"But Friday is Valentine's Day."

"I don't care about that, do you?" he said almost flippantly.

His words cut through me. "Yes, I do."

"Oh, really?"

"Yes," I said, knowing my voice now had a steel edge to it.

"Well, Joel, I'll get back to you. Yeah, I will soon. See ya."

He hung up the phone and turned to look at me. I could tell from his expression that he saw I was not happy with his response.

"What is wrong with you?" I said.

"What do you mean?"

"Valentine's Day doesn't mean anything to you? Do I mean anything to you?"

"Of course you do. It's just that Valentine's Day is another example of how holidays are commercialized. It's all about what people buy, not love—another excuse to spend, spend, spend. It's disgusting."

"Well, let me tell you how I feel about it."

"Okay, please do." He sat down across from me, folding his hands in his lap.

"I love you. I'm here because I'm trying to make a life with you. We've loved each other for so long and there have been few Valentine's Days when we've been in the same place to celebrate together. I've been looking forward to celebrating this day with you since you first asked me to come here."

"Oh," he murmured. "I know what you're saying. I just don't much like any holidays. But I really want to do this trip."

"Why?"

"Because…well…it's a male thing…fighting with the elements and all that."

"You can do that anytime."

"But, you know, I'd like to get to know Joel better."

"Why did I come here? You're brain-dead—just like your ex-wife said. If you think it's okay for you to go off and do this on Valentine's Day weekend, then you must be brain-dead."

He chuckled uneasily, "Maybe she was right."

By this time I was so angry and hurt, I could feel the heat in my face. I continued to glare at him and then realized what I needed to do. "Okay, Neal, it's okay for you to go on the trip, but I want to go, too. I'm not going to stay here by myself without transportation while your housemates feel sorry for me because you took off on Valentine's Day."

His mouth dropped open. "You want to go?"

"Most certainly."

"Well, I'll have to ask Joel."

"Okay."

"You know I need some time away from you. I can't spend every minute with you. I need to be with the guys sometimes."

"I understand, but this is on Valentine's Day."

"But it's hard work sailing. I mean, I couldn't entertain you.

You'd have to stay out of the way."

"That's fine. I understand."

"But it's going to be very cold and wet, not very pleasant. It may take three days. That's a long time to be miserable."

"I don't care. I was a Girl Scout. I'm tough. Either you stay here with me or I go on the trip or else I walk out that door and never come back."

"Okay, you can go," he said, but his dejected tone of voice told me I wasn't really welcome, "I'll check with Joel, later. I need to take a walk."

After he left the room, I cried. What was the point of my staying in Seattle any longer? His attitude was shocking, and I realized there was still much about him I didn't understand, but by the next morning, I had cooled off and decided to call Gladys before I made any drastic decisions. I was surprised when she said, "It's beneficial to stay. Both the conflict and good times are reality. He's feeling inadequate to deal with the relationship, so he sees himself as inconsiderate and selfish."

On the following day, he and I talked again. "I'm not feeling very good about the way I handled this," he admitted, "It was a shock for me to realize I could be so selfish. I didn't think I was like that."

"You can choose not to be like that."

"I don't know if I can," he said, looking away. "I think you need to face the fact that I may not change. I'm not even sure I really want a relationship."

By the following morning, Neal had thought things through, so we talked quietly and came to some point of harmony. I thought we were okay, but it was difficult, especially because I was trying to decide whether I should take the sales job I had been offered the same day Joel had called. Of course, feeling that the relationship was tenuous, I decided I couldn't afford to say yes. I depended on Neal for a place to live and transportation, and perhaps he was feeling that he had overextended himself. I saw his point about holidays, but I also believed they were whatever you made them.

During this time together, I'd seen a soft, vulnerable side of

Neal that I hadn't often seen. Despite his need for independence, he really did like to be loved, hugged, and kissed frequently, but he had built strong defenses against needing any affection from anyone.

Once we began the trip, I was truly excited. This was my first sailing adventure and I was perfectly happy to serve as the galley slave. I had hoped to learn to sail, but before the first afternoon was over, a storm hit and we had to motor until the afternoon of the third day. The men struggled with the elements on deck, and I stayed in the cabin out of their way, taking them maps or tools and preparing the food. Fortunately, Neal had had the foresight to insist that we cook chili and soup ahead of time. It was a lifesaver because we had to moor in a residential cove the first night and stay on board. As Neal and I crawled into the sleeping area under the bow, I snuggled up to him, glad to have a close moment, but he didn't respond.

Still, I was glad I went. The sky, water, and changing tides were beautiful. It was magical in the early morning, slipping through the passages between tiny mounds of islands, disappearing into the fog like creatures silently invading another dimension. Frolicking seals escorted us in open water, and we fed the ducks that approached the boat with enthusiastic quaking. It was heavenly being so close to nature on the open water, but I never appreciated food, warmth, and dry clothes as much as I did the night we docked at Kingston. It was a luxurious delight to stand in a hot shower after sailing in a storm for two days and never feeling dry. We devoured our dinner of hot salmon, potatoes and green beans as if we hadn't eaten for days.

Had I done the right thing? Perhaps I should have let Neal go alone. I had hoped somehow the experience would bring us together, but he kept his distance and subordinated himself to Joel's wishes, which was not an easy task with the storm and Joel's temperamental behavior. On the third morning, as we slipped out of an inlet, we hit something underwater, and I was thrown into the bulk head striking my head so hard that I literally saw stars and became nauseous. The men hardly noticed when I went below to lie down. I spent most of the day in misery, but by late afternoon, the nausea subsided. Throughout the trip, I was tolerated, and what sharing took place was between Neal and Joel.

By the time we returned home the evening of the third day, I wanted only a hot bath, food, and about two days of sleep. Walking up behind Neal and putting my arms around him, I said, "I'm so glad we shared this adventure, Neal. I really admire how patient you were with Joel."

"Thanks," he said, pulling away.

Finally, the next day he started talking as we sat by the fire. "You know, up until last week, I was operating on the assumption that marriage was a possibility for us, but when I completely disregarded your feelings about Valentine's Day, I realized that's how I am. I probably won't change, and I don't want to be responsible to you."

"So, you're not willing to make any effort to change. You don't love me enough to even try? How can learning to be more thoughtful be a bad thing?"

"Look, this relationship isn't going to work. Our differences are just too great."

"Maybe so, but no relationship will work for you if you don't show a woman consideration."

"Not everyone demands as much as you do."

"Really? What would your perfect relationship look like?"

"It wouldn't be as hard as this," he said adamantly. "I'd have someone to be intimate with when I wanted it, which wouldn't be very often. She would be there to help me with daily work and other burdens, but not expect me to be close all the time."

"So you don't want to have to help me, but you want me to help you."

"I want you to be successful so I don't have to feel responsible for you."

"I've never asked you to be responsible for me. I want you to be responsible in the way you treat me, not take care of me."

"You say that, but it isn't true."

"What if I decided to stay in Seattle? Would you even want to see me?"

He thought a minute. "If you were in Seattle, I'd probably want to spend a couple of hours with you during the week and one day on the weekends, but not every weekend."

"So, you don't really want much sharing, not the daily sharing I want?

"No, I want to keep my life just as it is. I don't want to share much of it with anyone."

Later, Neal decided he wanted just a platonic relationship. During the last few weeks, he had began to see me more as a whole person and liked what he saw, but he decided he didn't want to be sexual.

"Sex is my weakness and I don't want to deal with it. Women always use me."

I had to bite my tongue to refrain from pointing out that he had used sex to manipulate women. Instead I asked, "Do you feel I've used you?"

"No, not you. I haven't felt used by you," he admitted, but he couldn't explain either why he was making this choice. I had no doubt that he made it out of fear because he was doing what he'd always done when it was time to make a commitment. He still couldn't let go of his image as the lone cowboy on the prairie.

I started crying and couldn't stop. Even breathing was painful. I knew it was over. Neal held me, rocking and stroking me as if I were a child while I cried far into the night for all the times I'd hoped I had found my life partner and all the times I'd been disappointed.

He tried to wipe away some of my tears and said, "I didn't want to hurt you this much, but you have too many illusions about our relationship. You need to let go of them."

What I saw as hope, he saw as illusions that needed to be destroyed even at the expense of being cruel. I had nothing without hope. I felt despairing, empty, and deeply sad, and his frequently changing his mind about us made me crazy because there were other things he said that indicated he wasn't so sure he didn't want the relationship. When I questioned him about this, he said, "I don't know what I'm feeling. I've told you what I'm capable of right now. It isn't much, but it's all I can do."

"Well, it's not enough."

Maybe I was screwing up again. Maybe I didn't need an answer about where we were going; everything could turn out all right. Maybe I was challenging his fear too soon. I was sad that I forced him to give me answers. When I'd done that in the past, I'd always lost. But did it matter in this case? We had known each other for almost eight years. I was tired of waiting for him to value the good between us enough to make adjustments for me to be in his life. And I was tired of begging him to give us another chance. I'd begged Gary to stay, and in the end, it had been to no avail.

One evening, his friends Jessie and Tad stopped by. Jessie and I sat in the kitchen drinking tea. She asked me why I was going back to Denver. I hinted it was in part because of Neal. She said, "I love Neal, he's a dear, but I wouldn't wait around for him. Of course, maybe if someone hung around long enough she might catch him." She was warm and joking, and I knew she meant no harm, but it did hurt. It was difficult to come so close, yet still be so far away from where I wanted to be with him.

I dreamed that Neal, as a teenage boy, and I were in a dark, underground labyrinth where there was little light. It was damp and like a tunnel with low ceilings. There was another Neal somewhere in the tunnels who had killed a woman with auburn hair. I saw her body, and I knew he was going to kill me too, but the Neal I was with protected me. That was how this felt—one side of Neal was destructive, the other was loving. Every time we talked about our love, he seemed very confused. For days, I vacillated between wanting him out of my life permanently and trying to be just a friend. According to Gladys, he felt inadequate to deal with the relationship and was still making adjustments. She thought I should stay, but I didn't understand why.

One day it was clear to me that I needed this to be over. I had done everything I knew to do to make the relationship work. We were standing in Neal's work area talking, and he was throwing tools around as if he were trying to pack a small tool chest. On the workbench sat the Valentine's Day card he'd never finished. I was trying to discuss the positive aspects of our relationship, but in a mean tone of voice he snapped, "Yeah, there were good times, but I have to put up with this all the time too."

"Oh, you mean my crying and grieving when you push me away and reject me?"

"Everything makes you cry. It doesn't matter what I do."

I turned and walked away. If nothing had changed in the next week, I'd fly back to Denver. I wanted to be sure I was making the best decision and not making it out of anger or fear. Later in the day, when I told Neal about the deadline, he said, "I do want to change some things. I feel like I need to deal more realistically with you, and it will take several months to do the things I need to do."

"Like what?"

"I don't know how I feel about my art work or where I really want to be. If I decide to go elsewhere, I could make arrangements to do that in a few months."

"What do I do? I have to start making money to pay my bills right away. If I get a good job in Denver, I can't just up and leave it."

"I don't think this is as inflexible as you see it, but our relationship does depend a lot on what we're each doing with our work."

"So we're right back to the same argument. You can't accept and respect my working in a system. If I were self-employed, you'd be okay with that, right?"

"Yes, but…"

"No, there aren't any more 'buts'—you still don't get it. I've tried for years to be self-employed, and it hasn't worked well for me, and I don't have parents who will lend me thousands of dollars to buy a studio. I have to work for other people."

"But I want you to be happy."

"No, if you truly did, you'd accept my reality and be supportive of what I need to do."

I scheduled a return flight to Denver. In Seattle, I'd become a more loving person and developed more patience and the ability to do my share in developing a relationship, so I was at peace with that. However, with every conversation we had, I felt that Neal was more of a stranger.

The night before I left, we curled up in bed under several quilts, the place where so many deep discussions had taken place. "Neal, before I go, I'd like to know what you actually feel about me. Clearly, it's different from what I've felt about you."

He was silent for a moment, then sighed. "Apart from the physical feelings I have for you, I don't feel any different than I feel toward my other friends. I love you, but I'm not in love with you."

I was surprised. "Then why were we even thinking about marriage?"

"You're the only woman I know with whom it seems possible."

"Oh." I didn't know what to say. I was a practical choice. That certainly took all the romance out of it. As he'd said before, for him, there was something missing. Was this love, free of illusions? Even Gladys had pointed out that I created illusions in my relationships.

"I really meant it when I said I wanted to change some things. I know I've been sloppy about the relationship. I haven't had the integrity or strength I wanted to have nor the discipline. I feel bad about it, and I know I need to change these to have a good relationship with anyone."

He sounded sincere, but I didn't believe he'd follow through.

Turning Over New Leaves

Back in Denver, I reflected on my time in Seattle. I would always miss the honest communication that Neal and I shared, for I had had none of that in my marriage. Although it was sometimes painful, it made it possible for us to be good mirrors for each other. I began to see my survival pattern more clearly. This was the behavior pattern I acted out when I experienced fear. With Neal, I became emotionally involved with the things he said and took them as a rejection if they didn't fit with my ideas. Then I tried to make him feel bad about what he was doing, and I succeeded, so he didn't feel adequate to deal with me. That was how I defeated myself. When he didn't feel good about himself, he withdrew and I felt abandoned. When we argued, he heard his ex-wife saying she was going to control him, and I heard Gary saying he was going to leave me. Not only did I need to forgive Neal, I needed to forgive myself for the part I played in this disaster.

Gladys warned me not to think of going back to Seattle until Neal and I determined the values and difficulties in continuing the relationship and were committed to changing the difficulties. However, by the time Neal came through Denver on his way to see his parents, my intuition was shouting, "Look at the reality, end it now, break the cycle." I had no faith that he would make the changes he promised. When he needed me, he told me what I wanted to hear, but when he didn't need me, he pushed me away. Sitting on the living room sofa, we talked carefully for a moment, then I turned to him, my stomach burning with dread, knowing I had to end this. "Neal, every contact I have with you leaves me feeling angry or diminished in some way. You aren't supportive of me emotionally because your constant ambiguity leaves me never knowing what to expect from you. I wonder if you'll be there if I need you. I just can't go on with this."

He pulled back, looking shocked. "Well, that's certainly honest." He was very quiet for a moment avoiding my gaze.

"There's really no point in my staying, is there?"

"No, there isn't." I choked back the tears, praying I had the courage not to reach out to him.

He quickly gathered up his bags and left, not angrily, but sadly. I too felt sad, but peaceful and strong. I had ended my addiction to him.

Although I ended the relationship with Neal, I knew I wouldn't be able to really let go until I understood his behavior, so I talked further with Gladys.

"Gladys, I know Neal's erratic behavior is fear-based, but…"

"His survival pattern is selfishness," she interrupted. "That's what he uses to protect himself. Like most men, he thinks that feeling what you feel is a weakness. He only does what he needs to do to make himself happy. He doesn't worry about others. What you need to do is to live each day fully—to experience as much value as you can without getting into the 'buts' and 'what ifs.' That doesn't mean to live without responsibility or concern for others, but don't analyze what each day is."

"So did Neal have trouble with our relationship because I expected him to be responsible and other women didn't?"

"Yes, that's right. When you were upset about his lack of concern on the sailing trip, you were looking for things that proved he rejected you. It wasn't that he rejected you. He never accepted you. His fears stimulated your fear that he rejected you, and your abandonment fears from childhood became a part of your present fear."

"But I wasn't ever abandoned as I child. I had a lot of loving people around me."

"The abandonment fear doesn't actually have to be related to an actual event; it could just be a perception of fear. Often, that is worse than an actual rejection, and all one can do is keep adjusting the mind to release the fear."

I was puzzled by her comment, but later I remembered all the times my mother left the house, angry with my father, and drove around for an hour or two while I feared she wouldn't return.

"But what is so confusing is that he was often very loving, and he accepted things about me that other men haven't accepted."

"In Neal's case," she explained, "it was the relationship he had trouble with, not you. He didn't want the relationship on the same level that you did and that created the conflict. If you had accepted the relationship on the level he wanted it, there could have been value for you, but for a relationship to work, both persons have to contribute to it."

"So my expecting respect and consideration was too much?"

She looked at me very seriously. "Don't be hard on yourself. I don't think it was wrong of you to want something different than what he wanted. If you let go of your fear, the reasons for hanging onto Neal will be gone."

I knew it would take time to release the false sense of security Neal gave me, so I tried to focus on finding a job, my most immediate need. Most of the permanent jobs for which I interviewed had set hours, low pay, and the managers seem manipulative or downright dishonest. Most sales jobs were commission only. With the weak economy, good jobs were scarce, but I quickly found a temporary job with a mortgage company. When I thought about my future, I wondered whether moving to New Orleans to be near my family would be wise. Gladys advised there might be fewer difficulties there in the job hunt, but there would be other restrictions.

After working at a temporary job for six weeks, I was hired as a loan service clerk at a mortgage company where most employees were women. I began with great enthusiasm, believing I would be treated with more respect there. The work was less demanding than the art school so I had the energy to start writing, something I'd wanted to do since I was a child. To stimulate my creative juices, I took a modern jazz class and a writing class.

It was good to have structure back in my life with the challenge to learn new things. I was amazed by the process I'd been through and how beautifully my mind was working. Over the previous few months, when I was confronted with decisions, the information came to me as I needed it. I weighed it and dealt decisively with each situation. When I was dealing with other people, I paid more attention to my interactions and how my words affected others.

At work, I observed the interpersonal dynamics, even sympathized with others in a conflicted situation, yet remained somewhat uninvolved, especially because the other women gossiped a great deal and tried to pull me into it. When I didn't respond and participate, I could see they thought I was unfriendly. Fitting in was tricky because they also took the attitude not to let their work interfere with their lives. With time, the situation became more difficult. I tried to practice letting go of my fears, but there was something about my mind that tenaciously clung to the fear. Breathing into what felt like the connection between the mind and the fear sometimes helped me to let go, but the process wasn't automatic yet.

Thanksgiving at my grandmother's house in Arkansas was a delightful change. My brother and I revived a family tradition by climbing the back side of Pinnacle Mountain, the site of many pleasant hikes in our childhood. My sister-in-law, niece, and nephew joined us. Like a little mountain goat, my six-year-old niece scrambled over boulders and rocks, almost always seeing the trail marker and following it. When she slipped and scraped her knee, she paused for a moment, decided it wasn't worth crying over and rushed ahead, leaving behind her father carrying her toddler brother. I loved her fearlessness.

After a while, we stopped to rest and I remembered the joy I always felt on the mountain. As a child, I loved being surrounded by the energy of all living things. I liked hiking in the fall, hearing the crunch of leaves beneath my feet, smelling the pungent odor of pine, and admiring the red, yellow, and orange of the leaves. As we hiked, my parents taught my brother and me to identify the birds, trees, and rocks that we saw long before we studied them in school. At least once a year, we climbed Pinnacle Mountain, a steep climb up the front path where we had to stop several times to catch our breaths.

One Sunday afternoon, when I was still in elementary school, we finally reached the top of the mountain, and my father decided to climb down the back side. We had never done this because it was very steep with only a hint of a path, and farther down, we had to scramble over a large area of boulders.

Mother protested, "That's too hard for the kids. They'll get hurt if they fall."

My father looked at her disgusted. "They're not going to fall. I'll go first and show them the way."

As we approached the edge of the mountain and looked down, it looked pretty rugged to me. I felt anxious and wanted to back out of this, but I didn't want to disappoint my father. At first, there was a tiny path, then we had some trees and large roots to hold onto until it became so steep we couldn't stand upright. Eventually, we stopped in front of a rather precarious crevice. My father studied the spot carefully then called to me. My heart beat faster.

"Okay, Anne, after I get across, you start across."

"Okay," I agreed, trying not to show my fear.

My father stepped across the crevice and turned to me. "All right, that rock right below you is secure. Step on it and hold onto the branch above."

Shaking inside, I did as he said. "Good, now you're going to have to stretch down with your left leg quite a ways, so bend down and hold onto that big root. It was strong enough to hold me, so it'll hold you."

The stretch was almost too far for my leg to reach, but then he was there to help lift me down. "Good girl."

"Thanks, Daddy." My father was a great mountain-climber, and I was very proud he approved of my climbing. It didn't seem so frightening after all. Smiling to myself, I realized my heart was beating normally, and I felt stronger somehow.

Calling out that he was ready to move on, my brother broke my reverie. Leaving this warm memory, I wished now that a strong hand would reach out and help me step across the crevices that appeared in my life's path. Watching my niece heading up the mountain, I prayed that she would retain her fearlessness into adulthood.

After a delightful Christmas with my Nebraska friends, I returned to Denver to begin 1987. Celebrating my new friend Jane's fiftieth birthday with her exuberant women friends was a great way to begin the year. We ate, danced, made collages, exchanged our gifts, and soaked in the hot tub. Jane read what I had written for her and everyone thought it was beautiful. My writing gave me much pleasure, and although I hadn't written poetry in a long time, I wrote two poems in one day.

Economically, I was in a better situation than last year, but it drove me crazy that the men I found interesting showed no interest in me, and the ones I didn't like, liked me. What was that about? My heart went out to another friend who now, a year later, was finally letting go of the man she loved and to Jane, too, as she struggled to let go of the need for a man in her life. It was such a shame—here we were, such loving and interesting women who had to condition ourselves to the idea we might never have a healthy relationship with a man. That was a tragedy. Would the men catch up in time? So many men still wanted a woman to subordinate all her needs to theirs. Would they grow and change quickly enough that we would benefit from their changes?

Facing the hurtful memories of last year's Valentine's Day made this February extremely sad, but it was even more devastating because, despite all my efforts to please my employer, I was laid off. I had trained a new employee to do everything I did, supposedly, so we would have a more flexible office. When she was fully trained, they let me go because I did not, in their words, "fit in." Facing unemployment again in an unstable economy seemed like a nightmare from which I'd never awake.

Most of the time I was peaceful, but it was hard to understand why, with that centeredness in place, life continued to be such a struggle. "Don't let being laid off destroy your faith in yourself or others," Gladys warned. It all came down to my mind and how I perceived the situation. I just had to keep doing what needed to be done.

Fortunately, a wonderful critique group grew out of the writing class I had taken. I sent my first short story off to a contest I didn't win, but, if nothing else, the story made the people in my group laugh, and that made me happy. A nice friendship developed with Frank, one of the men in the group, and I quickly found a job at another mortgage company as a loan clerk working on the processing side of the business.

Frank called one afternoon and we talked for over an hour about religion, poetry, and being in love. He was a short, teddy bear of a guy with thinning gray hair who had his own financial business and was funny and open. When he started talking about his negative feelings toward institutions and authority, I felt a knot in my stomach because he sounded like Neal. However, when I released my fear, I realized I didn't have much good to say about them either. Then, in the critique group, I was surprised he related to my poem about a woman's transformation.

"So how do you feel it relates to you?" I asked.

"For me as an accountant, transformation is cyclical. I feel reborn after tax season every year."

We all laughed knowing he was serious but couldn't resist making a joke.

"You know, I wasn't sure that particular poem would translate for men."

"Men do have a lot of feelings, you know, but we've been taught not to show them, so they come out in physical ways."

"How do you mean?"

"I express them in my stories. Although when I write about women characters, I'm always concerned I'll offend women."

"Oh," all the women sighed together the way we did when we thought something a man said was sweet. He blushed and looked down shyly, but unconvincingly, making us laugh again.

At the next meeting, Frank shared a bottle of wine that a client had given him, making the evening more special than usual. We were all engaged in our usual joking and repartee.

"Aren't you reading *Mists of Avalon*, Frank?" I asked.

"Yeah, I'm almost through."

"What do you think of it?"

He hesitated, searching for words. "Well, I think it's really a woman's book. I can see how it's very empowering for women to read about women with power."

We all shook our heads in agreement. "And I'm really enjoying the King Arthur part, but that other stuff ... that's scary."

"Scary? You mean the goddess stuff?" He nodded his head.

"Why?" I had trouble following his answer, but it had something to do with how he found most women and men were going back and forth between the old and new ways and were having a very difficult time.

"But," I said, "I find it hard to understand why, when we have both female and male aspects, developing those can't make us feel more secure and comfortable."

He gave me that blank stare men give women when it's clear the woman understands nothing about what it is to be a man. "That's very intellectual."

I just smiled and shrugged, "Oh, well."

When he left that evening, he made a point of reminding me he was moving into my neighborhood.

"Have you received my welcome letter yet?" I asked.

"No," he said, looking puzzled.

I couldn't help laughing. "Call me when you get it." That definitely piqued his interest. In the letter I welcomed him to the neighborhood and humorously pointed out a few of the local sites like the gang of aggressive squirrels in Cheesman park and the enormous sheep dog whose owners let him run rampant down the street early in the morning, knocking over garbage cans and people, while they sauntered along drinking their coffee. It was only a few days later when he called laughing.

"This was very nice of you and very, very funny."

"Well, I thought you should be forewarned about those squirrels. It was the least I could do for a friend."

"I'll tell you what. If you'll show me the crazy squirrels in the park, I'll tell you about my new short story."

"It's a deal."

We took a walk around the park, then he came in for tea. We talked about writing and relationships, but didn't get into the kind of sexual joking we sometimes did. It was all pleasant and safe. When he left, he said that it was nice to have a friend in the neighborhood, and we'd have to do it again.

Because Frank and I lived so near one another, we started riding to group meetings together. Among other things, I discovered he loved the blues as much as I did. I kept asking to be guided to take the steps that would allow my friendship with Frank to grow. I hadn't experienced too much insecurity, partly because every time I'd reached out, he responded positively. Soon, we had some patterns established, like riding to the group together or taking a walk. With our writing, we'd had moments of very personal sharing. I could see pain in him just as I was sure he could see it in me, but so far we hadn't burdened each other with it and that was good.

One day he agreed to look at one of my stories. "Well," I said, "I'm really pleased you like what I've done with the male character."

"He's a real man's man. It's hard for men to be friends sometimes. Most of my own friends are women."

"Why is that?"

"I guess because I've always been kind of a loner. I've never been into sports very much, at least not enough to really be a man's man."

"I can see where that would be hard if you don't fit the old stereotypes," I said.

"Definitely." I was glad he trusted me enough to be so open.

The downturn in the economy worsened. My company reduced its hours and hoped that the lower rent in a new office and staying on a tight budget would help us survive without layoffs.

Often I felt that the business world didn't value my real talents, but *I* liked who I was. I was grateful for the few people with whom I could connect on a deeper level, including Frank and a couple of women friends. I found it difficult to be around most people, so I felt very alone much of the time. I knew that the strength and belief I needed could only be found within me, not without. Frequently, sharing with others was limited and superficial, and I was filled with a deep longing that was never satisfied.

I wasn't sure where things were going with Frank, and I tried to remember that I shouldn't ask him for proof, but just present him with choices, and if he didn't make the choices I wished, I shouldn't take that as a rejection. He was mature in many ways, and I loved him for saying that he wasn't attracted to young faces anymore. I felt secure with him because he always let me know he wanted to see me again.

The next week was difficult covering for two people at work, trying to complete a great deal of computer work and emotionally dealing with the fact that the company had to cut our pay and hours in order to keep the office open. The anticipation of going hiking with Frank on Sunday kept me going. He had too many good ideas about where to go, so I spent a lot of time organizing the trip and trying to accommodate what he wanted. When he decided he wanted to do a more difficult hike than the one I had planned, I adjusted and ran downtown to get the topographical maps. He was so enthusiastic, I didn't want to disappoint him.

On Wednesday, he called, "I've got some bad news. I got hurt playing volleyball and I'm not sure I'll feel like going on Sunday."

"What happened?"

"I'm so sore I can't move. I played an extremely hard volleyball game to impress a woman who was watching the game. It was stupid of me because I don't exercise often, and I'm so out of touch with my body that I didn't realize how much I was overdoing it."

"Why don't we take the easier hike?"

"I'm not sure I can do that one either. I don't know how I'm going to feel so I want to give you an out if you can find someone else."

I said I'd call friends and see if anyone was available because I desperately needed that time out of doors, but in a little while, he called back, "Georganne, I'm not being fair to you leaving you up in the air, so I need to tell you I'm definitely not going. I'd love to go with you another time."

I appreciated his letting me know about the problem in advance, but I had hoped he would suggest brunch or something else if I couldn't find someone else to go. Besides I was hurt, angry, and surprised that he ruined our plans by trying so hard to impress another woman after I had gone to so much trouble to prepare for the hike.

Struggling to survive the pay cut was stressful, and I lacked the resilience to deal with anything else. The Siren's call to write was pulling at me and both my mother and Gladys warned me to curb my risk-taking tendencies. Playing it safe wasn't my strength. On top of this, the summer heat was oppressive, and without an air conditioner, I wasn't sleeping well. Then, the news I dreaded came —the mortgage office would be closed down in August.

It had been seven years to the month since I arrived in Denver, and the day I received the bad news and the next were the Harmonic Convergence. The timing of the news seemed significant as a cosmic cycle was completed at the same time a cycle in my life was completed. The Harmonic Convergence was the fulfillment of a 5,200-year-old Mayan prophecy, the completion of the separatist, competitive, materialistic age and the beginning of a global consciousness and cooperation guided by spiritual values. At this time, an energy was being sent to the earth to help mankind find balance and make the choices that would lead to the survival of the earth. It was also time for me to reevaluate the path that would lead to my survival.

At dawn, Carol, another friend from the art school, and I joined a circle in a downtown park, encircling six Zuni dancers as they performed dances and rituals, greeting the sun as it rose from the East, sharing their music and wisdom. A Zuni brought incense to each of us, and at the end we all joined in a dance. Soon after Carol and I arrived and were standing behind the circle, I realized that a friend was standing in front of us. When he recognized us, he opened the circle to let us in. As I took other hands, a powerful surge of energy passed through me.

Afterward, Carol and I ate breakfast at Racine's, outside in the sun and breeze, talking of the usual personal things. I told her about a recent conversation with my mother and how, as always, she told me that they were there for me if I needed them, but then my mother had said she hoped I would find work that would use my intelligence and education and provide me with a good living. She was very proud of me, of my persistence and my strength, and what a special person I was. I had no idea she felt that way about me, and I was deeply touched. Her words were very healing.

Carol had to fly to Philadelphia, so I taped the Harmonic Convergence radio broadcast that afternoon for her and anyone else who missed it. It was beautiful and inspiring and increased my sense that I belonged to a global family consciousness. During the first hour, a friend called to tell me about the Convergence, and we talked for an hour or more about how she had used visualization to draw a wonderful man into her life. Later, as I listened to the last hour of the tape, the day moved toward sunset, and I felt centered and powerful. I meditated and visualized health, prosperity and peace for the earth, others, and myself. I felt the full measure of my strength in the visualization, with no intrusion of fear. That was the feeling I wished to maintain. Then I visualized the man I wanted in my life and sent that message out, using my friend's advice about how to do it. Afterward, I meditated a while longer.

Over the next few days, I moved from one phase into another. I could understand and practice what Gladys had taught about releasing the fear, but I needed to go further and visualize exactly what I wanted. Then I needed to work on creating as much value in each day as I could and taking the steps that were there each day. It was time to take a bold new step because it was the dawn of a new age and a privilege to witness the change.

For a while after the hiking incident, Frank and I were uncomfortable, but eventually a new ease and openness grew between us because we had so much in common. We progressed to hugging when we parted, so I thought we had taken another step toward more intimacy. But when I gave a party, I was surprised by the lovely blonde who came with him. It was clear they were fond of each other, and one of my friends observed, "She seems very secure. She knows she's got him." Because I liked her, I didn't feel jealous, only sad and disappointed that he wasn't available. Now I understood why he kept some distance between us.

In the last few months, lower downtown Denver had become a ghost town with rows of empty business spaces. The occupancy rate of newly built high rises had plummeted. Every business in Denver was affected by the oil and gas disaster. After the mortgage company closed, I took a commission-only job selling an employee benefit, the cafeteria plan, but it soon became clear I was unlikely to sell this plan in a sinking economy. The stress was wearing away my health, and my friends were leaving. Carol was transferred to Pittsburgh; Jane was leaving and didn't know where she would decide to live after she traveled around the country for six months, and even Alan was working in Santa Fe most of the time.

My brother's family and our parents were living together, and when my brother offered me a place to stay until I could get a job and settle in, I accepted. I longed to see my nephew and niece grow up. I knew there would be restrictions, but the economy in Louisiana was beginning to improve a little. I had never wanted to live in New Orleans, but I had to admit that its charm and exotic culture were intoxicating for a writer. Perhaps walking through the streets of the French Quarter that inspired Tennessee Williams, William Faulkner, Kate Chopin, and Anne Rice, I would find my muse.

Co-Creating with the Divine

Arriving in New Orleans just before Thanksgiving, I discovered that no one was interested in hiring, only in celebrating the holidays to the extreme. After all, this was the Big Easy. When I did start job hunting, I felt I'd been transported back to the years before age and gender discrimination laws. Many companies weren't interested in employees in their forties, and others blatantly asked illegal questions about marital status and children and didn't care what the law was. I was fortunate to find a sales position with a company that was an agent of a major regional company selling and renting pagers, car phones, and voicemail. My brother and sister-in-law were successful in sales and thought I would be good at it. More importantly, it would provide me with a good income.

Living with my family for several months and seeing old patterns repeated was challenging. I spent most of my youth giving my mother emotional support, then I had to learn what I needed to know about life that she failed to teach me. Sadly, she still hadn't taken responsibility for her own happiness, but at least she was getting out a little. My father also worried me because he seemed depressed, but he agreed to see a counselor to get some help.

Little by little, some things improved, and I could see the changes that Gladys had anticipated coming true. There was hope and light again. The first six months of 1988 were good times on the job. Being a sales person meant that sometimes I was a hero, and I closed a huge deal with a car dealership after a few months. Although generally my selling wasn't great, I was promoted to agent manager, supporting the sales staff and doing product training. The manager explained that this position would support my desire to move up into management. I was grateful for his support and felt that a new cycle of success and prosperity was ahead.

When one of the sales people closed a huge deal, we all went out to celebrate. I dreaded these occasions because the group drank and played pool, and conversation never went beyond the superficial and banal. Drinking with my Nebraska friends had always included serious conversations that bared our souls, but I had nothing in common with these coworkers other than the job.

What a week. Anger, endings, depression. Suddenly, business was down to a very low point after two really good months. I stared at the numbers day after day and they never moved. The stress was unbearable. People were at each other's throats, and it was impossible to keep the sales people in the office long enough to train them on voicemail. I had little resilience for their lying, cheating, and abusive anger. I was beginning to feel that this business wasn't where I belonged. More than ever, I missed the passion I felt for dance and education. It had felt so good to know that what I did helped and inspired others.

I wanted to continue teaching one class of dance a week, but the pay was a quarter of what I earned in Denver. As it turned out, I worked long hours, especially after the manager discovered that an employee was stealing, and I was promoted to office manager. When I discovered that the two top sellers of pagers were regularly selling to drug dealers, I expressed my outrage, but no one cared. I learned that it was better for me to keep my emotions under control. I couldn't change the people with whom I worked. I could only change myself. The major lesson was how to maintain emotional balance and always be harmonious with others regardless of their attitudes toward me.

As I put on my nylons and heels each morning, I often felt as if I were putting on a straitjacket. Now, as I sat listening to Mozart, I felt my soul and heart open. The passion within wanted to burst forth. What a terrible price I paid to support myself and succeed according to society's standards. And New Orleans was a strange place. I was like a fish out of water, trying to breath in the air when I was created to breathe in water. I needed to get back to my writing.

It was nice turning forty-four and having the family celebration to look forward to on the weekend. I was relieved there was no card in the mail from Neal. It seemed longer than two and a half years since I had ended that relationship, and I'd come a long way in the last year. I had the best apartment I'd ever had, had more money than I've ever had, was a manager, and experienced joy and peace much of the time despite the challenges. Unfortunately, I still hadn't found friends with whom I could share my values and thoughts.

A week after my birthday, I received a card from Neal. It was very strange—a Norman Rockwell drawing of Rosie the Riveter. He said that I was remembered for the good things I had given. Carolyn had seen him and said he was depressed, which is why he had sent the card. I was afraid to write or call him because I didn't want that old feeling to come back. When I thought of him, I wanted to remember the good times, but I also remembered the pain when he pulled away. I knew I was much stronger emotionally and spiritually. Perhaps I was even healed and ready for a relationship, but I was also determined to make a better choice the next time.

On February 14, 1989, I felt terrific—solid, clear, peaceful, and joyful. Life was very mysterious. Three years ago, the relationship with Neal was quickly sinking in a little sailboat in the middle of Puget Sound. I wondered how he was doing, so I impulsively decided to call him. After hearing the news that he was engaged and actually talking to him for the first time in three years, I felt relieved, released, and excited again about moving on with my life. I felt the best was yet to come, a feeling I used to have, but that I had lost track of.

It didn't surprise me that Neal, tired of being alone, had decided to get married. It was the same with my ex-husband. They thought they wanted to be free, but the freedom eventually turned to loneliness, and they didn't take the time to learn how to be at peace alone. Maybe I wanted too much in a relationship by wanting more than just companionship, but Neal had spoiled me, because when it was good, it was fantastic. I always saw the freedom and potential, but he always saw the limitations and restrictions.

The day that I talked to Neal, I thought I'd resolved my feelings about him, but later, as I began crying, I realized that I was finally letting go of the residual anger and expectations I had had about him. Soon after we talked, he sent me a picture of him and his wife-to-be. She wore the same silly sunglasses he wore and appeared as eccentric as he. I was furious at his insensitivity in sending the picture but realized that he believed what I said, that I was happy for him. The truth was that I was lying to him and to me. I cut the picture into little pieces and sent it back to him without a message.

He had destroyed my fantasy. Disturbed that I had harbored the idea in the back of my mind that Neal would appear one day and want to marry me, I broke down. I thought he would mature and stop being Don Juan. I had expected to grow old with him and have a hell of a good time. I thought he saw me as the "love of his life." I had never accepted the idea we wouldn't be together some day. How could I have been so stupid?

One morning I had an early appointment at a business, and when I returned to our office, the manager from the main office was there. He had fired the general manager, made the woman who was the sales manager the new general manager, and gave me a choice. I could continue as office manager, a position that was not part of a management track, or if I wanted to be on that track, I could go back to selling. I asked for a raise as office manager because I was working twelve hours a day and was refused, so I chose to go back to selling. I was extremely angry, of course, that the former manager had misled me about being on a management track.

The unrelenting need to adjust my mind in this competitive environment was exhausting and depressing. It never stopped—the change, the abuse, the conflict, the humiliation. The sales manager, fifteen years my junior, didn't have the maturity I had and didn't really care about anyone who couldn't make money for her. I had no respect for her as a person, but she was the one who had power over my future. I'd never seen any indication that she was willing to help anyone else along. My only alternative was to go back to teaching, but the pay in Louisiana was the worst in the country.

Life was strange. Its twists and turns surprised me. Was I really so different from other people or did they think like I did, yet played the roles they needed to play to get through each day? I'd been an actress playing a role this year. Not even my private life was quite my own. The pursuit of money had been empty and actually hadn't brought much to me, but I guess the lesson was that the pursuit of money didn't make me happy; having money wasn't what it was about. Being with this company was an opportunity, but what I'd discovered was that the pressure brought out a greedy, competitive side of my personality that I didn't like. That wasn't the person I wanted to be.

On the other hand, it was a trial; I'd been forced to choose which way I wanted to go and to learn to restrain my overly emotional nature. I'd learned diplomacy and compassion and that everyone needed to have power over her (or his) own life. That was what appealed to me about teaching—I could empower the students and strengthen them for life. Besides, this was an amazing time to be alive. By May 1989, we were witnesses to colossal changes in the world. The Soviet Union was moving toward democracy, and students in China were protesting for democracy. Imagine, China. Who would ever have thought this could happen? The world was shifting so rapidly, and we each, in our own lives, could choose to play a part in that change. I wanted to be a part of it and make a difference, something I could do by teaching students to think. With what I'd experienced the last few years, I had even more to share.

During my first year in New Orleans, I had discovered the Unity Church of Practical Christianity and began to practice the metaphysical principles they taught. If thinking "right" and being in the right place spiritually was the key to having what I needed in life, did I not have what I wanted because I was not aligned spiritually, or did I have everything I needed and didn't know it?

Being back on the street selling was helpful in looking for

other work because I controlled my own schedule. I filled out teaching applications and looked for other jobs in business. I tried to have faith, to surrender to God, and let her be my guide. In my heart, I felt teaching and writing were my calling in life, but I was open to the idea that I might be wrong. There certainly was a reason for my coming to Louisiana. Perhaps it was to become reacquainted with my family. Perhaps it was to see the poverty and how desperate life could be for people. Perhaps it was to learn to create some stability in my life. As I took each step, I experienced new spiritual growth and took a step closer to the next door that would open for me. What I learned from the Unity Church prepared me for the next step, but I didn't know what path to take. God had to work through me. I only knew my path had to benefit, not only me, but the people around me.

I continued to practice denials and affirmations, though I was not entirely clear about the whole process Unity taught. The denials released from the mind the negative aspects of a situation, and affirmations were positive statements that programmed the mind to believe positive ideas. Because I didn't know what to do, one affirmation was a great comfort: "God works with me to will and to do whatsoever she wishes me to do and she cannot fail." I had begun to embrace the feminine image of God as mother, and because I always worked better with a partner, she became my partner. I no longer felt isolated.

A prosperity workshop presented me with a new concept of prosperity: all the good things that came into my life were abundance. I learned the steps to creating prosperity. The first step was to pray and be one with God. The second step was to set goals that were worthy of a child of God. The third step was to pray with affirmations and thanksgiving. The fourth step was to let go of fears and distracting thoughts. The last step was to put real actions behind the goals I'd set.

I was impatient for the divine plan for my life to evolve. I understood that Unity and Gladys were saying the same thing. For a need to be filled or an affirmation to be manifest, conditions had to be right. The people and situations had to be present, but first I had to be open to the possibility, put aside old thoughts, and create circulation so that the new people and situations could come into my life. Were things moving slowly because the elements weren't in place, or did I still need to let go of outdated beliefs?

By reviving my meditation practice, I found a place of silence and stillness. I wanted to hold onto that feeling forever, always to be suspended there, to be that peaceful. I felt reluctant to move forward, knowing I might face chaos again, but I tried to believe even the chaos would offer beneficial lessons. Except for the doubts about finding a job, I felt a deep peace most of the time. Other things were changing in my life. I'd stopped smoking and felt strongly that I wouldn't start again. Surely that was a sign that my good would come to me.

Things that were stuck opened up with three interviews in two days. For each interview, I saw myself as successful, competent, creative, and innovative. When I was offered a position teaching tenth-grade English at an excellent Catholic girl's school, I was excited. It was a tremendous relief to return to education where I always felt competent. I liked the principal—she was funny, and we hit it off, and the school was excellent academically. I couldn't wait to teach world literature, especially Greek mythology.

On the first day of school, the combined sound of so many high-pitched female voices was deafening. They poured into the classroom, hugging friends, and shrieking with delight at being reunited. Before class started, I was nervous about meeting the students. When the bell rang, they tumbled into their seats, but with only a little prompting calmed down for roll call. If I mispronounced a name, someone invariably rolled her eyes or giggled. After passing out a syllabus, I tried to be honest with them and explained that if I didn't know the answer to a question, I would admit it and then find the answer. That seemed to please them, but I could see that trying to understand the minds of fifteen-year-old girls wouldn't always be simple.

As I began to teach, I loved the tired, excited feeling I had every night when I planned the next day's lessons. I was immersed in literature that I loved, doing something worthwhile, and receiving enormous pleasure from it. The word for the year was *giving*, and I felt as if I were overflowing with good things to give.

It was November 1989, and the world continued its rapid change as I witnessed more events I never expected to see in my lifetime. The fall of the Berlin Wall and democratization of Eastern Europe were changing the world structure. There was actually talk of cutting the national defense budget by billions, and the abortion rights issue was changing politics. When I talked to Gladys on the telephone one night, she commented that our own lives were slower to change. The change would come, of course, but we were anxious and impatient for it.

Good changes were also taking place at work. The administration finally acknowledged real problems in the sophomore class that they had not been addressing. One problem was that a group of girls had lied to the counselors about my grading policy on a major project. When I produced the specific guidelines that I had given the students in writing, the counselors realized they were being manipulated. This shaping of young minds and their values was an interesting challenge.

One of the most nerve-wracking parts of being a new teacher was being observed almost every week by the assistant principal. Although I dreaded her visits, she gave me almost immediate feedback, and the new methods she taught made my teaching more successful. When I had taught years ago, I usually lectured; now the methods were more activity-oriented, such as small and large group discussion, projects, and presentations. These methods were more successful in engaging the students in learning and were fun for me as well.

Ten years earlier, I had moved to Denver to start a new life, and in many ways, it had been the real beginning of my spiritual search. I was at peace in a way I hadn't been for a long time and made peaceful friends from my spiritual community. During the last few years, my concept of God had changed from the traditional Protestant one to a loving energy that permeated all creation. The secret to staying balanced was to keep my spiritual link strong and have faith, for when I did this, God helped me navigate the choppy waters. When I was in touch with God's love, I loved myself and was able to love others. No link in the universe had so much power for me, and it helped me be the person I wanted to be.

Navigating the Inner Landscape

Life cycled through its seasons, bringing endings and beginnings. We expected the oldest to go first and lived in fear that their going would be full of suffering, but at least we knew it was an end. But my great-aunt Eva was somewhere between living and not living, brain damaged from a stroke, out of touch with reality, and no longer able to care for herself or my grandmother. As we moved my grandmother to New Orleans to live with my parents, I grieved for my aunt, who had been like a second grandmother to me, who lovingly massaged my tiny aching legs when I had rheumatic fever, and who took me to lunch at Frankie's Cafeteria every fall to celebrate the start of school. I would never know that woman again, but I was thankful that my mother's cousin, whom my aunt had reared, would care for her and love her like we did.

Despite any difficulties in life, one thing was absolutely good and true—my relationship with God, who guided me each day. When I affirmed and prayed and didn't receive what I wanted, I knew to look for anger within. If it was there, I had to release it; otherwise, it blocked the manifestation of what I desired. I also knew that I might not receive what I wanted because it wasn't appropriate or the time wasn't right. I tried to remember what Gladys had said: "You will always receive what you need, but it may not come in the form you expect or at the time you wish."

During the summer, I took a literature class on the 1960s to renew my teaching certification, and it brought back the memories of that time when my generation thought we could change the world. Now, I tried to do that through my teaching, especially teaching young people to think for themselves. I was always shocked when people said that teachers didn't need better salaries because they worked only six hours a day. The actual working day was ten to twelve hours with all the planning, paper grading, extracurricular assignments, and meetings. When had I ever had a weekend off? Like many teachers, I often worked in offices during the summer to make ends meet.

Working in a private school meant there were no limits to what could be required of me, but at the same time, there were few discipline problems. I could actually teach, and most parents were supportive. Still, not being a Catholic or graduate of the school meant that I was an outsider. Most of the teachers at lunch clustered around one table where there was little room and only a couple of friends ate at the larger table with me. In general, people in New Orleans formed friends based on what high school they had attended. If you were not from New Orleans, it was difficult to fit in.

In December, just before Christmas, my second nephew was born, a little angel with a head full of golden curly hair. The other kids had become curious toddlers before I lived near them, so it was a joy to interact with this child from the very beginning of his life. Whatever restrictions I experienced in New Orleans, they were worth it to be near my nephews and niece.

In the spring, when I read about a workshop retreat titled "Journey to the Underworld," I felt very drawn to it, for I loved mythology and always wanted to learn new things to make the sophomore classes more interesting. This workshop focused on the myth of Inanna, a Sumerian goddess, who journeyed to the underworld where she was stripped of all her power and left to die. Instead of dying, she was saved and took back the power she had lost. I hoped that by exploring her story I would gain deeper insights on power issues in my life.

Finding this workshop on Inanna seemed to be in divine order, and the school paid for me to attend. At the camp where it was held, I was happy to be out in nature, meeting new people, and exploring my feelings. The first night was mainly social and an introduction to the myth. During the second evening, we worked with ritual, identifying our correspondences with the four directions. We identified the West as the place of darkness—the home of the witch or magician. I related this to my experiences in Denver with Sarah, ceremonial magic, Gladys, and unemployment.

The South was the place of naiveté, innocence, and passion where I spent my childhood. The North was associated with the rational, cool, and creator and was not a place where I felt comfortable. The East was the place of light and enlightenment where ancient spiritual practices originated and where intelligence and education were highly valued.

We also brought personally symbolic items to use in a ritual. Just choosing these items reminded me of my strengths. Already Inanna's story was empowering me. My favorite picture of my grandmother, mother, and me represented our family tradition of strength and survival. A figure of the goddess of change reminded me that I was fluid like water, traveling through cultures and experiences, learning from them, changing shape like Proteus to accommodate the situation. A sea shell symbolized my depth and ability to travel through layers of consciousness like waters flowing through the layers of a shell. This depth was the inner strength that connected me to the significant mysteries of life. Robert Johnson's book *She*, about the myth of Psyche and Cupid, suggested that I was willing to undergo many trials to find true love. Finally, a small piece of amethyst represented the channel of light, for I was God's child, a willing receiver who shared freely what I knew and learned.

After enacting the ritual of descending to the underworld and being stripped of our power as Inanna was, we gathered our mattresses together on the floor of the community room and slept. We awakened the next morning to the heavenly sounds of "The Beauty of the Night" from *Phantom of the Opera*. As we came to consciousness, a leader sat by each of us to receive whatever dreams and thoughts we had to share and to usher us back into the land of the living and our place of power. By the time I returned home, I no longer remembered what I had shared that morning; I only remembered the profundity of Inanna's story. Although we might be stripped of our power, we could transcend that darkness and rise again into a greater power as the result of what we learned in the darkness. Inanna's story empowered me, and I hoped would also empower the girls I taught to believe we could all rise above our difficulties.

The Jung Society of New Orleans became my intellectual oasis and enriched my teaching in the midst of this perpetual party land. From the programs and workshops, I learned more about mythology, psychology, and dreams, and that knowledge provided a deeper level of insight in my relationships as I explored the inner landscape of my own psychology. I also read everything I could get my hands on about the psychology of men and integrating the masculine and feminine aspects of my psyche. Knowing I needed help in order to heal, I began to work with a therapist.

In therapy, exploring my feelings toward my parents brought major issues, such as power and love, to the surface. One day, as we discussed these relationships, my therapist Catherine asked, "If you could say anything to your father, what would it be?"

I didn't have to think long about that. "I would say, 'I know you love me, but it's hard to remember when you've only said it once or twice in my whole life. I know your way of loving is to do things, but now that you're sick and you can do little, I don't hear the words or see the demonstration and feel I'm not loved at all. Right now I'm really angry at you for throwing away your older years. You've always looked so young and were active until you retired. Then you decided you were an old man and became one. You're a burden for mother when she's still young enough to enjoy life, and now she has to care for you as well as Mama. Even now, you could still volunteer in the community and be useful, but all you do is to feel sorry for yourself. Well, I don't feel sorry for you because the doctors told you long ago to stop smoking and you didn't. I know it isn't easy to quit, but you were already sick. Now you're practically an invalid. Why did you do this to yourself and to us?'"

"And to your mother?" Catherine asked.

I took a deep breath and could feel the tears filling my eyes. "I would say, 'Mother, I'll never understand why you stayed with Daddy when he was so mean to you. You say it's love, but I think it's codependency. As you get older, I'm afraid of the time when

I'll need to take care of you. I love you, but this love is painful. I feel sad and tired when I think of loving you. It wears me out wanting you to be happy because you never are. You never feel loved enough, but your life is the one you've chosen. It's too much for me to go on trying to care for you emotionally. Teaching is exhausting. I hardly have the energy to take care of myself now.'"

I brushed away the tears and continued. "Your love for me has always confused me. You either smothered and over-protected me or pushed me away if I disagreed or rebelled. Despite your being so unpredictable, I did feel I could rely on you most of the time until I was divorced. Then you turned against me, and I learned I better not ever rely on anyone but myself. You and Gary both deserted me at the same time."

"Is there more?"

I thought a moment and continued. "Mother, why did you always support me in school when I succeeded, but in life you've ignored my greatest accomplishment, becoming a dancer? You're always supportive when I'm failing, but not when I'm succeeding. Are you jealous? I just want to have someone stay in my life and be supportive of my success or to have someone I love actually contribute to my success. I feel that to succeed I've had to turn my back on the people I love because you're all untrustworthy. You don't keep the promises you make."

"I thought that by coming to New Orleans I would always have a family who emotionally supported me, and you certainly did when I was living with you, but since then you're all too busy. You think you have to be available to my brother's family every moment and have no life of your own. You won't even go out to lunch with me. This is wrong. Your son will always take care of you because he loves you, and he has the means. His love isn't conditional. You don't have to sacrifice your life to him."

We sat quietly for a moment, and it felt as if a great burden had been lifted just by speaking those words out loud and having Catherine witness them.

Therapy continued to help me understand what caused my frequent depression. Because of my mother's sacrificial devotion to family, I wasn't always clear about the difference between nurturing and martyring in relationships, for I frequently felt I wasn't loving enough. When I mentioned this to a friend, she said she thought I was very loving without being gushy or getting into the unnatural, extreme compassion that many women expressed. Her support was reassuring, but I was still often haunted with the idea that were I truly loving, I would be in a relationship with a good man. Only one of the men I had dated seemed capable of a relationship, but he was too much younger.

Despite the emphasis on fun, family, and food in New Orleans, there was a darker side. Most of the people I knew came from families that could claim drug or alcohol addiction or histories of abuse. In the apartments where I lived, I was exposed to problems I'd never encountered before. When I reported a hostile neighbor to the manager and police for playing his music extremely loud at night even when he wasn't in his apartment, they did nothing. I discovered later that he was the person slashing my tires every couple of weeks. I moved.

Two years later, I had to move again. I had a drunk neighbor who fell asleep at night with the television's volume much too loud. Across the courtyard was a screaming man who beat up his own mother. Meanwhile, the war in Kuwait had begun and the first American pilot who was shot down was the father of a student at my school. I was devastated by this girl's loss and the loss of my dream that this generation would never have to know war.

The violent energy in the environment invaded my dreams. In one dream, I was unable to move, lying trapped in my sleeping body as a snapping and snarling wolf ran toward me. I was terrified he would attack, but at the last moment, he leaped over me and ran away. I was relieved when I found a small apartment building where most tenants were retired and led quiet lives.

In addition to the therapy, I read books that evoked powerful insights about relationships. One of these was Sam Keen's *The Passionate Life: Stages of Loving*. Much of what I had revealed in therapy in my imagined conversations with my parents related to issues he discussed in the childhood and adolescent stages of life. But what really caught my attention was what he wrote about the third stage, a shockingly accurate statement: "The making of an adult is a complex process that systematically cripples, reduces our consciousness, our compassion, and our potential to love. The decisions required for maturity exclude from care all except family, friends, and fellow citizens. The circle of love is small, the circle of hate is large. Tribal consciousness is formed more by negation than affirmation, more by fear than by wonder, more by dis-ease than by health." That was the great struggle—having to conform in order to survive. I needed the symbols of settled adulthood for security because it was easier to live like everyone else. However, the untamed part of me wanted to ignore this reality and rebel against such narrow mindedness.

My fears that I was shrinking my life and losing my inner vitality surfaced in a dream. Men surrounded a woman in red, and as I woke I knew they were going to kill her. She was the intuitive, creative, passionate, committed me. Was my desire for a relationship or my own assertive, masculine quality sabotaging me?

I often dreamed about the men in my life. My therapist Catherine, in order to work with these issues, asked, "Who are you dreaming about?"

"Mainly Neal and Gary."

"I want you to choose one of them and tell me what he would say if he could tell you how he really feels about you?"

I frowned. "I'm not sure I'm going to enjoy this very much."

She smiled, "Who's first?"

"Neal, I think." I thought for a moment. "He would say, 'Just let go—don't try to hang on to everything. Accept people as they are, enjoy what you can, but don't try to make the relationship rigid. Nothing is permanent any more, you know. You enjoy one person for a while, for a while it works. When it stops working, let it go and move on. Don't get angry and hate the other person because he doesn't love you anymore. Say thanks for what you had, value it, let it go, and move on. If it didn't last, it wasn't as great as you thought it was.'"

Catherine looked at me as if asking what I was thinking.

"He's right, you know. I couldn't accept how he was and trying to change him certainly didn't work. But I don't want someone for awhile; I want a long-lasting relationship. I know now that if I need to change the other person, it isn't the right person."

"Who's next?"

"Gary. He would say, 'You need to be aware of how strong you are; you're like a bulldozer running over people with your ideas and enthusiasm. You get so hooked on your own goals that you forget that other people need your attention. We aren't as strong as you are. We men need a woman to make us feel important in her life. You put on this front like you're one way, sweet and innocent, then you come on with the anger and criticism, and the other person isn't prepared for that. It's shocking. You need to remember not to intimidate insecure people. It made me want to hurt you because it made me feel diminished.'"

I added, "Actually, Gary did say most of this to me."

"Anyone else?"

"Charles—the relationship was short, but I feel he wants to speak to me. He was the much younger commercial artist I dated."

I sat with my thoughts for a moment, then spoke for Charles, "You think I'm too feminine, but that's what you also seem to like—my kindness. When I'm nice to you, you melt. I see it. You're very afraid of being vulnerable, like you will shatter if you give yourself to another man or another dream that doesn't work. But you won't. You're stronger than you think, but the kind of man you're attracted to doesn't treat you well. Don't let love blind you."

"Is that true?"

I hesitated, not wanting to admit this weakness in myself. "Yes," I murmured. I had spoken truthfully in each case, but it was hard to hear the truth. Knowing how to release fear had not been enough to overcome these fears.

In a dream, my Unity friend Theresa and I were swimming in a lake in the country. It was clear and beautiful, but we eventually came to the edge of an area filled with sargasso. We decided to turn around and go back because we didn't want to swim through this undergrowth. When we turned around, it was there too, and we had to swim through it to get home. As much as I wanted life to be easier, this dream reminded me there was no way to swim around the entangling garbage of life; that was part of the journey too.

Suddenly, it seemed, it was the beginning of another year. My affirmation for 1994 was "I am successful, prosperous, loved and loving." In February, Theresa and Diane, another friend I had met at Unity, went to the beach for a vacation with me. Diane had a chronic illness and her activity was limited, so it was good to have Theresa join me as I roamed along the shore collecting shells.

I had an interesting dream on our first night there. I was sitting on the edge of a large bathtub and said to the person near me, "I wonder if there are any fish in there?" I stuck my finger into the water as bait and a large fish mouth appeared level with the surface of the water. My fluffy black cat Daisy then attacked the fish and won the fight, but I didn't feel the fish was destroyed. There was also another fish in the tub (both were catfish), and it had large fangs and swam around continually.

At breakfast the next morning, I asked Theresa, who was a counselor, to interpret the dream. "Well, fish are symbols for the divine, so I think they represented divine ideas coming to the surface of the unconscious, but a part of you was the cat trying to attack or work against them. Does that make sense?"

"Yes, in a way. I don't follow through with the ideas that do come up because I don't have enough time to work *and* write, or I get distracted with the practical problems in my life. So, many creative ideas just disappear." The dream identified a significant problem: I often had difficulty moving forward with a project because I had difficulty making decisions and staying focused. I needed to listen more carefully for those divine ideas and act on them.

The trip to the beach was a pleasant distraction from the frustration at work. The school had a new principal. She let me teach a drama course this year, and I was designing a new senior English course, focusing on drama, women, and multicultural literature, that I would teach next year. In my impatience to teach more creative courses, I had expected the principal to also allow me to teach the new fine arts survey, but she gave it to a teacher with fewer qualifications.

One of the divine ideas to which I had responded the previous summer was to take a course called "Teaching the African Novel." Responding to the students' desires, the professor who taught it had written and received a Fulbright-Hays Travel Abroad Grant to take teachers to study in West Africa the following summer. I was wildly excited when I was chosen for the trip. As a child I had been inspired by Albert Schweitzer's work with the lepers in Africa and read many books on Africa. It had been my lifetime dream to visit, and by some miracle, I had manifested this means to fulfill my desire. Thrilled, I rushed to the new principal with my news. "Oh," she said, "I'm so jealous. I've always wanted to do something like that." In that moment, she destroyed what little respect I had for her. Instead of announcing my good news to everyone as she did with other faculty members, she ignored it, but as I told my coworkers and students, they rejoiced with me.

About this same time, I asked the principal for a raise so that I would be paid for all the years of my experience. I needed more income and hoped the new course I was developing would justify it, but she refused. I could no longer survive on my current salary, and I wanted to do more than teach privileged children. The New Orleans Public Schools would pay me much more, and I could teach gifted children in need, so I applied for the next school year. The African trip was the perfect preparation, and I was confident that I would be hired.

Butterflies

The trip to Africa was empowering, for I knew dreams that seemed impossible could come true, and I returned home feeling connected to the rest of the world in a way I never had. I had learned what it felt like to be hated because I was a different color, but also what it was like to be embraced as an equal by people totally different from myself. I had learned that art could speak as a universal language across continents. I saw the face of abject poverty and the terrible price we paid for allowing it to exist. I saw its children, begging far from home. And I knew how the sheer joy of living transcended it all through music and drums echoing through a desert or cathedral. As a citizen of the world, I knew we were all one. My life had enormously expanded, and it was time to move on.

With newly found courage, I asked the principal again to pay me for another year or two of service, and again her answer was no. Within two weeks, the New Orleans Public Schools hired me as an itinerant gifted English teacher for ninth through twelfth grades. I traveled to three schools a day, taught one to six students in a class, and made $8,000 more a year. With more money, I could enjoy plays and concerts, pay bills easily, and afford a real vacation. I felt showered with abundance. Traveling each day gave me time to relax and think as I went from one school to the next. There were no duty or committee responsibilities. I prepared individualized education plans for each student because the gifted program was under special education, and I could have only a maximum of twelve students on my rolls. Having fewer students was balanced by having to prepare for four grade levels or sometimes more when individual students had diverse needs. Only one student wasn't African American so the African trip was a perfect segue into teaching literature to African American students, many of whom knew little about their African heritage. By this time, Chinua Achebe's *Things Fall Apart* was required reading in the tenth grade.

I ushered in 1995 eating black-eyed peas and cabbage with my family and soon afterward began taking gifted classes at the University of New Orleans to earn a gifted license. My first year went well although all the students were working below their potential. With poor study habits, raging hormones, and problems in their families, they had many distractions. I couldn't motivate some at all. Despite a few victories, I was emotionally drained and grateful to finally have time to take care of myself when summer arrived.

During the school year, Ricky, an art teacher at one of the schools, and I had developed a close friendship. He was a tall, slender man with intense green eyes and a head of thick, wavy, dark brown hair. He was in transition and healing from a break-up with a woman he had hoped to marry. We had great times walking along the lakefront, going to the Greek Festival, and talking. I felt a deep affection for him developing, but I didn't know whether he really returned it, and I was fearful. I could tell by the way he looked at me that there was some attraction, but I didn't know how he felt about my being older or if he were dating anyone. Moving from just being friends at school to friends outside of work was a big step.

Before long, one thing became clear: Ricky didn't want a relationship because he had failed at the last one and had no confidence he could succeed at another one. When I first visited his apartment, it was a wreck, and it was clear to me that this was a sign of his inner confusion. I kept telling myself to accept the fact I could only be his friend.

Then he asked me to spend a week with him in northeastern Alabama, the closest place we could find mountains. Just below the cabin where we stayed were trails and a beautiful stream. I slept in the bedroom, and he slept in a bed in the front room where he could stay up late watching television without bothering me.

Throughout the week, I watched him dance with the mountain as we hiked, moving with the balance of a mountain goat and the grace of a tiger, finding a clear path through the bushes and over rocks. I followed his lead willingly as we created a natural pas de trois with nature that led us to places in the heart where stillness and peace resided. I rarely saw him misstep, and when he did, his equilibrium quickly saved him from falling. He flowed over the rocks in counterpoint to their slips and shifts, showing me the easiest way. I matched my rhythm to his, dancing with the mountain and with him, accenting and improvising to his choreography.

Within this dance of nature, there were moments of silence—breathing with the wind, feeling the birds sail on an updraft, following the fluttering Tiger Swallowtails as they landed weightless on the leaves of trees. We listened to water trickling over the stones, followed its path downstream to hidden pools, baptizing ourselves in the cool pleasure of its depths, washing away the fatigue of our climb.

It was hard to say whether it was Ricky I loved at those moments or simply being one with nature. We were quiet as we calmly tread water in a green pool where a baby copperhead joined us or lay on the grass at night, dreaming separate dreams beneath the stars. Deep within our cocoons, the mountain nourished us daily with its strength and beauty, teaching its dance of peace, urging us to grow toward more than what we were, exposing our hearts to a new and shared reality.

But we never talked about our feelings. We always watched for the butterflies, and after having gone with Ricky on a butterfly count with the Audubon Society, I had learned to recognize a few. Miraculously, we saw a Diana that wasn't supposed to live in that area and took pictures to prove to his friends that it was real. The outing was like returning to my childhood, swimming in the mountain stream near my grandparents' house in northwestern Arkansas.

At night we watched old movies and looked at the stars. It was a beautiful time luxuriating in nature. It was very romantic, but we were strictly platonic. Ambiguity hung heavy in the air.

One night, we were talking about high maintenance and low maintenance partners, and I commented that most the men in my life had seen me as high maintenance.

"Are you kidding?" Ricky said, surprised, slathering peanut butter onto a piece of bread for a snack. "I think you're low maintenance—you haven't complained once about falling over rocks or getting drenched by thunderstorms."

I smiled and stopped myself from kissing him, "Thank you, that's one of the nicest things a man has ever said to me." Finally, I'd found a man who appreciated my strengths.

Returning home again, I had difficulty separating the Ricky I saw in the city from the Ricky I had seen in the mountains. He finally told me he loved me, and I could see it in his eyes, but because he still wanted us to be platonic, I wondered whether he loved me as a friend or as a man loved a woman. I wasn't sure and couldn't bring myself to ask. He was the only man I'd met in years with whom I could envision a life, living together day by day, because we shared such a richness of experience with our teaching and love of art and nature. He was immature in some ways, but no more than most men I'd known. It was often a challenge for me to be loving—to not let anger enter the relationship because I wanted his feelings to be what I wanted them to be. I often felt cheated that he wouldn't take the next step. I had to accept him as he was, but not harm myself in the process. This was new territory, and I had trouble hearing my inner guidance because I wanted a relationship so much.

Determined to work out my relationship problems, I continued seeing the therapist I had seen previously. It concerned me that Ricky was friendly with many women, all of whom he insisted were just friends, so I asked Catherine whether she thought he was capable of a relationship.

She shook her head. "Considering his butterfly nature and the intimacy issues he has, I think it's unlikely. You see, he gets along so well with women that he gets positive responses, and he likes that. If he wants a relationship, the way he relates to these women will need to change."

"I just feel confused all the time. He says he doesn't want a relationship, then he becomes more affectionate. "

"Sometimes we have to say no so that we can allow something to move forward. By saying no, he feels safer."

"But what is he so afraid of?"

"The greatest fear a man has is that he can't please his woman. So, if we're constantly critical or make him feel inadequate, he'll go away because he feels he's failed. A man needs to be reminded a lot how wonderful he is so he will feel he's pleasing us. Remember, men respond with the flight or fight response much quicker than we do."

I cringed, remembering the times I'd been so critical of the men in my life. "So we have to be really careful not to trigger it."

"Right. And as far as his flirting is concerned, it would be good for him to see you interact with other men and see them attracted to you. When he's flirting, he won't acknowledge it's flirting because it feels good. If he sees you flirting, he may get the point quicker, but, because making others feel good is part of his nature, when he wants to make you feel good, assume he's sincere unless he does something weird like standing you up. Don't analyze it."

"I don't know what to do with this. Should I give up on him?"

She laughed, "This may surprise you, but I think it's beneficial for you to see how this evolves. You seem to be learning a lot. It must be good for you in some way because you're more sexy, vibrant, and full of life than I've seen you in a long time."

"Really?" I thought about that for a moment. "Well, I am learning a lot. I haven't issued any ultimatums."

"That's a good change."

"When I talk about problems, I don't attack. I treat it as a problem we need to work out."

"Good."

"I also try to do nice things that will make him feel good and let him know I really appreciate him."

"You're on the right track."

Soon after this session, Ricky and I were together, and he was very affectionate, saying he loved me, Georganne, his friend. His affection was more than friendly, but I decided to let things evolve.

But a few months later, I knew I couldn't handle the ambiguity any longer. It was like the craziness with Neal, so I told Ricky I couldn't see him anymore. Our separation was agony to me. I hated him one day, loved him the next, but underneath it all, I felt deeply sad like some bright butterfly had deserted my garden.

Our last conversation before I pulled away haunted me with its familiarity. He said, "It's like the butterfly, you get a little love here and some there, but if you try to pin it down, it dies." So, love or commitment was like death to him. When my therapist heard this, she looked at me very seriously, "He isn't likely to want a relationship."

"It's so sad that he can't envision a love that expands a person as the love opens and grows and develops."

She looked at me sadly, "What you need isn't going to happen with him."

I started smoking again and hated that I had, but I was depressed and knew there was nothing I could do to change Ricky. If I became who he needed me to be, I would compromise who I truly was, so that wasn't an option either. Nothing dulled the pain and sadness, but somehow I could at least still function, and I realized I'd grown stronger.

I was often haunted by the memory of that week with Ricky in the mountains. In the midst of this distress and confusion, I was convinced we had been at our best in the woods, seashore, or bayous. But, at home again, we were not good with chaos—the complications of our friendship confused and tired us. Now, he walked the levees at sunset alone while I walked through the early morning rain, both pursuing different paths to fend off the terrors of growing old, of trying not to fail again. His dance led him down paths where I couldn't follow, disappearing into the darkness and failing to light the way for me as he had on those nights when we climbed down the mountain to the river. We had seen our togetherness on the mountain as an illusion, but it was not an illusion. It was the reality. Our illusion was of our separateness.

In the middle of summer, I excitedly dressed for my favorite art event, "White Linen Nights" when everyone wore white linen, a good protection against the smothering heat and humidity of July in New Orleans. Several streets were blocked off in the gallery district downtown, and jazz, classical, and rock music filled the air. It was pleasant to wander from gallery to gallery, sipping wine and nibbling on hors d'oeuvres, with a woman friend because we always had a good, stress-free time together, and I needed an evening to let go and celebrate life.

About halfway through the evening, we entered a gallery where a jazz guitarist was playing. As we moved toward the group surrounding him, I stopped. Ricky was standing behind one of the women he had assured me was just a friend. His arms were wrapped around her, and he pulled her closer against his body to whisper in her ear. She turned her head, and as he tilted his face toward her, he looked in our direction. Quickly pulling away from her, his smile changed to shock as he realized he'd been caught in his lie.

Despite what I knew about Ricky, I eventually made the mistake of trying to be friends with him again but found his lack of consideration intolerable. Arguing at my apartment one day, I again confronted him with the way he had lied to me about Maria.

"I'm not lying to you," he insisted. "I just don't know what I'm feeling. When I told you I was just friends with Maria, I was telling the truth. At the time, I felt she and I were just friends. Later I felt something else."

"Do you want to know what really makes me crazy?"

"What?"

"It's the feeling that the way I experienced the time with you last summer wasn't the way you experienced—that I thought you loved me, and we were sharing this deep, magical time. I'm beginning to think I imagined it all."

He took me by the shoulders. "Oh, God—that's not true. I felt the same things you did. There wasn't a day that went by that I didn't think about taking things further, but I had no faith that any relationship could work. All mine have failed. Why would I think this one would work? Besides, you're not the kind of woman I could go to bed with casually. I couldn't treat you that way."

All I could do was cry.

I was thankful for my therapist. "Georganne, don't doubt the reality of your own experience. It was real for you."

"How do I get past this grief?"

She smiled sympathetically. "Every night, ask the universe for what you need, for that loving male energy that makes you feel secure and that you will be willing to accept it in whatever form it appears. You see, the reality of life is a series of joy and despair, but you don't accept this yet, and you need to."

On Saturday, January 20, 1996, I returned home after visiting with one of the other gifted teachers for several hours. There was a message on the answering machine from my brother that our father had died suddenly two hours earlier. A blood vessel burst in his chest, his lungs filled with blood quickly, and he was gone in ten minutes. He had trouble breathing because of his long history of smoking and lung disease, but we didn't believe he was in imminent danger. This was a shock.

The funeral was the following week and two of my uncles attended. My father's death was particularly difficult for my nephews and niece, with whom he'd lived for most of their lives. At the burial site, my youngest nephew spontaneously and gently placed his new gold ID bracelet on my father's chest. When he did, I thought I would collapse with grief. Although Daddy wasn't expressive with his feelings, I felt secure knowing he was always there.

Days afterward, it still seemed like a dream. Although I was at peace with his passing, I was very aware of how alone I was. I had taken the time after I moved to New Orleans to try to understand him and to accept him the way he was. I loved him very much and was pleased to see that as he grew older, he started reaching out to us and tried to express his love. When he did this, and my mother pushed him away, it hurt him deeply, and it hurt me to see her reject him. I suspected that she would regret it, for she certainly was not at peace with his passing.

Ricky came to the funeral and later to the house and stayed

until 7:00 pm. As we sat on the couch, with his arm around me, my youngest nephew walked up, looked him directly in the eye, and asked, "Are you going to marry Aunt Georganne?"

Ricky and I both were speechless, but I recovered and stammered, "We're just friends, Sweetie."

"Oh," he said, looking disappointed, and turned and walked away. Ricky and I just looked at each other.

He called me every night that week. We were together on the weekend, and sitting on my couch as he held and kissed me like he used to, I carefully tried to learn more about his fears.

"Ricky, you're acting like you used to, but what are you feeling?"

"I'm sorry. I do love you." He pulled me close again. "I know I'm not being fair to you, and I know that many feelings you struggle with are about me, but I'm still afraid to have a relationship."

By this time, I was curious to discover if there was more to this issue than he was telling me. Was he being nice out of guilt?

"Why?"

He sat back and looked down as if he were gathering the energy to tell me. "I'm terrified of losing myself in another relationship, of disappearing into it until I don't know who I am anymore." This had been one of Neal's issues too.

"I thought you were feeling stronger?"

"I am—I do feel that I'm more of myself again. Maybe someday, I'll even be strong enough to have a relationship."

"Why don't you get some help? I have a friend who is a wonderful therapist."

With a deeply sad and haunted expression, he looked at me, "Can she heal the crack in my soul?"

For a moment, the pain I felt for him overwhelmed me.

I knew I was on dangerous ground with Ricky. But like every relationship in which I had invested so much emotion, it was difficult for me to admit defeat and let go. In a short while, he decided that he was only moderately attracted to me, not enough for a life partner, and my age bothered him a little, but he was mainly concerned about the difference in our lifestyles, a comment that made no sense to me. Once again, he hadn't been truthful.

The next time I was at his apartment, I asked him, "Is my age the reason you've never taken me around your friends?"

"I don't have any other friends you haven't met," he answered quickly.

"That's not true and you know it. You usually get together with a group on Sunday nights. What's that about?"

"It's some people I went to high school with. You wouldn't like them." He was clearly uncomfortable, crossed his arms and wouldn't look me in the eye.

Reluctantly, he admitted, "We usually go to a club where everyone smokes pot."

"Are you serious?" I was shocked. What was wrong with a man in his forties who still wanted to go out and smoke pot? No wonder he couldn't get his life together. And I was wasting my life thinking he would change.

"You're still doing that? No wonder you have problems, Ricky." I gathered up my coat and left for good.

On a beautiful, sunny winter day, a Cloudless Sulphur floated by me. Realizing that I would never look at butterflies with Ricky again brought tears to my eyes. At my therapist's, I told her how foolish, rejected, and distrustful I felt, but that I still needed to understand him so I wouldn't choose someone like him again.

"All right," she began, "One way to understand this is that there is an archetype of woman—the temptress—that he's attracted to, but she isn't good for him. He could work out this attraction in therapy, but the problem is that he's acting it out in real life. That creates a problem for you because there are always these other women with whom he becomes entangled."

"That makes sense."

"In addition, he's like Sleeping Beauty, waiting for the right woman to awaken him. He expects you or some other woman to fix him."

"Well, it's very clear, I didn't awaken him."

"No, but no one else can fix him either. He has to fix himself."

In March, I was still grieving the loss of my father and Ricky. At fifty-two, I felt old for the first time and became depressed, unhappily contemplating the possibility that I might never find a partner.

Therapy had helped me understand the dynamics of the relationships I'd had, but I knew only I could truly heal myself. Turning again to meditation, the following images appeared like a dream. I was at a workshop in an old warehouse. There were ledges on each side of the second floor level with an open space between them that dropped down two floors. I was walking across a plank between the two sides, focusing on Ricky, who was on the other side. He was supposed to guide me to cross safely, but instead kicked the plank off his side, and I fell two floors. I landed on a padded cushion, but the plank fell on me and it hurt. "Never again," I thought, "Never again."

A deep ache of abandonment often surfaced when a relationship failed. I remembered that Gladys had said that it was often only the perception of abandonment that caused these feelings, not literal childhood abandonment. Hoping that inner child work would perhaps heal that pain, I turned again to meditation, and profound images related to this issue surfaced. I was riding the Minotaur, the Greek mythological creature with the body of a man and head of a bull. He tried to shake me off, but I held on. I understood intuitively that to gain control of my fears so that I could face another relationship, I had to tame the bull and integrate the male energy within.

My inner child felt vulnerable to the male bull energy, so I needed to nurture her. I imagined her crawling into the arms of my higher self, an angelic figure with long red hair wearing a white dress. The little girl went to sleep while the higher self nurtured and rocked her like a baby. As the little girl felt warm, complete, and totally peaceful, she knew she was protected from the dangers of life by the higher self. Then a man came into the picture. He was tall, slender, and broad shouldered with brown hair and glasses and wearing a blue shirt and brown pants. He gently took the girl in his arms and held her while she slept, and she also felt safe with him.

Then the Minotaur reappeared, but this time, I was riding him peacefully, and both he and I wore samurai gear made from gold brocade, like spiritual warriors working as one. I felt deeply at peace and free of my fears. Soon I began dreaming dreams of transformation. My inner landscape was being redecorated.

Hurricane Season

The school year was over, and with it, came a flood of overwhelming fatigue the moment I allowed myself to rest. I had known the previous spring that I was out of balance physically, but I refused to consider that I might be ill because I was afraid of losing the opportunity to go to Africa. Unfortunately, during the past year, losses and disappointments took their toll as well. I woke up every morning as exhausted as when I went to bed. In addition to the fatigue and aching joints, I also frequently had the sensation that my face was going numb or that my skin was crawling. My doctor's tests revealed nothing, so he concluded I was having anxiety attacks and prescribed anti-anxiety medication. I saw other doctors for other problems, and they were all fixated on the idea that I had contracted a bug when I was in Africa, but their tests were negative.

I knew it was time to make a radical change. Living in New Orleans wasn't healthy for me because of pollen, mold, and chemicals from the chemical plants upstream. The violence of such a drug-ridden city with its constant carjacking and random murders had taken a toll on my psyche. I often had violent dreams. In one, I sat in a red sports car convertible on a city street waiting for someone to come out of a building. A hippie in ragged jeans was crazily muttering and screaming in a threatening manner as he walked unsteadily toward me. He carried several hand guns and threw one of them into the back of my car. Then, many young men ran into the street from all directions, screaming at each other. I was terrified they would start shooting, so I started my car and sped away.

That summer, my dear friend Diane, whom I had met at the Unity Church, moved back to the North Carolina beach where she had grown up. I was thrilled when she invited me to visit later in the summer. I missed our deep conversations and thought that getting away from Louisiana would relieve some of the tension of living in Hurricane Alley during the hurricane season.

Diane's family's cabin was located on the inner banks along a quiet wooded cove. Being near woods and ocean calmed me. I had been on anti-anxiety drugs so long that I'd forgotten how it felt to be normal and was convinced the pills were dangerous and contributing to my depression. Perhaps in this peaceful place with a wise friend nearby, I could get off them. Meditating on what path to take, I received a strong message to drop these drugs, and when I was off them, to take only Buspar, stop using Nicorette to cure my smoking relapse, and drink only a small amount of caffeine. I stopped taking the other drugs the first day I arrived, but had great difficulty sleeping.

Unfortunately, the quiet of our lazy summer days was soon interrupted with the news that Hurricane Bertha was heading straight for us. I had to laugh at the irony that what I had come here to escape had followed me. Unable to resist my attraction to the drama of a major natural event, I felt an adrenaline rush. I trusted that Diane and I would survive this just as we had survived many others in New Orleans. Perhaps the hurricane winds would not only unearth trees and boat docks, but also sweep away the blocks that kept me attached to ways of living that no longer served me.

Diane and I quickly abandoned the idea of leaving because it would take hours to pack up all the supplements, food, and equipment she would need. The chronic fatigue syndrome she still had made traveling extremely stressful, so we made a quick inventory of what we would need, and she reassured me that the sturdy cabin had withstood many serious storms. Knowing we would lose power, Diane and I threw every vegetable in the refrigerator along with some chicken into a cold rice casserole that would be nutritious and keep well in an ice chest. We ate a fairly heavy lunch and read and talked during the afternoon as the wind force and speed steadily increased.

About six or seven hours later when Bertha arrived, we lost power and gave up trying to sleep, for the sound of the wind and constant plummeting of tree branches on the roof was intense. We lit candles and Diane curled up on the other bed in my room. When the eye of the storm brought peace and quiet, I read to her from a book on *A Course in Miracles*. This was our version of a grown-up pajama party without the popcorn and stories about boys. Late in the night, after Bertha's last rage calmed, I fell asleep and slept better than I'd slept in several days. It felt like the drugs were finally out of my system.

The next night, I dreamed about Ricky. I was teaching on a campus, realized I had missed a class, and ran into him as I was rushing about. In the middle of our conversation, he said, "I love you." I said, "You love me?" Taking my face in his hands, he said, "I finally realized how much I love you." When I woke up, I felt love opening my heart again. What had hurt so much was the feeling that he really didn't love me, but I knew now that he did in his own way. Reading about *A Course in Miracles* reminded me that peace and love needed to be my guides. If what I was doing didn't bring me love or peace, I wasn't doing the right thing, so I could love Ricky, treat him with love, and still choose not to be with him because he wasn't good for me. When I remembered love was the center, everything happened in divine order.

After one week of being off the anti-anxiety drugs, the remaining anxiety symptoms were slight and infrequent. I'd also read that eating sugar depleted the adrenals and pancreas, and a diabetic friend said that fat also stressed the pancreas. Over the last year, when I'd been so upset and stressed, I had comforted myself with too much fat and sugar, and those unbalanced my system. I suspected the anxiety disorder was really a blood sugar problem and had once mentioned this to my doctor, telling him that my mother was diabetic, but he refused to consider it.

Fortunately, Diane's cabin sustained no major damage, and I returned home from the shore drug free. Eating a mostly macrobiotic diet while I was there and talking with Diane about spiritual matters was healing. She convinced me that it was possible I had chronic fatigue syndrome too. I no longer trusted my doctors or my own inner guidance, and because Gladys had recently made her transition into the next life, I had no one to whom I could turn for help. It was time for me to see Diane's doctor in Tucson and find out what was disturbing my body and mind.

Suddenly, the summer was over, but I wasn't ready for school to start. I longed to read for days and immerse myself in new characters, cultures, and language. Instead, I plunged back into welcoming new students and making lesson plans. I loved the African American literature I was teaching, especially Zora Neale Hurston's *Their Eyes Were Watching God*. Its richness and depth of feeling touched me deeply, especially in Hurston's depiction of Janie, the main character. Janie's dignity and strength to carry and overcome burdens spoke to my isolation, my sense of being different, of being a minority in a world where the majority didn't share my values. It was also a joy to teach this to mostly African American students who were so bright and to encourage them and develop their talents. I wanted them to feel good about their intelligence, to give them joy and access to the world. I wanted the joy of learning to sing in their hearts.

It was December before I finally called Dr. Aaron Stromberg in Tucson. Because I couldn't travel to the clinic until summer, he ordered tests in March to be done in New Orleans so he would know about my condition in advance. When he received the results, we talked on the phone and he informed me there was good and bad news. I liked his warm and direct manner.

"Georganne, the bad news is that you have nine things wrong with you, but the good news is that we can cure them all."

"Well, I guess that's good news," I said with some doubt.

"The problems are mainly chemical imbalances or vitamin or mineral deficiencies and absorption problems."

I was shocked by the vitamin deficiencies. I'd always eaten a healthy diet. How was that possible? The doctor went on to explain, "The deficiencies indicate there's damage from free radicals and low amino acid production. This results in poor absorption of nutrients. When amino acids are low, the body can't make the protein it needs. Because enzymes are 100 percent protein, it's possible that the enzyme deficiency you have is a result of the body not being able to make enough enzymes rather than a problem from something you ate. Only time will tell. Also the bacteria that cause ulcers are in your stomach, and there's an overgrowth of candida in the colon."

"No wonder my digestion is terrible!"

"That's right. Also, I think that the crawling sensation in your face is probably caused by hypoglycemia or low blood sugar. Some of your weakness is due to low sodium, so one thing you can do right away is to increase your salt intake."

"Thank you, it's such a relief to know what's wrong. All I've heard up to now is that it was anxiety or my imagination."

"No, no, we can fix this. Don't worry. I look forward to meeting with you. I wish I could start now, but I'm not allowed to prescribe treatment without seeing you, but I can give you some guidance that will help you get started in the right direction. Eating organic food as much as possible would be a good start."

"At last," I thought, "someone finally believes me. This isn't all in my head." There were tears of gratitude in my eyes when we ended the call.

Finally, in June, I spent three days at the clinic in Tucson in appointments with a variety of health-care professionals. Lying in bed at my motel after a long first day at the clinic, I was struck by how different the desert was from the swamps of Louisiana. Like New Orleans, the desert was a place where I would never feel at home, and I longed to find my home, a place to put down roots and have friends I'd known for years, friends on whom I could depend. Finding my heart's home had been an issue for some time.

In the spring, I had dreamed that I was downtown in a city and needed to go home, but walking was too dangerous, and I had only enough money to take a taxi a few blocks. I knew where my home was but didn't have the transportation to get there.

I lay in bed thinking about my arrival at the clinic that morning. The minute I walked in, a nurse handed me a water bottle and said, "Drink water constantly while you're here. If you don't, you'll get a headache," she emphasized, "The temperature will be over 100 degrees today." She was right. Despite drinking what I perceived to be a huge amount of water, I had a slight headache anyway.

When Dr. Stromberg arrived, he was dressed in a Hawaiian shirt and lei and had come straight to the clinic from the airport because his return flight from Hawaii was late. When he greeted me with a warm, generous hug, I knew I was in the right place. Everyone at the clinic was just as nurturing and kind as he. Little did I know that I was beginning a lifetime journey toward a level of health and well-being beyond my imagination.

I had read about acupuncture, but avoided it for a long time because I feared needles, a result of too many painful penicillin shots as a child. Reluctantly, I agreed to a session and the acupuncturist was so gentle that the insertion of the needles hurt minimally on only a few points. Miraculously, I slept deeply throughout that first night, something I had literally not experienced since the beginning of menopause. The next day, my energy was higher.

Because Dr. Stromberg was both a medical and a homeopathic doctor, he understood my wishes to heal naturally without drugs. His clinic provided a holistic approach, so I also met with a chiropractor, nutritionist, and therapist. The therapist, a Jungian, created a crack in my self-image when he insisted, "Because of your perfectionism, you expect a great deal of yourself and others, but you need to be kinder to yourself."

"I don't feel like I'm so hard on myself—I just want to do things well. Why is that a bad thing?" I countered.

"It's a matter of degree. I'd like for you to read *The Spirituality of Imperfection*. I think it will be enlightening."

"Sure," I murmured as tears began to well up. "It's just overwhelming—all I have to deal with right now."

"Remember, there's always light in the darkness, and even if it's a small glimmer, pay attention to it." His words comforted me.

Later, I saw the nurse practitioner who was supposed to do energy work, but talking to her was so helpful that we dropped the energy work. She, too, told me to be kinder to myself and not to expect to be perfect. I didn't see myself as a perfectionist, but by the time I left the clinic, I saw it was true and it was hurting me.

The highlight of my last day was a luxurious hot stone massage offered free of charge because they were auditioning a new therapist. With the warm, smooth stones and oil being spread over my body, I fell into deep relaxation, feeling most grateful.

In contrast with all my other experiences at the clinic, my last appointment with a Cherokee medicine man was disturbing and disappointing. Normally he worked with his wife, who was also a healer, but she couldn't be there. At first, his blond hair and white face startled me, and he spent too long telling me about his life on the reservation. Finally, he turned to my issues.

"You are like two people," he said, "because you have healing and intuitive powers that you've shut down and are afraid to use. Because you are so shut down, I won't be able to do any spiritual work with you today."

"But that's why I'm here," I responded, shocked. His attitude was incongruent with the others who worked in the clinic. "I had assumed you would work with me wherever I was spiritually."

"We can still do some work, but not the main work I do."

"Well, what do you mean I'm shut down?"

"The main area that is shut down is your third chakra. This chakra is related to issues around money, power, ego and reputation."

I nodded my head, knowing he was right about that. Maybe he would be able to help me after all. "Where do those blocks come from?"

"They came from religion, and you need to let go of them. Until you were five years old, you were in touch with your intuition. Then, something happened that made you afraid, and you learned to hide what you knew."

I tried to remember what happened that traumatized me, but no event surfaced. He continued talking about this for some time and emphasized that we couldn't let go of negative attitudes until we took responsibility for them.

"You are a natural healer and should do that work." Then he

asked, "Who is an Aries in your life? Why don't you heal her?"

The only Aries I knew was Diane, and I said, "I don't know how to heal her."

"Of course you do. Ignore the people who tell you that you need this training or to know a certain thing in order to heal. You don't need to be trained. You can do it naturally."

I didn't know what to think about this. He also said I should teach adults and that I might like to teach on an Indian reservation, but that I needed to find the right one. He spent the rest of the time talking about his own life, but I couldn't listen because I felt he had been judgmental, and I was angry he wouldn't even try to help me become unblocked. When he finally stopped talking, I told him I didn't want to continue, and I left an hour before the three hours was up. I concluded that it was probably his wife who was the real healer.

My last appointment was with Stromberg to receive instructions on what I needed to do in all areas of my healing. When I stood up to leave and turned toward the door, I saw that a two-foot high statue of Yoda from *Star Wars* stood in the corner. I turned, grinning broadly at the doctor, "I see the Force is with you."

"And with you," he said smiling back.

Paths to Healing

That summer began a three-year odyssey that required me to overhaul my entire life. Fortunately, I was self-disciplined and dedicated to healing as naturally as possible, but I often felt overwhelmed with so much new information and developing a new and restrictive daily routine. The changes I made related to sleep, food, supplements, and spiritual practices.

Sleeplessness had been a problem for years. After I began to go through menopause several years earlier, I spent an entire summer during which I only slept two hours at a time. I lay awake for hours, slept for awhile, and woke up again. By the time I visited Stromberg's clinic, I was exhausted all the time despite the fact that my previous doctor had prescribed hormones that allowed me to sleep several hours at a time. Stromberg changed my prescription to safer bio-identical hormones that were sustained release. With this change, I felt more peace of mind and my moods leveled out.

The major change, however, was that I had to go to bed at nine o'clock every night. This was necessary to rest my stressed liver. Even with sleep medication, I was never sleepy that early. After so many years of working in theater and dance, rehearsing and performing well into the evening, going to sleep early went against my natural inclination. My most creative time was late at night. When the school year began, this became more of a challenge because my chattering mind couldn't let go of the day's challenges.

By this time, I'd stopped smoking again, given up alcohol, and sex was only a distant memory. Food was the last sensual pleasure I had left, but the restrictions placed on it destroyed my enjoyment. As time went by, I learned to take pleasure in feeding my body what it needed to be healthy and energetic, but at first I felt only deprivation and stress. I had to travel across the city to find organic food, rotate a variety of vegetables, eat some animal protein at every meal, and add gluten-free grains to my diet. I was used to reading food labels because of my gluten intolerance, but now I had to read more carefully in order to also eliminate all preservatives, chemicals, sugar, refined products, and dairy. My diet consisted almost entirely of fresh food that needed to be cooked every day.

All day I thought about preparing the next meal or taking the next supplement. Fortunately, most of the nine problem conditions Dr. Stromberg had identified could be cured by supplements and a good diet. I took several types of vitamins and minerals, amino acids, items to improve absorption, digestive enzymes, ayurvedic teas, homeopathic remedies, DHEA, and glandulars. I took them at meals, in between meals, and at bedtime. I kept a list as a guide because the brain fog I still experienced made remembering the schedule impossible.

I had to continue working full-time because my insurance didn't cover the alternative treatment. After teaching basically the same classes for two years, I had good lessons prepared for all the levels and only had to adapt them to individual student needs. With small classes, I could easily grade papers, plan, and take care of the required paperwork. Even traveling to two or three schools a day was a blessing because I used the traveling time as a brief vacation during which I practiced quieting my mind. Work kept me engaged with life. If I hadn't been working, I'm not sure I would have been able to get out of bed.

I was thankful for Diane's friendship and two other women, friends of hers, who had chronic fatigue syndrome because virtually no one else understood this condition. Most people, including my family, doubted that I was really ill because I didn't look ill. This had been a blessing and a curse throughout my life. Most people thought I was just whining. "Well, we all get tired," they would say.

I meditated often, for I knew I wouldn't heal unless I also gave attention to my mind, spirit, and emotions. I often threw the Healing Runes created by Blum and Loughan that had been recommended by the nurse practitioner at the clinic. Along with the runes was a book that contained inspirational messages for each rune. Many spiritual questions haunted me, so I read a number of spiritually oriented articles relating to mind and body. Why did I become ill? Did I create my illness with my thought patterns? Had my perfectionism contributed to this? Was God testing me for some reason? At least I needed to release the old "God punishes us for our sins" message, clearly an idea from religion that caused a block to healing, according to the Native American medicine man I had seen.

One night, I had an amazing dream with many layers. My students' mothers fixed food for a celebration to honor me, or maybe all the teachers, and it was in my schoolroom. I took a helping of fish stew made from salmon, scooped out blocks of fish from it and pinned them on the bulletin board, covering it. I planned to gradually eat them, but I thought, "I've taken too much, I'll never eat it all." Then I wandered around, eating and visiting with people.

Next, the room became a store with a counter of antique jewelry, and I sold an old pearl pin to a girl. She planned to take the pearls out and make them into something else. Then the room became a large outdoor place. A little black boy who looked African, but had on western clothes, was near the salmon board (now outside), and I knew he wanted some fish. I went to get him a paper plate, and when I returned, there was a crowd of African-dressed people by the board. I said, "No, we can't feed so many people," so they left. Then I saw that the salmon board was empty, and I realized they had been fed, and I was very happy.

This felt like a very powerful dream. If fish represented divine ideas, then I had plenty of them to "feed" many people; perhaps my ideas fed my students, particularly my African American students; perhaps what I gave them were pearls they could make into something valuable. As a teacher, one could evaluate one's success only in hindsight. In the dream, I was successful. Perhaps these divine ideas would guide my healing as well.

I was amazed at the end of the school year that I had made it through two terms working full-time and trying to heal. It was July, the middle of summer, although in New Orleans most of the year felt like summer. My energy was better but still out of balance, and the natural remedies for sleep weren't working. The regime was still stressful. I had to rest, read, and take it very easy in the evening. Affirming that I was well put too much pressure on me, so I began to affirm that I was getting well. Even thinking positively stressed me out.

One night when I couldn't sleep, I cried for hours, finally realizing that I was grieving for the loss of community and family I had experienced during the past year. I had virtually no social life. A close woman friend had stopped communicating with me. I had no man in my life and couldn't help but envy the other women I knew with chronic fatigue who had men in their lives to love and help them. Even my family kept their distance. Although my mother paid for someone to clean my apartment twice a month, and I appreciated that, she felt she had to be available around the clock to help my brother and sister-in-law. This was her choice, not their requirement. Raising kids and building a new house took all their time, but I knew they would have supported anything she wanted to do to help me.

In indulgent New Orleans, putting good health first made me odd. I didn't fit the image of the sacrificial mother who was queen in New Orleans. Women's voices, except for mothers, weren't valued much. I wasn't a nun either—that would have brought me respect. So who was I and how could I fit into this world? I wanted to belong so someone would want to be with me and help care for me.

Because I meditated regularly and was able to remember most of my dreams, I was in touch with the unconscious, but I didn't always understand the messages of the dreams. A very powerful one explained partly why I had trouble in relationships with men. In the dream, two friends, introduced me to a man who was tall, slender, gray-haired, and very nice. The man and I sat at a table talking and my mother was in the room. Suddenly, she tripped and slid down a hole in the floor that opened onto an incline that was full of white gravel. This interrupted my conversation with the man because I had to rush to rescue and drag her out of the hole. Afterward, I apologized to the man. My mother then sat down at the table to look at the newspaper, holding it up in front of her so that it blocked my vision and was between the man and me. When she lowered the paper, the man was gone.

That dream recalled the way my mother used to take my friends' attention away from me with her vibrant personality. It suggested that she played a part in my inability to have a relationship with a man or perhaps with my mature masculine side. Maybe I wanted to be rescued the way she needed to be rescued, but how did my emotional connection with her interfere?

I needed to leave New Orleans soon for my mental as well as physical health, but I loved my family and didn't want to leave them. If I left, I was afraid they would be too busy to visit me because that had happened before. Once again, I thought about Asheville, North Carolina, where I had visited various friends over the years. It appealed to me because it was in the mountains, but also because it represented a spiritual path, a way to a higher consciousness and better life, but its relatively wet climate concerned me. Although I was afraid the drive would be too tiring, I decided to take a vacation there the following summer.

Finally, with the arrival of summer, all obstacles dropped away, and I headed for the Appalachian Mountains and a vacation in a cozy cabin just outside Asheville. The frilly curtains and white iron bed reminded me of my great-grandmother's bed and the times I took naps there, falling to sleep as she repeated the stories of her childhood. Geese and ducks honked and quacked quietly as they waddled around the yard. Their voices blended with the chirp of crickets and the sound of the stream behind the cabin. The energy was so different, so peaceful and serene, and the fresh air was laced with the fragrance of honeysuckle. No one locked their doors. Although the trip had been exhausting, peace filled my heart.

Everything I'd read about Asheville sounded ideal, but I still wondered whether I would feel isolated because it was so small. Every day I drove into town and walked the streets, visiting shops and usually eating where I knew the food was healthy and organic.

Deep healing was taking place because my dreams about men continued, and in them, the men were friendly. In one dream, Gary, a little girl about eight or nine, and I went to the movies to see an Anne Rice vampire movie. We went to a private screening room where we could lie on the floor. After a few minutes, I realized that Gary and the girl weren't there. I looked out just as they were coming back from the concession stand. He brought me a little plate of sausages that he thought I would like, but I didn't want the sausages. I wanted popcorn and refused to take the sausages because I was mad he hadn't asked me what I wanted. Then I realized I had hurt him by refusing. He was trying to be nice to me, but I didn't appreciate the way he expressed his caring. That was at the core of the problem in our marriage—we didn't understand what the other needed. He needed me to help him create financial security, but I didn't value that—my creativity was more important to me, and he didn't understand my need to be creative. It was all so clear to me now. The dream was a wonderful gift, and I finally let go of my underlying anger and forgave myself and him.

By the time I left Asheville, I felt renewed and put it at the top of my list for a place to live; however, I was used to an abundance of arts activity and wasn't sure I was ready to sacrifice that source of inspiration in my life. I had also considered moving to Albuquerque because it was a larger city. For years, I had subscribed to *New Mexico Magazine*. I was fascinated by the beauty of the landscape and southwestern art and inextricably drawn to the concentration of Native American culture there, but I had never been there and needed to visit and explore the possibilities.

In August, another school year began, and soon afterward, I received the transfer I had requested to go to a new home base school. The previous year, students often set fires in the bathroom near my classroom and ran through the halls disrupting class by banging on doors. A class of four students who were totally unmotivated and disrespectful also frequently cursed me. Even suspension didn't affect the behavior of these students. I was relieved to be leaving, but when I told the students I had had for two years, they were disappointed, and one of my favorite boys dashed from the room hiding his tears. At that heart-wrenching moment, I almost changed my mind, but I knew I couldn't tolerate more stress without it damaging my health. Once I arrived at the new school, I was relieved that all my students were respectful and eager.

As I gained more energy, I was able to participate in classes and workshops sponsored by the Jung Society. At the last moment, I decided to attend Ginette Paris' workshop on mythology and psychology based on James Hillman's work. One thing she said was exactly what I needed to hear: when we do something wrong, we aren't sinners—we're just stupid; we don't know the right thing to do, so the situation blows up in our faces. Her words touched me deeply because I still felt inadequate dealing with relationships and business. In that moment, I was able to release the anger I felt toward myself because of my difficulty creating peaceful relationships. Who I was did not naturally fit the business world. Those jobs didn't allow me to express my gift, but teaching about life and spirituality, making literature come alive with meaning, and feeding the minds and souls of young people—that was my true gift. I had made the mistake of believing that I needed fixing when what I needed was to express my gift.

As Paris continued and discussed how spiritually empty many people were because of our emphasis on physical things, the words of the medicine man again flashed through my mind to let go of the old religious ideas that no longer served me. I understood more deeply why Native American and African religions held so much appeal for me. I saw God as spirit—pervading the universe, me, all life. The god of traditionalism was too limiting and didn't allow for expansion. God was personal for me and that made the dogma of the church unnecessary, for if people respected each other, the earth, and spirit, we didn't need the kind of rules the church established.

During the workshop and afterward, I felt a great release. Able to see my flaws as ignorance, I could forgive myself for failing and applauded myself for how hard I tried to succeed in difficult situations. I began a new journal because this week felt like a turning point, a new beginning. I vowed to celebrate the positive *intentions* of the choices I had made.

In December 1997, I crashed emotionally. The stress of living this restricted life for six months was too stressful. Although I was getting better, the pain, fatigue, low blood sugar, and isolation were still taking a toll. I was still upset that, in October, when I had crashed the last time, no family member was available to help. No one even took me seriously. I felt abandoned, shocked that even if my health was in jeopardy, no one could interrupt his or her routine. They said they loved me, but what did that mean? One Sunday afternoon when I was at their house visiting, I tried again to get through to my mother.

Standing in the kitchen while she started to prepare dinner, I approached the subject I'd often hinted at. "This is so nice not to have to cook. I feel like all I do is cook and think about what to cook next."

"Well, I'm glad you could join us," she replied smiling.

"You always cook healthy meals," I began, feeling uncomfortable about expressing my needs, "so I was wondering if you could help me out. If you're cooking food I could eat, would you save a little extra and freeze it for me? If you could do that even once a week—you know, just put away parts of different meals, it would help me so much."

She was quiet for a moment, then with resistance in her voice, she said, "We don't eat organic food. I wouldn't know what to fix you."

"I don't have to eat organic for every meal. I eat simply. You could freeze a piece of chicken from one meal, some vegetables from another. Whatever is easiest for you. Even one meal a week," I begged.

"No, that wouldn't work. I'd have to cook other things for you."

"Mother," I shouted, losing my last ounce of patience, "why do you have to make everything so difficult! This is simple!"

"Hey, what's going on?" my brother asked, walking into the middle of our conversation.

Using her most martyred tone of voice, "She wants me to cook for her as well as you. I can't do all this cooking."

My brother looked at me questioning. I shook my head and rolled my eyes, then explained what I wanted her to do.

"Mother," he said walking over and putting his hand on her shoulder, "Georganne needs your help and you only cook one meal a day for us. I think you need to help her out. You can do this." He looked back at me. "We'll get it done."

As a result, she started preparing two meals a week and brought them to me frozen or had my brother drop them off. Although she insisted on making more work for herself and cooking them separately, it was a relief that, on days when I was exhausted, I could eat a healthy meal and not have to cook it. But it hurt that she helped only after my brother insisted she do it.

Around Christmas, the friend who had kept her distance finally admitted to me she had stopped being friendly because my illness frightened her. Before I had become ill, I ate healthy food and exercised regularly, so how could someone with good health habits become seriously ill? The reminder that life was uncertain terrified her.

Through testing and telephone calls, Dr. Stromberg treated me long distance. When I crashed, I called him, "Aaron, I can't handle this regimen anymore; it's too strict and it's wearing me out."

"Okay, we'll have to take another approach then. How are you feeling?"

"Weird. My body feels like a paper thin shell filled with powerful energy surging through it, like it will suddenly burst through my skin. I've never felt anything like this."

"I know exactly what's going on. That is a perfect description of a condition described in Chinese medicine. Based on that, we'll start by eliminating the amino acids, and I'll send you a crock pot recipe for congee, a rice and vegetable dish, that will actually heal your liver. You'll eat a little several times a day. Then I need to look at your most recent tests, and I'll get back to you about the other things you can eliminate. Does this sound manageable?"

"Yes, thank you so much."

"Good. I've got to go, so here's a big hug," he said with enthusiasm, making me laugh as I hung up the phone. I liked the idea of food as natural medicine and was beginning to think of it as healing nourishment.

When depression and blood sugar problems returned, I turned for help to Unity teachings. To manifest the good health I wanted, I needed to write down what I wanted. Then I acknowledged that God was in me, and I would receive God's good. I expressed gratitude with emotion and then stated to the subconscious, writing this and repeating it often, "I want to totally accept this belief." I still didn't fully understand how this aspect of New Thought spirituality worked, but I was grateful that it sometimes did.

The craziness in the schools and the violence in New Orleans were becoming a permanent part of my psyche. There were fights at lunch every day, even among the girls, and certain children were chosen for harassment on a regular basis, including a student of mine. He was a small boy, quiet and respectful in class, but he was a member of The Hot Boys, a group that had just signed a recording contract. His success made him a target. In later years, he would develop a performing gangsta persona known as L'l Wayne, but at this point in his life he was young and vulnerable.

I couldn't imagine how students could learn under these conditions. I would never have survived emotionally in these environments. About this time, I dreamed that I arrived at my home base school very agitated and went to an administrator's office. Something bad had happened at the school while I was away. There was a student in the office, sitting in a chair to my left, but I couldn't see who he was. An assistant principal (who was black, but in the dream was white like a negative image) was standing behind the desk. When I asked whether I could go get things out of my room, he said, "Yes, but take a guard." Then he added, "Don't think you're going to get by with this. You can't nurture kids like that and not be reported for it." This was a reprimand as if what I had done to help a student was breaking a rule. I was upset, confused, and crying. I rushed out into the halls that were completely dark, and I felt it was very dangerous to go to my room alone. I was about to panic because I needed to get what was in the room and leave, but I couldn't find a guard. Then I found one putting things into a closet, and he accompanied me down the hill to my building. I felt relieved. Teaching felt like that sometimes—doing the things that really mattered were the things that would get teachers in trouble.

In February, spring arrived in this strange place, with azaleas blooming after a winter that was much like any other season. For a while, I dreamed of former men friends and groups of people. They were healing dreams, and in them I felt a part of something. A sign of good things to come, I hoped. My health had gradually improved to a normal energy most of the day and into the evening. Finally, I believed it was possible to fully recover.

When I used the Healing Runes, many of their messages related to my heart. I pulled the Love rune, and its message was to stop protecting my heart and let love in, for it could heal the pain I felt. To heal, I also had to find a community that would support and comfort me, and I needed to choose to see evidence of love in the world rather than its despair and disharmonies.

After this reading, the first thing that came to mind was my family. As much as I loved them, I had to face the fact that we didn't have the relationship I had envisioned when I moved to New Orleans. My expectations were not realistic. I needed single friends who were intellectually stimulating whose lives weren't totally immersed in their families, a situation typical of New Orleans where everything was centered on family. Being honest about this allowed me to forgive my family and myself for my life not being what I wanted. It was time for me to move on. I excitedly gathered brochures on New Mexico, the Land of Enchantment, where I hoped the dry climate would complete my healing quickly and where I could make a home.

Land of Enchantment

When I thought about Albuquerque, I was anxious to see the beautiful skies, landscapes, and art that filled the pages of *New Mexico Magazine*. Perhaps Asheville would be in my future, but it felt too small and isolated for now. I still needed what a city offered, and I hoped Albuquerque would fill my needs.

My week in Albuquerque was a real vacation, not having to cook or handle any personal business and waking up each day able to visit shops and galleries in Old Town and eat the Mexican food I loved. One day I took a bus trip to Santa Fe and fell in love with the art and adobe buildings. It was another place, like Boulder, Colorado, that touched my soul, but it was too expensive to live there. At the end of the week, though, as I returned home, I felt I had still not touched the heart of Albuquerque and felt uncertain about living there.

I continued to heal on many levels. Throughout the next month, I had many dreams about Gary. In them, we were always cooperative and getting along. Each dream brought me more peace as positive images of our relationship replaced the negative ones.

In another recent dream, I was a teenager walking home from a friend's house and came to a flooded area that I had seen before in dreams and knew could be very deep. A teenage boy came along and said, "I'll lead you through this if you want me to." I said, "Yes, thanks." Then I woke up. Even the youthful inner masculine was offering friendship and assisting my inner feminine.

On the following night in my dream, a man who was my boyfriend or husband was being pursued by gangsters. There was a struggle and the gangsters were gone, but at one point, my man hugged me and said lovingly, "I could never get through all this without you." Later, two girls, his daughters, hugged me with tears in their eyes and said they were so happy and touched when he said that to me. At the end, it appeared we were winning by outsmarting the gangsters.

These dreams were signals that my masculine and feminine sides were becoming integrated because the men and I were cooperating and caring for each other. In these dreams, I was willing to accept help and to acknowledge that the masculine side was trying to be helpful. When I became irritated, I calmed down and behaved more appropriately than I sometimes did in real life. The dreams were teaching me to be more at peace with men on a conscious level.

Then, two days before my birthday in October in 1998, I had the second most significant dream I'd ever had.

I was in a new apartment in a complex with several interconnecting buildings. Many rooms had unusual shapes and were on two levels. The first room had a continuous wrap-around window that filled the room with light. The lower level was a living room or den, and the upper level had mustard-colored vinyl benches with backs that ran along two walls. I also found kitchen items on a shelf to one side. Many of those items were from the 1950s when I was growing up.

I walked through the living room and opened a door into a dark cave-like room. It had an extremely high, domed ceiling, the floor was dirt, and it was empty. I felt it was a holy place, and unable to find a light switch, I left.

I continued exploring interesting new rooms and was very excited about the entire space. Other people were also there: women and the landlord, a bearded, slender man. I asked about the huge, empty room with the domed ceiling, and the landlord led me there. After we went inside, he turned on a light switch. The room was filled with light although I couldn't see a light source, and I saw that the walls were made of red sandstone. I was flooded with inner joy and knew that it was indeed a holy place—my own private cathedral.

We walked across the room, and the landlord opened another door to a bedroom also filled with sunlight. It could have been designed by Frank Lloyd Wright. It had a bed with simple, clean lines made from beautifully grained wood. I was excited because I liked it much better than the other bedroom.

Outside, I walked around the corner of the apartment building, which was on a hill, and looked out over a city. I was thrilled by the beautiful view.

The dream was a metaphor in which the rooms were areas of the mind or aspects of the psyche. Each door I opened led to a light-filled room and indicated I was entering into a more enlightened level of consciousness. When I was in the holy room, I was filled with love and happiness. This was the holy place within me, the heart at the center of my being, and I knew I was finally whole.

A friend invited me to attend a dinner at the house of her friend Frances, who was having the dinner in order to share the information she had received at a poetry workshop. She was a tall, regal, gray-haired woman with a cheerful disposition. Because she was a retired English and history teacher who also attended the Jung Society meetings, I enjoyed meeting her because we had so much in common.

A couple of months later, at the Jung Society's Christmas party, I walked over to her and asked, "What are you planning to do this summer?"

"I think I'm going to house-sit in Albuquerque and write," she said. "If I get away from home maybe I can actually start writing."

"What a great way to spend the summer!"

"You want to join me?" she asked enthusiastically.

"Are you serious?"

"Of course, we'd have a great time."

"I'd love to. I'll just have to figure out how to do it. You know I spent a week there last summer."

"You did? What did you think?"

"I loved it. The sky and the landscape were spectacular. I'd never seen such beautiful sunsets. And the art—I loved everything I saw."

"Did you get to Santa Fe?"

"Yes, I took a tour up for the day, and I also went to Acoma Pueblo. That was really interesting."

"Did you talk to the schools?"

"I did, but the salaries in Albuquerque Public Schools were so low. They give you credit for only six out-of-state years of experience. I couldn't live on what they pay, and I didn't have time to check out the schools nearby."

"You can make good money teaching on the reservations, but those can be difficult places."

"I really couldn't decide whether it would be a good place for me to live, but if I could be there a few weeks, I'd really get a feeling for it."

"Oh, I hope you can go. We'll have such a good time."

A storyteller was beginning his presentation, so I whispered, "We'll talk later." She nodded in agreement.

Later in that month and again in January 1999, I had several dreams in which I was in danger or had to face obstacles, but in every case, someone was there to help, or I easily handled the problem. Difficulties were melting away. My energy had improved enough that I could actually consider moving soon.

In one of these dreams, I was in a building packing for a trip I was taking with a group. I went outside, but when I returned, someone had scattered what I had packed, especially the jewelry. I gathered it back up. I then got on an elevator and rode it to the top, but it got stuck on the fifth floor. Luckily, an engineer got it running again and warned me to just get where I was going and stop playing around. Could the fifth floor relate to the fifth chakra, the throat chakra? That chakra related to choice, communication, the use of one's will, and surrendering to divine will.

In the same dream, I went back to the room where the leader was ready to go and gathered my things. We all went outside. We had to jump off a large rock. Other people had trouble getting down, but I jumped in slow motion and landed gently. We walked up an incline toward a bridge but didn't go onto it. Instead, we went to the bank of a ditch with little water. The group leader talked about how people could float down this river eating shrimp; I assumed she meant this had happened in the past because it was only a ditch now. The messages in the dream seemed to be telling me that taking a leap wouldn't be difficult and that I shouldn't delay. The path might look like a ditch, but it was a river that would take me where I wanted to go and nourish me.

In July, my arrival in Albuquerque was clearly in divine order and accompanied by auspicious signs: a double rainbow filled the sky, my plane arrived ten minutes early, and my rental car was upgraded to a larger one at no extra cost. As the sun set, the sky filled with a spectacular panorama of changing colors and shapes —gold, purple, pink, and shades of blue, dancing across space until the sun slipped behind the silhouettes of ancient volcanoes west of town, and I turned to realize that we were blessed by a full moon.

Frances picked me up at the airport, and when we arrived at the house to drop off my bags, I was delighted to see that it was centrally located and only two blocks from a large natural foods store that planned to open in two weeks. Frances gave a quick tour of the house before we headed downtown to get Chinese food. The air conditioning in the restaurant was broken, so we brought the food home and sat at the kitchen table, talking incessantly. As we finished eating and closed the food containers, a bulb in the lighting fixture hanging above our heads burst with a loud pop. We gasped, jumped back, then burst into laughter, both thinking the same thing.

"My, but we are powerful together, aren't we?" Frances said with a sly smile.

Neither Frances nor I wrote much that summer. There were too many fascinating places to visit. Most importantly, Frances and I developed a deep friendship, the kind for which I had been longing. Not only did we love going places, we also talked for hours, sharing our lives and thoughts, and explored our mutual interests, the arts, and spirituality.

Albuquerque offered countless alternative healers, several natural foods stores, one of the best writers' organizations in the country, and interesting free lectures at the University of New Mexico. Art was everywhere—on walls, the sides of buildings, hanging in galleries, at outdoor art fairs. New Mexico was called The Land of Enchantment, and I was truly enchanted.

Over the course of the summer, Frances decided it was time to move back to Albuquerque, where she had grown up, and began to look for a house. Because I loved looking at houses, I often accompanied her. The moment we entered one in particular, it felt like hers. In the back yard was a small fruit tree above what had once been a fountain, and in the tree, intertwined among the branches, was a cloth snake.

Frances turned and looked at me as if she were asking, "Do you see what I see?"

"It's a sign, Frances," I said, knowing that she knew snakes were symbols for the earth goddess.

Catching us by surprise, the real estate agent commented, "It is rather a Garden of Eden picture isn't it? Or of the feminine divine." We all laughed the knowing laugh of women who shared a secret and launched into a discussion of the garden's symbolism and spirituality that ended with an invitation to attend the agent's Religious Science church.

Excited by what the real estate agent had told us, Frances and I attended a service the following Sunday. We loved the music, the intelligence of the minister, his positive message, and the loving energy of the church. We grabbed a quick lunch and returned in the afternoon to attend a workshop presented by Alan Cohen. He was very funny, and the workshop helped me to decide that I wanted to live there where workshops to expand my spiritual awareness were abundant. Albuquerque felt like my soul's home—the place I was supposed to be.

It was the end of July and applying for a teaching position was a long shot because most jobs were filled before the summer. I didn't know how I would manage to write and teach, but I put it all in God's hands, knowing that if this were the right place and the right time for me to move, it would all work out.

Everything fell into place. Within two weeks, I found a high school teaching position at a relatively new school in a suburb where the pay was comparable to New Orleans. It was divided into four academies, and I was to teach sophomore humanities in the Fine Arts Academy. Although that academy had just hired a new dance teacher, the possibility for me to work with dance or drama was open. It was my dream job. I enjoyed the students, and considering it was the beginning of the year, they weren't any more difficult than I had expected them to be, and the academy and department heads were supportive women.

I found an apartment near the school although it was a long drive from Frances. Because I was hired only a couple of days before the start of school, my mother made arrangements to have all my belongings and car shipped but sent a few necessities like clothes and pots and pans ahead. Everyone in the family pitched in to help. I was grateful. Surely, this was meant to be.

When I was offered the teaching contract, I was warned that I was the last teacher hired at the high school. If there were too many teachers for the number of students when they did the major count, I could lose my position, but everything felt so right that I didn't take the possibility seriously. Then six weeks after school started, I received devastating news. There were too many teachers and I would have to transfer to another school in the district. I was heartbroken. How could this be when the whole situation was so perfect? I felt that the universe had played a really dirty trick on me.

At that point, I only had two choices: an eighth grade class or the new alternative high school that was just opening. I chose the high school, but within a few weeks, the principal made it clear that I wasn't "motherly" enough for his students. I suspected that the issue had to do with my setting boundaries for students who had poor ones. Sitting in a meeting of all women, including the Director of Human Resources, he was unable to clarify what he meant although he had no complaints about my actual teaching. Reluctantly, he agreed to let me finish the year.

Although my professional life in New Mexico had been challenging so far, I found inspiration and solace at my church. I took the course, Foundations of Religious Science, that delved more deeply into understanding the mind-spirit connection and how to use positive thinking to create my own reality. We explored extensively and deeply the mechanism of how affirmations, prayer, and meditation worked. It proved to be significant preparation for even more disturbing experiences I had later in the year.

At midterm, desperation overrode my intuition when I took a position teaching ninth grade humanities in order to return to the regular high school. During the years I taught in the New Orleans public schools, I often dealt with difficult but gifted inner-city students. Because I was an itinerant teacher, I had worked with many administrators over those years, and despite the challenges I encountered, I was treated with respect by administrators and faculty. The administrators always supported and advised me when I had discipline problems that went beyond what I could handle, and they held the students responsible for their own actions.

However, among the classes I began teaching in January at the regular high school, there was one class where the students were incorrigible. I followed the advice of the administrators in disciplining them and wrote referrals, but the consequences were so delayed they made no impression on the students. After a few weeks, the principal informed me that my classroom management was unacceptable, and I would be fired if it didn't improve. When I explained I needed disciplinary support from the administration, he considered my attitude inappropriate. At that point, I contacted the teacher's union and learned there was a procedure the school had failed to follow. To correct this, I was put on a professional development plan monitored by two administrators.

At this point I felt hopeful. They would be able to see that I was doing everything I should do, and surely they would see that the students I wrote up were disciplined. I also wanted to call parents about their children's behavior, but they assured me that wouldn't solve the problem. The whole situation seemed crazy to me, but I followed the plan they outlined. It didn't work, and although I did everything they required, they recorded all my actions as negative. Finally, I did start calling parents, and student behavior improved.

One day after a particularly difficult class, I was called to the office over the intercom and told that parents whom I had called had called the principal and complained. Therefore, I was being released from my position. I would be put on administrative leave and my contract paid in full. I was escorted from the building by security, in shock and trembling, hardly able to start my car and drive home. After so many years of successful teaching, how could this happen?

Even after a few weeks of rest, my mind was still cluttered with the absurd way the situation had played out. I'd never understood the need for a teachers' union, but now I did. Without union help, my entire career would have been destroyed. I would soon need to apply for a position for next year, but first I needed to sleep for days and remember what it felt like to be positive and joyful.

Looking ahead, I had several months with income during which I could return to my long neglected writing. I pulled the rough draft and research on a novel from my files, reviewed it carefully, and felt the surge of joy and energy that always filled me when I was writing. Determined to complete the book, I headed to the library the following week to research more information on certain aspects of World War II. It was the story of a journalist's spiritual journey to discover who she really was.

And that was my journey now—reclaiming who I really was, certainly not the negative, incompetent teacher my former colleagues tried to convince me I was, but a creative, caring, sensitive person with a holy center.

Dust Devils

Living on the desert, one always longed for rain, but often, in its place, storms appeared that pelted the land with sand and whirling columns of dust devils. Their brown curtains fell over the horizon, obscuring mountains, houses, and roads, blinding drivers and sanding away the shimmering veneer of the landscape, leaving dust and damage in its wake.

Living at the center of such a storm for three months had eroded my confidence, health, and joy. As the weeks away from school passed, my frayed edges began to mend, but my heart and trust of others was deeply damaged. I longed for rain and the company of green trees to heal my soul, but I only saw desert cactus and tumbleweed. It began to dawn on me that my enchantment with this land was an illusion.

During the past year, I had survived the psychological manipulation and abuse by meditating and releasing the endless fear that encroached on every moment of my professional life. Regardless of the chaos around me, I returned to my holy center each day, knowing I was one with God. But the grief that I felt each day as I failed to please those who held my future in their hands overcame any personal pleasure I felt in the successes I did achieve. I often cried with deep shaking sobs each time I felt the peace at my center, grieving for the lack of some small peace in my working day.

I had also survived because of my spiritual community. Each Sunday, I went to church and was inspired by the music and the messages that reaffirmed I could change my life by changing my thinking. On some level, I knew that all the powerful people at work who seemed to control my life, in fact, did not. I was in control even if I didn't always know what to do. The secret was to keep practicing the principles just as I had practiced how to release my fear and that had eventually changed my life for the better. At least now, I had time to recover, and I asked the universe for guidance, trying to remain open to whatever showed up. I was showered with blessings.

One of my lifelong fears had been the fear that I wouldn't have enough money, and now I feared getting another job would be difficult. Without my making a formal request, the universe seemed to know what I needed and a prosperity workshop at church appeared. It introduced a broader concept of prosperity that included more than money, and as a result, I saw less scarcity and more abundance manifesting in my life in many ways. Certainly, the continuation of my teaching income was one manifestation.

In addition, I was matched with a woman and a man in the workshop who became my good friends and role models. We were a small group known as a power pack within the large group. Letitia was a playwright and writer who had supported herself and her child for many years by writing, therefore disproving what I had always been told—that you can't make a living writing. Later, as a member of Southwest Writers, I would meet many people who earned a decent living from writing. In addition, I felt that my novel would make a better screenplay than novel, and Letitia had the expertise and willingness to help me.

The third member of our power pack was a social worker, Ron, an attractive man who worked in the public schools and would eventually help me obtain my next teaching job. He was kind and had integrity. He wasn't attracted to me as I was to him, but my attraction was at least a good sign that I was setting my standards higher for future relationships.

Over Memorial Day weekend, instead of frantically figuring final grades as I had done year after year, I treated myself to the First Annual Santa Fe Screenwriting Conference. Chris Vogler, who had worked at Disney, taught an all-day workshop on the hero's mythic journey and the mythic elements in our lives. It all corresponded to Joseph Campbell's writing about the journey, but Vogler put it in terms specifically related to writing a screenplay.

The next three days of the workshop consisted of nine hours of instruction on screenwriting by Rick Reichman, a mentor who

Awakening to the Dance

worked with beginners and taught in Santa Fe. As a novice, I was glad he dug into the nitty-gritty of screenplay structure. With exposure to other inspiring writers, I learned how to pitch to producers and format a page. At the end of the conference, I felt competent enough to begin a screenplay.

So often in my life I had wanted to do something and hadn't known how to go about doing it. For example, when I was younger, all I knew about becoming an actress was to go to school as I would for anything else. I had only the vaguest idea what one would do next. I'd felt the same way about writing, but in Albuquerque there were all kinds of writers, many who generously encouraged others. I could take workshops and classes on anything I needed to learn. From a writer's standpoint, moving here was the right decision, no matter how difficult it had been.

When school started again, my friend Ron helped me obtain a position at one of the better high schools to teach gifted students, but the program was very different from New Orleans' gifted program. It consisted of geography for the ninth grade and mentorships and apprenticeships for the older students. Only half my time was spent in the classroom. The rest of the time, I drove all over the city trying to set up jobs for the older students. The paperwork load was tremendous, most of it similar to what I had done in New Orleans. Because the public schools gave teachers credit for only six years of teaching out of state, the pay was too low to meet my basic expenses, but it was certainly better than having no job.

After my first pay check, it became apparent that I'd have to get a part-time job to supplement my income. I couldn't imagine where I'd find the energy for it, but that was another issue. Fortunately, a few weeks after school started, a high school in a small town near Albuquerque asked me to set up a drama program. They would pay for all my experience plus a stipend. When I asked to be released from the current contract, the principal wasn't happy but allowed me to leave.

At the new school, most students were Hispanic and Native

American, from five pueblos as well as from town. The principal warned me not to expect them to sit quietly for long periods like Anglo students because the students were from very community-oriented cultures. I taught many who didn't speak English well and who often missed school for church or pueblo-related religious occasions. I was instructed to never ask the Indian students (they preferred to be called Indians) why they were absent. This was considered intrusive because many pueblo-related matters stayed on the reservation. There were also students who at around age fourteen decided to follow their culture's ways rather than the white man's. They attended school until they could legally quit, were very respectful, but usually did very little work. It was certainly a challenging situation; however, I respected and felt a connection to this culture because of its relationship to nature.

The principal of the school was very supportive of the drama program. Half of the students previously enrolled in my drama class were in special education and had behavior disorders. They were incapable of sitting quietly while others performed, and one boy ran around the room constantly. Slowly, I was able to have the worst distractors rescheduled into other classes so that I could actually teach. Just as that class was settling down, I received the devastating news that the principal who had hired me was retiring immediately. I wondered what would happen to the drama program.

The many rapid changes taking place in my life were stressful and wonderful at the same time, and I worked hard to benefit from them. My attitude toward abundance had improved with my new larger salary although I sometimes slipped back into scarcity thinking. I had more faith in the universe to fill my needs, but I still went into a deep depression at times when old problems surfaced again.

One evening when Frances and I had dinner at her house, I asked her, "You're my friend and I need your help. I need to understand what's at the root of my conflict with people and why I'm having trouble making friends here. What do you see?"

"You know I love you," she began. I nodded to encourage her to go on. "I think the hardest thing is when you're defensive with people. Your response hurts them or scares them away. They give up because they don't know how to deal with you."

"I guess I don't realize when I'm doing that. I think it's almost a habit now because I've had to defend myself so much this year at school."

"I know, but people who don't know you don't understand. Sometimes, it's hard even for those of us who do."

"I'm sorry, Frances," I reached out and squeezed her arm. "Thanks for being my friend. I'll try to be more aware."

I couldn't help remembering when Juan, one of my students, said one day that I was like Dr. Jekyll and Mr. Hyde. One minute I was sweet and the next minute I was mean. I knew what he meant, and I didn't like that in myself. I had succeeded in manifesting more income, but I hadn't succeeded in releasing the fear that the experience from last year would repeat itself, and that fear led me to overreact to conflict. I had little emotional resilience left and was stressed from trying to fit in, first in New Orleans, and now here. Both cultures were very different from my background.

Working with administrators in this school was also stressful. One woman had only a corporate background, not one in education. In conferences, she acted more like a social worker than a disciplinarian, always sympathizing with the student and undermining my position.

Again the issue of power and misuse of power reared its ugly head. Were all the schools in New Mexico like this? Was there some cultural issue at work here that I didn't grasp because once again I was dealing with administrators who resisted holding students responsible for their actions? On a personal level, dealing with this issue over and over was torture. I couldn't control others. What was it that *I* needed to learn?

A memory surfaced early one morning. The image had appeared one night in Denver as I fell to sleep with Alan. I was wearing a black robe and golden snake headdress, holding a powerful wand that I was angrily misusing. Was that it? Karma from a past life when I had abused power? Was this payback? That was a frightening thought.

The drama class was still a challenge, and I knew I had to find something that would engage their attention. Reading plays was a problem because so many had severe reading problems, so I asked the class whether they wanted to write their own play and perform it. They were excited about the idea but not sure they could do it. I reassured them I would lead them through the process.

They improvised and wrote scenes that they performed for each other in class. They rewrote and discussed each scene and how it fit into the whole piece. In the middle of the process, Letitia visited the class so that they could meet a real playwright. She worked with them on dialogue and complemented them on how realistic the dialogue they had written was, but they seemed rather uninterested in her as a playwright and had few questions. Afterward, I realized most had never actually seen a play.

Although the play sounded like it had been written by adolescents, it was an honest story and reflected their life experiences. A week and a half before the performance, we had a completed script, and at that point I gave it to the new principal to read, feeling that we had successfully retained the real meaning and power of the play while avoiding the objectionable language the students wanted to use.

After reading part of the play, the principal burst into the classroom one day during my planning period.

"Why are they writing about these things?" he demanded, sounding very offended.

"What do you mean?"

"You know what I mean—the drugs, a girl gets pregnant."

"Because these are the things happening in their lives."

"I taught some of these kids in middle school…"

"They're not in middle school anymore, Mr. Santos. They're grown up. They need to express these concerns and issues."

"Ms. Spruce, you are not going to present this play, do you understand?"

"Why?"

"Because it's too upsetting."

"For whom?"

"For anyone seeing it. We had a student commit suicide at the beginning of the year. This could push an emotionally fragile student to do the same thing."

"What about the students in the play, Mr. Santos? What are they going to feel when they've spent the entire semester on this, and you tell them they can't present it. The pay-off for the work is to put it in front of people. Some of these kids don't know much about success, and some of them don't feel good about anything in their lives. They need to feel good about this, they need the applause. This will devastate them."

"You should have thought about this before you let them write something with all this upsetting material in it."

"Well, believe me, this is the squeaky clean version. It took a lot of diplomacy for me to convince them not to use objectionable language because that's the way they talk, but I convinced them we would definitely not get to perform this with bad language in it. Besides, the messages in the play are positive."

"Which ones would that be?"

"Did you read the whole play?"

"No."

"No wonder you're upset. What happens in the end is what's important. The messages to other young people are clear: don't get pregnant, avoid drugs because they can cause bad things to happen in your life, suicide isn't the answer to your problems because there is always help available, get an education and make something of yourself. Now what is objectionable about that!"

"It's still too upsetting."

"Mr. Santos, under what conditions would you consider letting us perform this?" I thought for a moment. "What if we had discussion groups afterward?"

"Well...maybe. If you had school counselors there to facilitate discussions and talk with any students who are upset by it."

"Okay, that's fine. What do I do? Can I just call the district psychologist and try to set it up?"

He looked at me as if he were trying to beam me away. "Go ahead."

"Thank you so much; the students will be so grateful."

Actually, the students were very pissed. They felt this was just another way the administration had shown them how little it cared. I called the psychologists, and because it was May and the end of the school year, they weren't available. Their supervisor intimated that this plan wasn't going to work because the principal didn't want the performance to take place. No one was willing to stand up to him. Even in talking to one counselor I deeply respected, I was surprised that he too felt some students were so fragile that identifying with the characters in the play could push them over the edge. No one seemed to share my feeling that this could be a healing experience for some students because the play had a positive message and encouraged good choices.

This was just another situation in which the students were described as being too fragile to meet what others would call minimum standards. I never doubted they were fragile; many were victims of abuse, incest, alcoholism, and drug abuse. I had cried for hours when one of my best students and a beautiful writer ended up back in jail because he couldn't stay away from his alcoholic and criminal cousins. I had found depths of patience I didn't know I had for a pregnant girl who appeared to be on the verge of an emotional breakdown who was sure I was out to get her whenever I tried to help her.

Because all my English students were seniors, finding a way to prepare and strengthen them became particularly urgent. They were required to write a four-page research paper, but few could write well enough to complete an essay, so I delayed the research assignment until the last semester when most finally had the skills to succeed at it. The principal accused me of setting them up to fail by giving the assignment in the last quarter.

When we were unable to find psychologists to work with us, the drama students were ready to stage a protest. I knew it would do no good, but I knew I had to find them an audience. Finally, the day before the original performance date, I called the principal with another idea.

"Mr. Santos, I have one last idea."

"Yes, Ms. Spruce," he replied, the tone of his voice making it clear that he had no more patience for me.

"I'd like for us to do a noontime performance for teachers only. Will you approve?"

"Yes, but how will you keep out students?"

"I'll get a couple of adults to man the doors—preferably not security."

"All right. Go ahead."

I knew he was agreeing only because the situation had become a matter of public discussion among teachers and students and he wanted it to go away. About ten teachers attended, and their positive, supportive responses were a great boost to the cast's esteem. The counselor I had consulted earlier offered to be there to help keep students from entering, and his calm manner helped defuse what could have been an ugly scene when some friends of the cast arrived and insisted on entering.

Not long after this, the principal made it clear that he wasn't expanding the drama program and that I was an English teacher. Then, in a conference with a senior and his parents, who were members of the family that founded this small town, he asked me to make special arrangements so that one student, who had made no effort all semester, could pass and graduate. I refused, pointing out that the seniors were out of school, and I would be unable to offer the arrangement to others who had failed. To do this for one student would be unethical. He became so upset and red in the face that I was afraid he would have a heart attack.

I knew I was fighting a losing battle. I was technically a short-term employee and could resign without ever receiving an evaluation. If I couldn't teach drama, I didn't want to just teach English to unmotivated students, many of whom were only waiting until they could legally quit. I knew my evaluation would be negative, so I resigned and mourned another closed chapter in my diminishing teaching career.

New Horizons

I had to believe that the difficulties I was experiencing in New Mexico were opportunities to learn lessons, for the idea of them being random acts of the universe was too frightening. It still wasn't clear to me what the lesson was unless I was meant to leave teaching and become a writer. When I boldly affirmed, "I am a writer and the universe supports this," a chill ran up my spine.

In a dream, a woman friend and I were traveling to see Gladys, but we didn't have an appointment although I thought we did. We drove across a hilly, meadow area, but my friend drove the car backwards because she was afraid of seeing what was ahead. This made me nervous. We got there, but I wasn't happy when she finally told me that we didn't have an appointment. In my life as in the dream, it seemed that things weren't going where I had hoped.

I had another longer dream, but I remembered only the end. I came home and was climbing a ladder up to the apartment. A little girl came out of another apartment and asked, "Would you rather have a dog or a baby?" The dog we had was sick, so I thought this was her way of hinting that the dog was better. So, I said, "I would have liked to have a baby, but since I didn't, I wouldn't want one now, so I'd prefer a dog." I was at the top of the ladder, and my brother came out at the story below me and said, "I'm really sorry, Georganne, but the dog committed suicide." I was stunned. I thought, "There's no way he would have done that."

The themes, doing things backwards, not getting what I wanted and the death of the loyal, protective dog all reflected the state of limbo I was experiencing. What did the loss of the dog mean? The dog was a friendly companion. He could sniff things out and find the right path. There was certainly no friendly support at work. Perhaps I'd lost my dog sense because it felt like my intuition had failed me. Albuquerque was feeling less like my soul's home each day.

At the beginning of the year, I had joined a spiritual support group with other people who were involved with religious science teachings. We met monthly, and sharing my life experiences with others who thought like I did was very beneficial. One night, one of the men, Don, asked me, "Is the universe teasing you or are you teasing the universe."

I laughed. "What do you mean?"

"You're always saying that you don't want to teach in schools anymore but want to write, but you just said you want the special education job you applied for."

This job was teaching English at the school in Albuquerque where I had taught gifted classes. "You're right," I admitted. "The universe gave me what I asked for. I'm afraid if I don't teach, I won't find another job, and at least the recent salary increase in Albuquerque will support me."

"So, you'd take this job out of fear. You don't trust the universe."

I frowned. "Yes, I realize that. I didn't have the courage to ask for what I really wanted. If I don't ask for what I really want, I can't receive it, but I need an income."

He smiled supportively. "It's good you can see that."

I remembered what my friend said in her psychic reading, "When you're happy, Georganne, you will have a career." To be happy, I had to define what that meant, but first I had to release the fear that blocked any happiness.

Later that month, I had another strange dream. I was sitting out in the open in a seat made out of a tree trunk. A park ranger, who was very kind, was with me as I gave myself a lethal injection in the thigh. Then I was with my mother. I wanted to put my head in her lap so I could die comfortably, but I couldn't because the way we were sitting was comfortable for her, but not for me. My mother was a teacher, but I was no longer comfortable with this version of me and needed to let go of it. Was I afraid my mother wouldn't approve? But in the dream I was choosing to end the life I had been living, and I was the only one who could do that.

In September, after school started, I was still waiting for the special education job. The school wanted me, but it appeared there was a temporary hiring freeze on the position. So on September 11, 2001, I was at home and called a friend in the middle of the morning. When she answered, she seemed distracted.

"Are you all right," I asked concerned.

"Turn on your TV," she said.

"What?"

"Just turn it on. A plane hit the World Trade Center." Her words didn't make sense, but I immediately turned on the television.

"My God," I uttered and sat down, stunned by what I saw.

For four days, I moved through my life like a ghost haunting familiar places. Time stopped. In those few moments when the planes struck the buildings, the world was irrevocably changed. Like the assassination of President John F. Kennedy, the consciousness of this country was altered. Both of those acts were unthinkable and unimaginable, destroying our sense of security and altering our reality.

Forty-seven hundred people were still unaccounted for. Under the eyes of the world, the generosity of New Yorkers became legend. Television and conversations were filled with heartbreaking and heroic stories. We processed them over and over with friends. I would never forget the little boy who made peanut butter and jelly sandwiches for the people waiting in line to see the list of the dead and survivors. In the plastic bag that held the sandwich, he put a note that read, "Be OK." Only a child could imagine that was a possibility.

The men on one of the hijacked planes, knowing they were going to die, decided to stop the plane from reaching its target, and gave us a new image for heroes. They succeeded in saving lives and giving meaning to their own deaths. And there was Barbara Olson, without fear, concentrating on what she could do to "solve the problem" before her plane slammed into the Pentagon. There was a man who was the only one to live out of the 700 people in his office who died, and in another office all 200 employees escaped. There was the woman who was alive because she had been laid off on Monday. There were the desperate goodbye calls between husbands, wives, and lovers before the lines went dead.

The images of firefighters crying will never leave my memory —so many men and women—so brave, so human, scrambling for days over the enormous pile of toxic broken concrete, bodies, and twisted steel, just living for that moment when they might find a human being alive. I remember being surprised by the enormous amount of paper floating through the air onto the ground, realizing with horror, that among it, people were throwing themselves to their deaths rather than burn alive.

I wanted to be there—to help lift the rubble and find living souls. I wanted to help, but I was frozen to the television for two days. I was numb. Then for two days I was able to turn off the television for awhile, able to cry, able to go about my life a little. By Friday when I went to the spiritual support group, I begin to *think* about what was happening. I became alarmed by President Bush's declaration that this would be the first war of the twenty-first century. The implication there would be others was disturbing, but I was glad he showed us his feelings. I was moved by his tears and by the moment when he stood on the wreckage with the rescuers and acknowledged their heroism. I was touched by the picture of the firefighters raising the flag on a pole in the center of the wreckage and how it shadowed almost exactly the sculpture of the Marines raising the flag on Iwo Jima that I had often passed in Arlington. What would our nation do in response to this? I feared this was the beginning of a terrible time.

Six weeks after school began, I was finally hired to teach English to learning-disabled students. It was challenging and interesting, and my department chair was supportive and helpful. In November, I received an excellent evaluation from the assistant principal. I was taking special education classes, working toward a license in that area, believing that, with more training, I could be an excellent teacher in this area. My department head concurred.

Then, one week before my formal spring review, the assistant principal who was my evaluator called me into her office and handed me a list of several offenses I had committed. I was accused of yelling at students, of giving students handouts to do instead of hands-on activities and discussion, and sending students to the Time Out Center for not having paper or pencil.

I was puzzled. "You've been in my room and seen the art and evidence of hands-on activities, and I often use discussion. And if you check the records in the Time Out Center, you'll discover I've only sent students there for disruptive behavior."

"Well, Ms. Spruce, the students say you're mean and unfair and yell at them."

"Well, they call any reprimand 'yelling.' One day I whispered to a student there would be consequences if he didn't settle down and stop aggravating others, and he said, 'Stop yelling at me.' And they're always complaining about how mean their parents and other teachers are, which means one thing: they aren't getting their way."

Most of the events that had actually occurred had been resolved during the first semester, so I wondered why they were being brought up again. A week later, during the formal evaluation, I was cited for not having corrected these situations. In addition, I was cited for not knowing the subject matter and not using appropriate methods. Any situations that had been resolved were ignored.

"Look," I said to my evaluator, "There is no way you can say I don't know the subject matter. I've taught English successfully for twenty years. I have copies of the positive evaluations to prove it."

"Oh that isn't the subject matter. The subject is special education."

"No, it isn't. I know you're new here and you've never done high school evaluations before, but at this level, the methods are adapted for special education, but we're teaching real English curriculum. We still read *Macbeth* and *Romeo and Juliet*. They're just simplified versions."

Ignoring this, she continued, "You aren't using special education methods."

"This spring, I took the ESL course the district required me to take first. I had no choice. I plan to take three courses or more this summer. Besides, I do use many methods that you listed. I've always used a lot of hands-on and art work."

"This is not what your students tell me."

"A couple of students are lying to you because they're failing. They're failing because they refuse to do the work. You can't believe them. They have their own agendas."

"Well, I feel that these issues, the content competency, and the methods are areas where you don't meet competency requirements. I need you to sign this evaluation."

"No."

"No, what?"

"I won't sign it. I can't be incompetent in a subject area that doesn't exist. There is no state curriculum in special education. As I said before, I am extremely competent in English—that is the subject area. The State Department of Education confirmed this."

"I don't agree with you. You do have to sign the evaluation."

"Not under any circumstances will I in any way acknowledge that evaluation is valid."

"Then I will have to indicate here that you refused to sign it and that you aren't recommended for rehire."

"In the district? That's outrageous."

"No, this only applies to this school."

"I don't think that's correct. This form is a district form and it goes to the central office."

"I'm sure I'm right."

"Fine, but I'm calling the central office and the union, and I intend to write a rebuttal to be attached to it."

"Do as you wish. I'm sorry you aren't open to the help we're trying to give you."

"Oh, please," I said as I left the office.

Talking to the principal was a waste of time because she totally supported the evaluator. I contacted the teacher's union and a lawyer was assigned to my case. Working our way up the chain of command, he and I eventually found an administrator sympathetic to my situation. I had been right about the content area being

English and that the evaluation marked "not for rehire" prevented me from applying for any positions in the district. An assistant superintendent agreed with the man with whom we spoke and called my principal, strongly suggesting that she "correct" the evaluation unless she wanted to face me in court. Reluctantly, the principal agreed to the correction and admitted that my performance wasn't bad enough that I should be banned from the district. The next day, the assistant principal appeared in my room anxiously requesting that I sign the revised evaluation, which I did, confirming that it would replace the inaccurate one. However, by that time it was May and the positions still open were the ones most teachers, including me, didn't want because they were with the most emotionally disturbed students. I knew I wouldn't last a month in one of those positions.

To make matters worse, President Bush's new initiative, No Child Left Behind, was in place, and districts had to fill vacancies first with people who had majors or licenses in the field they taught. To do this, Albuquerque had recruited special education teachers from out of state, something it had not previously done. Without a license, it would be almost impossible for me to be hired.

I couldn't understand why the school administrators had taken such a bizarre stand because they could have easily just not rehired me. It was my first year in that district full-time, so I was on probation, and according to the law, they weren't required to give any reason for not rehiring. Was this the principal's way of getting revenge because I had left my gifted position there last year when she was assistant principal? Or was this the universe hitting me over the head with a two by four trying to get my attention to change my life?

During one week, I received the same message, "change your life," from several sources. The film *Chocolat* emphasized the importance of being who you really were. Then Dr. Phil, on *Oprah*, talked about doing and being who you really were which tied in with the previous Friday's spiritual support group discussion. Only three women were there, and we all wanted our lives to be about who we *were*, not about what we *did*. In Isabel Allende's *The Infinite Plan*, the book I was reading, an Anglo man who grew up in the barrio couldn't change his life until he faced his fears. He spent most of his life repeating old patterns and not getting what he wanted while his friend transformed her life because she wasn't afraid to envision a different life.

On the last day of the 2001-2002 school year, I left the school feeling strangely calm, knowing that this was all in divine order. I affirmed that whatever happened was for the highest good of all. Most of all, I understood that God, not any school administrator, was the source of my supply.

Soon after school was out, I attended the church's summer retreat near Taos. It was a transforming time, and I received information that helped me see where I needed to go and what I needed to leave behind. In the transformational kinesiology workshop, the leader Orenda used kinesiology in a holistic balancing technique to release any obstacles that prevented the group from believing that our chosen goal was true. The goal was for each of us to believe "I am the Light of the World." By the end of the session, we were able to affirm and believe this statement.

This was a powerful experience to share with others and very freeing. Afterward, I could see myself happy and at ease in a relationship. I felt energized and empowered to finish my novel. As soon as I returned home, I intended to clean out my office and begin work. My daily mantra became "I am the Light of the World." With this moment of clarity, I was able to admit that teaching in high school was what I fell back on; I never intended for it to be my life's work. I was supposed to create art as a dancer or writer. The importance of this revelation became even more apparent in the Enneagram workshop.

The Enneagram is an ancient form of wisdom. Various personality traits are paired with numbers. According to the Enneagram, the characteristics that best described me related to a four: the romantic, creative, artistic type who needed to express these qualities through an artistic creation. The number opposite the four was a two, the giver, and my path of disintegration. Like my mother, I gave in excess and was disappointed when the giving wasn't reciprocal. To move toward integration, I needed to move toward the one and find the serenity that would allow me to accept that everything was perfect just the way it was. According to this, teaching that required so much giving actually led me away from integration and explained why it often felt like a burden. The clarity that this insight provided was a great gift.

After the retreat, I woke up every morning feeling strong, clear, and empowered. I repeated, "I am the Light of the World." I wasn't afraid to write. I was getting more of what I wanted. Although I didn't have a job, I had won the evaluation battle.

More good came to me through my neighbor. Ron, who was in the prosperity workshop power pack, moved into the apartment next to me. Although he and I were friends and nothing more, his attention and love were very nurturing to me. While I was at the retreat, he took such good care of my aging cat Pondy that I was able to relax and know she was fine. When I came home with a painful knot in my shoulder, he helped get my bags inside. Then he gave me a helping of a delicious gourmet meal he was cooking. As a result, I didn't have to get groceries until the next morning and was able to settle in and rest for the evening. Those little things meant so much to me.

Without Gladys, life felt less safe knowing I could no longer turn to her for help. Eventually, though, I decided to talk to a woman who gave spiritual counseling and was highly recommended by a friend. I liked her and gained two insights from working with her. First, I needed to notice where in my body an answer appeared when I asked for spiritual guidance. When I asked whether I should pursue teaching special education, the answer telling me to teach was in the back of my head, so that mind chatter was related to the past. This was not spirit speaking to me. The desire to write was something I felt in the body. That was significant. What I felt in my body, not in my head, was truth. I became aware that I had lost much of the mind-body connection I'd had as a dancer.

In the second session, I finally understood that just stating my desire wasn't enough to make it manifest. Emotion created form into which spirit poured life. When I meditated, I was centered, and the purpose was to see the blank slate—to feel the oneness, but the key was that I had to enter an emotional state in order to manifest.

The next day I had a dream that I was packing to leave my mother's house—deciding what to take and what to leave. Later in my dreams, an assistant principal was passing out the schedules for the next semester, but I didn't get one. It felt as if I weren't going to be there. Things were changing internally. I was thankful for this summer when I could explore the new direction I wanted to go while I was still drawing a pay check. I was thankful for each small thing that went well in my life.

Breaking the Block

Although the desire to write was compelling, I nonetheless had a monumental block. Several times, counselors or psychics had told me that spirit guides were speaking to me, but that I wasn't listening. My restlessness and the chatter in my mind made it difficult to meditate. Then I remembered that a friend, who was frustrated by learning to meditate, turned to Julia Cameron's "Morning Pages" from *The Artist's Way*. Those became her daily meditation, during which she wrote in a stream of consciousness style. On July 28, I also began each day with the "Morning Pages."

July 28, 2002—Morning Pages—My group of women friends and I plan to see "The Divine Secrets of the YaYa Sisterhood" tomorrow, but Mark, Kathy's husband, has invited himself, so Frances is inviting another one of the husbands, and I'm irritated because this was supposed to be a women's get together. With men present, we won't talk to each other the same way.

I wonder what I'll be doing this next school year. I don't feel panicked yet. I don't mind borrowing money from my mother to live on for awhile, but I wouldn't want this to go on for very long. I need to do more writing and research and want to know more about transformational or transpersonal psychology. What I would do with a psychology degree afterward, I don't know, but that will come clear from the doing of it. Physically, I really want to clear up my intestinal problems and resolve my shoulder, which still hurts.

I don't think I can stand another year of being a short-term employee. I hate being on probation and knowing I can be fired without a reason. I wonder if it's really true that they will only hire licensed special ed teachers before they hire anyone with waivers. They need so many teachers. That's so crazy if it's true. I love teaching, but I have to find a new way. Father, Mother, God guide me to do your work, to do what you need me to do. I know that will be the right thing. It feels right and I feel peaceful about it even though I don't know what the steps will be. Research energy work, schools, grants? I'm not sure what the right place for me to study might be.

I've talked to one psychic, but I wonder whether I should talk to others and compare what they say. Is that not having faith? When I talk with a psychic, they always tell me to move somewhere else, but it's so beautiful and inspiring here, and I love my church and community of friends. That's so important. How can I have an income that is not touched by the scarcity consciousness of this area? How can I stay unattached from this consciousness? I'll feel better when I have a plan, a specific goal. I'm so tired emotionally and mentally that I keep dozing off. I think I'll take a nap and then have tea.

July 29—I'm still feeling angry about Mark who wants to come along on our women's get together. He didn't get my hint and Kathy is going along with it. She should have taken care of it and told him this wasn't the time for a man to join us. Now I'm wondering whether this is going to happen often. I'm also irritated that Frances was so concerned about his feelings and that's why she tried to get another husband to go along. She just took it for granted it would be all right for the men to go along and didn't bother to ask anyone else.

What should I do about income for the next month and beyond? Have faith. What must I do? Look at art, dance, visions, research, find grants. Is there benefit in getting a job with APS? Yes, gifted. There's not a good chance to work for Home Hospital. I shouldn't let this hold me back—progress, move forward with art and healing. These are the answers I get when I talk directly to Spirit.

I long to be on my own, financially secure, doing good work that touches many people. I wonder who the man is that the psychic told me about. She said I would have a love partner and one to work with. Maybe the same person. There's nothing more to say for now. I look at my cat Pondy and some days she looks so old. She doesn't take care of herself much anymore. I can't imagine *not having her unconditional love. I have to have someone to love.*

I do feel new gates are opening. I've wasted so much on foolish self-indulgence. Years ago when I was in Seattle, what if I had borrowed the money to study Effort-Shape? What if I had gone ahead and gotten a physical therapy degree when I was interested in that? I could be in such a different position now. But all I ever do is dream. I never feel I have the strength to do these things by myself. I want a partner. Bouncing ideas off another helps me be more creative. But is that really true? If I do go to school in psychology, how will I get the income to pay bills? I really want money to come into my life unattached—plenty of money. Money I win? Maybe. I must spring to action. Wouldn't it be great if I could teach gifted this year—do Great Books and get the training for that.

The psychic said that my mind is so busy that the spirit guides can't get through. They're trying to help me. Who are my guides? Do they have names? Should I burn the sage and call the spirits of the four directions each time I begin to write? I have the feeling I should treat this as more sacred than I am. These pages are sacred. This communication is sacred, but I keep falling asleep. A moment ago I was wide awake and now I'm dozing again. When I sit for a long time I feel like dozing off. Should I give in?

July 31—I don't know exactly what I need to do right now except that when I ask Spirit if I should look for a job with APS, the answer comes back as a no. It's in my head. Should I ignore everything in my head? My guides say, "Yes." I check it and it comes back "no" again. Should I just write—"yes." As it turned out, only Frances, Kathy, and I saw "The Divine Secrets of the YaYa Sisterhood," and the men didn't come." Kathy did talk to her husband after all. After seeing that movie, I can't get the image out of my mind of my mother the night before her wedding.

She had been at her friend Buck's. He tells her he would never marry her because he's too old for her. It wouldn't be fair. Before this she loved a football player who was an alcoholic. She's now having second thoughts about marrying my father. She's upset. Buck gives her a drink. Eventually, she goes home. As she's coming through the front gate, her clothes catch on the gate and rip so her slip is hanging below her dress. She looks a mess. She opens the door and my father is there. She's clearly been crying, has liquor on her breath and her slip is hanging. It doesn't look good. He can't trust her. They get married the next day, but he throws this behavior into her for years. He had his pain too. The woman he'd planned to marry broke the engagement. Maybe he and my mother were both on the rebound. What do I feel about this? A lot of pain. I feel her pain. I feel his. Life is often not neat. Things are left dangling.

Where am I going? I think I do want to write and I want to study psychology. What is the fear that keeps me from beginning to write? Am I afraid of success or failure? I think I'm afraid of both. What step do I take today? Guides, speak to me, lead me. I can't see the next step. Perhaps it's to take care of the money I have now—to make it grow, to create residual income. I hear the music going round and round. I see myself with a man. I can't see his face, but we are working together. We have a good partnership. We are working with my manuscripts to prepare them for publishing. I now have that degree in psychology and the expressive arts and I'm giving seminars and writing a book. I have a wonderful relationship with this man. We're happy. He's my life partner.

I have everything I want and do all that I do according to the highest good for all. I serve Father, Mother, God. I help people repair their lives and grow and find their true selves. I assist with transformation. I use many tools. I have a beautiful house filled with beautiful things arranged according to feng shui. I am genuine—the real me. I am showing up in my own life. Who I am really is good enough. I trust God. I trust the path that opens before me, for I know God's guidance is always there. I can use all that I know in my work. It all comes together. It all contributes. It is all one. I have completed the circle and am back where I began. I begin my new life today. I am excited and enthusiastic. I feel lifted up. I know I will find the resources. I know I am complete and one with God. Love flows from me to others and changes their lives. My practice flourishes. My writing flourishes. All that I need comes to me. My life is good—it is growing. It is expanding. I have peace, joy, and respect in my new profession, but I still get to teach, which I love. Love is something I feel in my life every day. Love guides my life—a higher love—the love of God and my love for God. I am reborn into the person I have always wanted to be. I must not doubt. Everything is perfect. Everything unfolds with divine order. My health improves, my belief and confidence in myself improves. I learn that it is okay to do nothing—that doing nothing is sometimes the right thing. And so it is.

Aug. 1—How can I use all I know to make the world better one person at a time. What do I need to do to step up a notch—to lift the quality of my life, my work, my being up a notch? To know that peace and joy, to carry it with me always? To know I need not have fear. I wonder if anyone has ever written Gladys's story? Perhaps I am here to pass on how to release fear, for that has truly changed my life. Would it be right for me to teach what Gladys taught. YES! Well, I got that guides. Is that what it is? Part of it. So one piece falls into place. Will a channel open to guide me? Yes. What do I need to do to learn to listen to my guides? Be silent and know that I am God. That is all.

A month earlier I had spoken to a psychic, and she, like the others, told me that I was a healer whose purpose was to make souls more whole, but that I was still trying to heal relationships with men and "scorpion stings" from my childhood when my mother would unexpectedly lash out and hurt me. Through these people, I had opened myself to the darkness, and this energy went straight to my colon and caused my current problems with it. The psychic said that these were the energies that kept me from doing my work. Only doing the creative work I was meant to do would heal me. I had to learn it doesn't have to hurt to be a woman and to release the energy that drew these kinds of people to me.

Aug. 2—It's sometimes hard to write these pages. They feel like a diary, but I'm not sure that's what they're supposed to be. Now I remember. Cameron says, "Don't judge them. They can be anything." Okay, I got that. I look forward to this time each day because I love the Native American flute music I play. It's soothing—an air sound that is earthy. What visions does the music invoke? Standing among trees, birds singing, creek gurgling. That is heaven on earth.

It's perfect the way that Pondy is sitting in my lap during meditation. As I look at her, I know she's perfect. She is the story of love and its healing power. Someday I must write her story, how she was discarded as a small kitten in the mountains and gradually learned to love because she was so loved. Perhaps what I experienced with her is a metaphor for all love. You can't force it. You can offer it, you can be there and eventually that creates enough trust that the other person (or cat) can accept your love and eventually come to you, allow you to love them, and love you back. But her necessities had to be cared for first. She had to learn she would have food and water, and she would be safe and sheltered. I love this cat who has taught me so much.

My thoughts keep going back to the problems I've had teaching in the schools here. Someone pointed out that when you shine a light in the darkness, it makes those in the darkness fearful. I suppose I'm doing that in a way when I try to get administrators to see what is really going on in the school, but they don't like that. What has happened here doesn't feel like it has that much to do with what I do except that there is something about me that everyone I've worked for doesn't like. I don't fit into their cultural expectations. I have too much to say. Somehow my wanting to solve the problems that exist is a problem. There's always more a teacher can do because so much is expected, but I also have to take care of myself, and I have trouble doing both in these troubled schools.

Aug. 5—I understand that the next step I've been searching for is what I'm doing—healing myself. I affirm that I can see myself eating a normal balanced meal without discomfort. I can eat whatever I want in moderation and will not gain weight. The toxic fat across my stomach has fallen away. I am a size ten again and can wear a bathing suit or leotard without embarrassment. I feel good—strong and light but grounded. I can dance again.

Guides, am I being open to you? Am I listening enough now? No? I must listen more during the day. I must be mindful in all I do. Cats are always mindful. They can spring into action in a split second. Pondy has stopped sitting in my lap when I meditate. She looks, but she doesn't come. I've disturbed the pattern by writing while I mediate. She doesn't like it when I'm not totally still. Spirit, thank you for healing her. She seems happy now and healthy.

Should I stop worrying about borrowing money from my mother? Yes, just don't take advantage. Is my using this money part of the divine plan? Yes. Should I apply for any jobs I see in the newspaper? No. None of these jobs are beneficial for me? Yes. I feel I should be reaching out. Consolidate your energy for only the important stuff. We will guide you. Abundance will be yours—never fear. Peace be with you. Thank you for all good things. They come from the Divine and I accept graciously all that is good, right, and beautiful. There is only love and light. And so it is.

Aug. 6—It has rained and the earth is soft and beautiful. I love to smell the freshness of the rain and especially in this parched land, water is truly a blessing. I am thankful for the rain, for the candle and the sage I burn, for my shelter which is lovely, for the food, for the mountains, my friends, and my teachers past, present, and future.

I have to keep remembering just to be me—to show up as me—to take one day at a time, one healing at a time. Yesterday I started feeling panicky about a job, but perhaps I'm not supposed to work in the schools. What concerns me the most is whether some of the things that come to me are situations I should respond to, but I don't. Should I interview for middle schools? No. Should I look for other jobs? Yes. What kind of work? Nurse's Aide. That comes up for the second time. I don't know what that really is.

I still have difficulty believing that I am a healer and can do energy work. I'm out of touch with my body and have to bring back that awareness. I am so grateful for the guidance I've received about healing. What do I need to know about the energy work? It will all come naturally. So I have faith and believe that what I need will be revealed to me as I need it. I am the Light of the World. All will be revealed. I am a channel for God's will and through me others will be healed. I am the sacred vessel. I am the means by which healing occurs. And so it is. Today I learn what I can from the earth. Heal and research are my instructions now.

Aug. 8—There is a light burning in my mind—my mind is filled with white light. Father, Mother, God, guides, what do I need to do to feel and see this healing power I have? I feel it is abstract. It is not quite clear to me yet. Will it become apparent as I work on healing myself? I affirm I will not take any more abuse. I am an adult, I'm not a child, I do not like to be stung, I do not like the negative competition between men or with women. This is unacceptable. I want it all out of my life. I release this abuse from my life now. I feel so light and free. Only those people who are honest and mean well are drawn to me. Only those people who support me on the divine path will come into and stay in my life. It's time for my divine plan to manifest. It is time for me to know what step is the next step for today. Complete rearranging the office and start writing. I am the light of the world.

The affirmations I wrote or used during meditation began to feel powerful. I was always impatient for concrete proof, wanting the manifestations to show up quickly, but sometimes I was fearful of them. I wanted friends to be forever and always wanted to believe the best of everyone. Reluctantly, I asked that anyone who did not support the divine plan for my life be released from my life. When Kathy dropped me after she met and moved in with a man she loved, I was hurt. She always seemed overwhelmed with health or life problems, and he came along and fixed it all for her. Then, when she planned to move out of her house, she asked Frances and me to help her clean it. Frances helped even though she had also been hurt by Kathy's desertion, but she felt that Kathy's choice to ignore her women friends was understandable because a man should always come first. I chose not to help but felt guilty about my choice until my guides confirmed I hadn't made an error, but that I had done what I had to do in order to learn. I was supposed to release her from my life. The lesson was that if the friendship wasn't reciprocal, it probably wasn't good for me.

Aug. 9—Now feels like a planning time, a preparing time. I need to clean out the old, save what is good and make room for the new. The symbol of all this is my writing room. My whole life is in those files. Even the things that are relevant need to be updated.

My priority is to heal my colon. I'm working on it—I no longer accept abuse from other people, including my mother or my employer. I'm working on healing the fear of abuse the little girl within me has. I am an adult. I choose my life. My life is full of positive, successful people who are willing to help, teach, and encourage me on my journey. I am led to the situations, ideas, and circumstances that will help develop my divine plan. I know I am blessed. I know I am guided by guardian angels. I cannot fail because I am God's perfect child. I am the Light of the World. I'm still uncomfortable about borrowing family money. Some of it will be mine one day so maybe I just need to shift my thinking and see it as a loan on what I will receive in the future. Then it feels okay. Perhaps that money is payback for what wasn't done for me when I was young, the lack of violin and dance lessons. I don't know. I only know there is karma. There is cause and effect. Be cheerful, my guides say. Be cheerful. What you need, you will get.

Aug. 10—I'm flooded with ideas about how to make money: a website where I can sell lesson plans for teachers, posting my resume on job hunting sites, enlarging and selling some of the photos I took in Africa, writing articles. I'm not afraid of the future. I feel serene, surrounded by light, and that spirit is carrying me forward and showing me the way. As problems arise, I know the solutions to them will appear so that they don't feel like problems.

I pray that from this point on in my life I will learn from good experiences rather than from suffering. I know that there is meaning in suffering. It feels awful to think we suffer for nothing. Regardless of why the last principal didn't like me, the whole situation was a sign to change, to realize there was no acceptance of me there. I want to live where the people and environment are welcoming, not where they feel hostile. I want to live in love—love and be loved.

Aug.12—I feel nervous and anxious this morning as school begins for some people. It's hard to believe and have faith when I can't see what comes next. My neck and body hurt from the tension I feel. I need a massage. It hurts that my high school teaching career has disintegrated and that no one values my talents as a teacher. My plan was to work in the same district for five years and get some retirement. Sometimes I feel angry because the money and time I spent taking special ed classes the previous summer was a waste. The credit hours I earned put me in a higher salary range, but there's no benefit from that unless I have a job.

What do I need to do today? Cry, laugh, search. I feel the guides are wrapping their arms around me. I have to let go of the fear. I have to let go. I need to spend $800 on the car, but it is difficult to do that when I have no real income. I wish the money I'm borrowing were coming from an anonymous source, but I am grateful for it. I must remember that God is my source. All that I need will come to me.

One evening while watching a television program, I thought about Kathy and I began crying. I wasn't sure why. What she and Mark had was so beautiful—physically, emotionally, and spiritually, and I was grateful she had this because her life had been difficult, and she deserved to be loved. She finally invited a couple of us to see his place, where she was now living, and I was surprised by how carefully it had been decorated by this Vietnam vet who obviously had the sensitivity of an artist. Being in his house was a pleasure, and he shattered my stereotype of a man who was so politically conservative. I had felt judgmental about his views, but seeing his home made me consider that if I knew more about him, I could understand and not judge. Although I was repelled by the idea of a man rescuing me, I had to admit it would be nice to have a helping partner. I was growing impatient for my sacred relationship to appear.

An interesting part-time job to implement a new Youth Education Program at the church became available and it paid well. It involved training teachers to use the fine arts in their teaching of Religious Science principles, and I had the perfect background for it. Working with the children at church was another avenue of expression and service, and something in me shifted. Because of my mother's martyr attitude, I saw serving others as something I was supposed to do instead of doing what I really wanted to do with my life. I often felt burdened by the service work I did and finally quit doing it. But this time, I felt the love inside more often, and it moved me toward expressing that love through action. Training the teachers would be fun, and I looked forward to recreating my life into one that was more meaningful.

Aug. 16—Last night I dreamed I was at a school and I needed something on the other side of the campus. I kept trying to get there, but I ran into other people and had conversations. I also was changing clothes a lot. I realized that if I put on an outfit that wasn't comfortable, I could always put on something else that was. I was very excited about this so I redressed and repacked and went on my way. This dream is what I'm always doing—trying out different roles or vocations to find the one that allows me to really be who I am—that will be the one that is comfortable.

I was awed by the people in my spiritual support group. They put themselves in growing situations, stretching and impacting others positively. I felt the change also. I no longer *believed* all was perfect and that I would receive what I needed to move forward with my plans; I *knew* what I needed was there. I *knew* that if I was hired for a teaching position, it was the right thing. I *knew* that if I wasn't, it was the right thing. I *knew* that however it unfolded was perfect. I *knew* this was the path, a very peaceful path. It felt good to have an open heart, but also centered and protected so I could easily choose love as my motivation for acting. I didn't feel I was giving too much away; I felt there was enough for me and whoever needed my love. I gave, and that place in me that used to be empty was filled.

Aug. 18—These "Morning Pages" do seem to be helping. Last night I dreamed that my mother was manipulating someone—one of my Nebraska friends, I think. Thinking ahead to Christmas, I want to tell Mother there better not be any more manipulations like last year when she created an argument between my brother and me, and then she went around telling people, even my sister-in-law's mother, how badly my brother and sister-in-law treat her. They treat her extremely well, so evidently, she'll say anything to get attention. I wish the family could be with me sometime on Christmas, but I never have a place large enough for them to stay comfortably. I would like for them to go to church with me too.

Aug. 19—"I am love," is what the guides say I need to know today. Love fills my being and my soul. I know that what I need will come to me. What do I need to do in order to find my sacred relationship? Love others. Practice love, be love.

Maybe my difficulties in the schools were a part of a spiritual contract, but I could now see how I had not always been wise. I was arrogant believing that I could disagree with administrators because I knew what was best for the students and that they would appreciate a different point of view. I also broke a contract to go to a better paying job, and although I saw how much it upset the principals, I thought I could return to that school without any hard feelings. I was very naïve about how things work and foolishly thought I would be treated as I always had been in other places—as a valued professional. But the psychic with whom I had spoken saw these experiences as spiritual contracts I had created before coming into this life and which I had now fulfilled. The purpose was for the other people and me to learn from each other.

Aug. 22—Dear Creator, help me to get out of my own way so that I can hear and follow your guidance. I know this is why I haven't made good choices. I try to listen, but when I make a point of listening, I don't hear anything. I'm still not clear when it's

Spirit and not my ego speaking because I often don't feel the message in my body. I think I've forgotten how to listen to my heart. Help me listen, receive the words, and act on them.

I couldn't stand the chaos in my home office any longer, and over time, I established a pattern that every day I would organize the paper files, computer information or begin to feng shui my apartment. As a result, the heaviness I felt about writing changed to a lighter energy. There was order and I could find things easily. I felt calm. Perhaps I could create some light in the darkness.

Aug. 23—This weekend I pulled myself out of a depression. Maybe the crying was just what I needed to let go. I want to let go of my anger toward my friend Kathy and Mark. I don't think my anger is just about them; it's about the resentment I feel toward men who only want women who are helpless or weak, who only want women they can control. It's that old feeling that the world is unjust that haunts me still. I acknowledge the anger and send it away. It is done. I release this anger and send blessings to these two lovely people. I need to focus on release and healing.

The dark sky was ablaze with stars as Frances and I sat in the Santa Fe museum plaza, a cool breeze gently caressing the audience. As I watched N. Scott Momaday's play *The Indolent Boys*, a story of clashing Anglo and Indian cultures, I was reminded why it would be emotionally wrenching to leave New Mexico. It was a magical night, as all nights were in New Mexico, surrounded by ancient mountains and the spirits of those who lived there long ago. When the character John Pei talked about feeling "beside himself," losing the sense of who he really was, I understood.

Duality again. Duality was an illusion. The root of the problem was that I didn't trust my own decisions. I didn't trust that I was one with the Creator because, if I did, all things were possible and duality didn't exist. So I declared that I was confident and trusted in my ability to make responsible and correct decisions that would produce success, happiness, prosperity, and health for me and others.

I continued to ponder Momaday's theme of feeling split. In his Pulitzer Prize–winning novel *House Made of Dawn*, there was a sad moment when Abel was out in nature and wanted to sing a song to nature, but he no longer knew his own language and therefore couldn't sing the song. I felt like that. I no longer knew the language of dance and the joy using it gave me. The self-discipline that had always helped me persevere through difficulties was inadequate. I needed to get up earlier to write and go to bed earlier or write at night and sleep in. What kept me from moving ahead? I was haunted by the shadows of past experiences when I made poor choices, and I was afraid I would err again. Releasing the past would free me. I had to surrender to this moment because the moment was all I had, but that was what confused me. How did I surrender and still take the action that was necessary?

Aug. 29—Someone said, "Our desires are God's guidance." God wants us to fulfill our desires. As I write, I'm filled with the peace that comes to me as I listen to Native American flute music. I want to know more about the ancient spirituality that is here, and I don't understand why people keep telling me that this isn't a good place for me to live. Must I leave here in order to succeed and have a real life? I'm hungry to talk to people about psychology and mythology and I want to share this with the man I love. I want us to make love with our minds as well as our bodies.

I'm not happy to admit that one of the ideas I need to let go of is that I have to have a relationship first before I can really be successful in a career. This suggests that I don't really believe I can make this change by myself so I continue waiting for my partner to appear. But this isn't right. I don't need a man to take control of my life. My neighbor and friend Ron is building a private therapy practice and is a wonderful role model. I see him rushing about, really dedicated to building his business, and I keep hoping that his attitude is contagious. I should be acting the way he is. Therefore, I affirm that I will complete the organization of my office and set aside a certain time each day to write. I release my fear of failing or succeeding. I am willing to receive success, prosperity and love.

Sept. 5—I'm not writing every day, but on some days I do write. I'm able to make some decisions. I've been reading Richard Gerber's Vibrational Medicine in the 21st Century *and learned that the Reiki work I thought I wanted to do involves channeling the energy of the other person through you. That's not what I want to do. I would rather do what he describes as tapping into the universal healing energy and channeling that into the person.*

The psychic with whom I spoke this week had a much more realistic approach than the last one.

"I seem to have a permanent block writing the novel," I explained.

"Why don't you write a book about all you've learned spiritually?"

"I don't have any credentials. I'm not a minister or coach or anything."

"But you've lived through such a fascinating time for women and you've learned so much and healed so much. People could learn from what you've learned, especially if you emphasize relationships. The book would lead to your teaching and speaking to large groups of adults, and the energy work you're supposed to do is the work you'll do teaching groups." I felt goose bumps on my arms as she described this path.

"I'd love to do all those things, but won't I need training for the energy work?"

"No, you've been learning it for years. You already know all you need to know," she said enthusiastically.

This was my dream, and it gave me such peace that I knew I could begin.

About the same time, I read Carolyn Myss's book *Sacred Contracts.* I'd never read much about chakras because I considered them esoteric elements of Eastern religions and not integral to my journey. However, as I read, I realized that many of my troublesome issues related to the third chakra. It dealt with issues of self-esteem, trusting our intuition, integrity, codes of honor, and "where you stand" in a particular situation. I followed the exercise she outlined, and it must have worked because afterward I actually wrote for an hour.

The block was broken.

Letting Go into the Flow

I dreamed I was waiting to take a trip with my mother after she finished teaching a class. Waiting by a picture window, I looked out at a beautiful sunset. Its light was reflected over the entire city below. It became clear my mother wouldn't finish in time, so I left. I had no map, but I knew where to go. After I decided what street to take, I could see a sign with the name of the highway or road, and I knew I'd gone the right way. I woke feeling confident that my intuition was leading me in the direction I should go.

I moved slowly through my writing block and actually began writing my memoir even as I struggled to find the right style, whether to write the book as diary entries or a straight narrative. I felt clearly that the worst of my life was behind me. As the psychic said, "The rest will be easy." I was amazed that the minute I sat down and actually began writing, I felt clear, unafraid, and committed, knowing I would succeed, knowing I would love my new work.

After I had written some of the introduction, I began reading through the diaries and journals I had kept for years. It was strange how the dark times I'd experienced made me forget what it was like to be carefree. Reading about the sixth and eighth grades was a reminder of the fun I had during my teenage years. Like all teens, though, I agonized over who liked me, how I looked, and the betrayal of girlfriends when they started being attractive to boys. Going through the 1970s journals was much more painful, reliving the divorce and the painful years of job hunting.

Sept. 22—This is a good way to start the week, getting up earlier. I need to do the pages today. I do love the quietness and the dark and the coolness. I see gold coins showering me this morning. I feel that all the money I need will come to me. I keep thinking about my brother. We've never really talked about his having polio when he was two. I guess we talked about it one time when we were riding the train to northwest Arkansas to see our grandparents. He was trying to understand why he was saved. It's clear in his life that he searches for something spiritual, as I do. That's one thing my mother did for her children. She gave us spiritual lives and set us on a quest to understand who we are in relation to God.

Two weeks earlier, I had attended a workshop in which children, parents, and adults played together to demonstrate how the arts would be used in the new youth education program at the church. I had loved it. Charlotte, a friend from the spiritual support group, had designed the program and asked me to take the position as director. I accepted and started working immediately, but two people interested in the position complained that the minister hadn't advertised the position. Neither person was qualified, but I was put on hold until the minister interviewed them. At the very least, this was awkward, but not surprising.

From the time the board approved the new program, there had been controversy with one group of members committed to stopping this change. It required courage on my part to move forward, but I believed the new structure was meant to succeed, and I knew it would enrich the children's lives. The program was organized so that the teachers at each grade level formed a pod of eight teachers who rotated responsibilities and planned together. They were supported by specialists in art, music, drama, dance, and other areas. It was my responsibility to train the teachers to integrate fine arts activities into their lessons. From the beginning, it was clear that the children loved the activities.

The first month working as youth education director passed quickly. Our first training session went well, and the new teachers were successful in applying the new methods; some who had been in the program a long time, however, were reluctant to use new curriculum and attend planning meetings that were crucial to the program's success. At the training session and at the self-mastery class I took, I was amazed when people said I inspired them. It was humbling and satisfying to know that I could make a difference and do for them what others had done for me. I was truly blessed.

The synchronicity in life always awed me. A woman friend who had cancer told me that it was more serious than she thought. On the next day, my neighbor gave me a tape on a man who had cured his cancer. I passed the tape on to my friend and also told her to contact me anytime she needed a ride. She didn't look sick, but I knew how misleading that could be because I hadn't looked sick when I had chronic fatigue. I asked God to help me to live up to my best in love by being there for her, to help open my heart and release the fear that always engulfed me when I was around anyone ill.

Being paid well for the part-time position at the church relieved some financial anxiety, but I wanted to eliminate the rest of the obstacles that prevented my moving forward in all areas of my life. Because I was so impressed with Orenda, who had facilitated the transformational kinesiology workshop at the church retreat, I attended several sessions with her.

Working with a small group of women in her quiet home, Orenda began to muscle test one person as we all held hands. This cleared our energy and prepared us to identify the limiting beliefs and energy blockages that limited our potential. On this evening, as well as on others, I was amazed that all the women had similar issues.

The first woman spoke, "My biggest issue is the idea that you can't follow God and make money."

I sighed. "That message also came from my childhood." Others nodded. Indirectly, the message I had received was that wealthy people probably didn't get their money honestly, and there was always virtue in poverty, an idea from my Christian upbringing. I thought I had released this from my consciousness long ago, but clearly I hadn't.

A second woman spoke of her frustration. "I keep asking, 'When is God going to give me what I need?'"

A third woman, looking fearful, offered her issue. "If I show who I really am, others will criticize me."

All these ideas were also a part of my consciousness. Because we all also had difficulty focusing on what we needed, Orenda suggested, "How do you feel about using 'I am experiencing a clear, quiet mind' as your goal or intention?" We nodded in agreement and she began the next step, applying a balancing technique to the process. As we began, I received an important message: "I want to follow God's guidance."

As we worked on removing blocks to accomplish our goal, I felt a shift of energy, and by the middle of the session, was perspiring heavily. Afterward, I felt very clear, like another chain binding me had been released. When we began to integrate the changes, it happened so quickly that I could feel the kundalini energy shoot up my spine and over my head and body. The process was completed in a flash.

At the next session, I felt my guides applauding. This powerful image originally surfaced when a psychic doing a reading said that angels were giving me a standing ovation for trying to help my mother change her negative attitudes. At one point, I could no longer tolerate hearing her litany of the things that were wrong with her life and had begun to consciously work with her to develop positive attitudes.

As I continued this work, flashes of intuition started coming very quickly, but I was amazed how I could receive messages from Spirit but discard or ignore them without realizing their importance. In many situations recently, the answer to a question came a split second before the question or as it was being asked. I learned to trust the accuracy of these answers.

At another session, our goal was a very powerful one for me, "I express myself as I really am." Blocks I didn't know I had were cleared, my fear left, and it felt as if there were no impediments to writing the book and succeeding as a teacher and speaker. This was powerful energy work.

I had a dream in which I was in a large building with many people, including one of the youth education teachers, and strange things started happening. I moved a few things from my old desk to a new desk, and when I returned to the old desk, everything else that belonged to me had disappeared. Strange things, not belonging to me, appeared on the new desk as if someone else had moved to it. That kind of thing was happening everywhere, and people in the office were panicked. Later in the dream, I was in a car at night, and we could see the outline of lions and other large cats in the distance walking back and forth across the road. I interpreted the dream to be about letting go of the old and accepting that new things I needed would appear. The cats were a reminder to pay attention to my instincts or intuition. Later, I would realize the dream was also a warning about the future.

Early in the week, Kathy cancelled another dinner we had planned. In the middle of the week, I called her because I needed to get the reading binder I loaned her when she had started teaching earlier in the year. It included an interest inventory I could use for the teens on Sunday. I had promised the minister I would start off with this. She agreed to bring it to the spiritual support meeting on Friday, or to call me if she couldn't, but she did neither. When I called her after the meeting, she said she'd bring it to me Saturday, but seemed irritated about coming into town. On Saturday, she called early in the afternoon to say that she was leaving home and would see me in a few minutes. Again, she didn't show up, and around 3:45, when I still hadn't heard from her, I finally called. She was at the grocery store and agreed to bring it over as soon as she checked out, but became angry with me for being demanding. She took no responsibility for what I perceived as inconsiderate behavior. We parted in anger.

I didn't understand. She had her partner to help her—he was even grading papers and cooking for her and her life was chaotic as ever. It hurt to lose her friendship, but I remembered how hard I had worked to get the friendship started. It suddenly dawned on me that perhaps she'd never been very interested in being friends to begin with and had only responded because I pushed it.

In addition to dealing with daily challenges, there were days when I doubted that I could continue writing the book because I relived each painful, past relationship, facing its failure all over again and spiraling into endless self-analysis. Why had I never realized Gary was unfaithful? Why had I continued my relationship with Neal for so long? If I saw him again, I knew I would still have trouble walking away. Was that an addiction or some bizarre, karmic connection? The understanding for which I longed was slow in coming.

It was Thanksgiving 2002. I went to Houston for that holiday rather than Christmas because I couldn't stand another combative Christmas, which the previous year had been. Unfortunately, of course, the same problems still existed there. The only time everyone sat down together to eat was at Thanksgiving dinner. The kids came and went, involved in their own activities. The house was full of people, yet I felt disconnected from them, having to catch someone here or there for a few minute's conversation. My mother's only topic of conversation was her Bible study class, but I was grateful she was getting out of the house to be with other people even for one activity. We went shopping and I enjoyed helping her find things she needed.

What I really missed were the times when my mother and I, and often my brother or grandmother, would sit around the table after we ate and have long discussions. We did this for a while on Thanksgiving Day, but it became tense when the topic turned to religion, which it invariably did, and evolved into an unpleasant debate with my brother over original sin. Despite our differences, we eventually found a couple of points where we could see similarities in our beliefs, but it always made me sad that our spirituality, which meant so much to both of us, was always a point of contention.

When I returned home, I discovered that others in the spiritual support group felt as disconnected from their families as I did, and their pain was very deep. The difference, however, was that they were in committed, meaningful relationships and received the love they needed from their partners. In fact, Kathy and Mark were getting married in a few months, and she wasn't going to work after that. What would that feel like? To have someone provide for all your needs? To have someone who understood and loved you?

Running the youth education program was a challenge because so many involved people had their own agendas. Don, Charlotte's partner, would soon be on the board as a liaison for the program, and Charlotte mentioned that he was doing it because of his interest in the program and their friendship with me. I appreciated this but still felt a distance there. Some deep discomfort I couldn't identify kept me from feeling really close to them.

Every Sunday, I collapsed at the end of the morning, amazed at everything I had done and learned. It was an incredible experience and a delight to be around the children. I was empowered and felt I had helped others to be empowered. I was always cognizant of how I used my power. Perhaps this was the end of that karmic issue I had glimpsed when I was with Alan years ago.

Then the minister surprised me by setting up a meeting to discuss the complaints he'd received about me.

"What are they saying about me?" I asked.

"They say you're angry, controlling, and loud and that you frown all the time."

"Who said that?"

"I can't reveal that or people won't come to me."

"Well, I know who it is anyway. You know about the caroling incident? The woman became angry when I explained I would have to consult the teachers before I could agree to let the children participate in the event."

"Yes, I heard. But Reverend Marsha also received letters from several people complaining about hateful emails sent to teachers."

"You've got to be joking. Who said that?"

"She didn't tell me, but she's going to give me a copy of the letters."

"Do you believe this stuff?"

"Don't worry, I support you all the way, but I do want you to look at those perceptions some people have."

"I will, but most people have been responding very positively to what I've done."

"I think that's true, and I'm aware that there are people who wanted your position, as well as those who didn't want the program to work. I had a conversation the other day with a teacher for the high school group who didn't think he needed to plan the class in advance. I made sure he understood the importance of doing that."

Despite his reassurances, I was very upset that once again I was being attack when I was doing a successful job. I began to realize that, despite what the minister had said, some of the most negative people were people close to him.

As it turned out, there was only one letter complaining about me from a person and his partner who refused to attend the planning meetings because they thought it a waste of their time. They had no interest in being a part of the teacher community. When the minister read my emails, he found nothing wrong with them. The other complainer was the woman who wanted me to force the teachers to include the children in the caroling program. What bothered me was that the minister treated these incidents as if they were major problems and hadn't bothered to investigate before talking with me. In the midst of sorting the situation out, I talked to Charlotte, who warned me not to trust Reverend Marsha, who in turn warned me not to trust my assistant. I was so sick of the politics.

I woke the next morning with the thought, "To choose the best team is the way."

It was January 1, 2003. I felt very lonely and had cried for the previous two weeks as if I were letting go of something enormous. I wasn't sure what that was—unnecessary protection, grief, old ideas, disappointment? All my friends were in relationships except Frances who was always traveling, having company, or taking classes. But on the days when I wasn't depressed, I was proud of myself for writing so much and envisioned the success I would experience by finishing the book and finding my soul mate.

On the other hand, I was deeply disturbed about my mother. The day after Christmas, she had a stroke, and I felt guilty and sad that I had chosen not to be with her during the holiday. Although she was doing well, I wanted to see her, but she would soon go into physical therapy and be too busy for visitors. It would be better for me to visit when she first came home, so I prayed for her recovery. She had been so active despite the diabetes that it was hard for me to grasp that she might be near the end.

Life continued to move along nicely, and I gave it a nudge with an affirmation I would do for thirty days for more money, a relationship, and new friends. Abundance began flowing immediately. My friend who recovered from cancer took me to dinner at a wonderful French restaurant to thank me for giving her rides when she was sick. Then a friend who was a psychic did a free Tarot reading. That reaffirmed that Albuquerque was as good a place to live as any while I was in transition and that when I opened up completely I'd know where to go. The third thing that happened was that I did a thirty-minute phone interview for a job at the design school. I really wanted to work there, training artists how to teach. The next interview would be with the director, so I went shopping for interview clothes and found a nice dress and a Larry Levine dark purple suit for forty dollars. By the time I returned home, the school had already called to set up the next interview.

I dreamed that I was a man in a car, driving on a dirt road, and couldn't tell where the road went. I had to cross railroad tracks without a ramp, and on the other side, there seemed to be several dirt roads to follow, but the one I was on had run out. Was this a premonition?

During the next week I tried to reach my assistant for the youth ed program several times, but she never returned my emails or calls. This was odd. When the minister asked me to meet with him, I became suspicious. One of the practitioners whom I respected was sitting in his office.

After I was seated, the minister began, "We've tried to give you time to work with the youth education program, and I know it has been challenging. You're doing a good job in many ways, but there's a general feeling that the program and you aren't a match. I hope you understand."

"Well, I don't understand. I thought you understood there are some people who will do anything to undermine me and the program. I thought you weren't going to allow that. Who's complaining this time?"

Again, mysterious people who couldn't be named or counted said I was angry, aggressive, or uncooperative despite the fact I'd gone out of my way to speak calmly and kindly to everyone. By the end of the meeting, the minister and practitioner had convinced me that this was a valuable learning experience. Listening to them, I almost believed that their accusations had some merit and even left thanking them for helping me look more closely at my life. Later, seeing again the secrecy and vagueness with which they discussed events, I realized that the minister had probably listened to his disruptive friends again and simply made the easy choice. I let them make me the victim again. Why couldn't I stop that? I still lived with the fear that even if I got a nice job, these problems would reoccur. I had no faith that I would be treated fairly or appreciated in any workplace. I had hoped the church would be different.

Before I went to sleep that night, I asked Spirit to help me understand the things the minister had said. I woke up the next morning and a big sign in my head said, "The words he says others say about you are what he feels about you." He was the one thinking I was too loud, aggressive, and angry. That made sense, especially when I remembered that he liked women who were compliant. I hadn't realized that he really didn't want a leader. He wanted me to be more dependent on him. The woman who eventually replaced me was decidedly compliant.

I was fortunate that friends reached out to me during this difficult time. On Wednesday night, I had dinner with Frances and talked. I had left a message for Charlotte and Don, and Don offered to come over or talk with me during the week. I also talked to a woman who used to go to the church who confirmed that the way the minister handled this wasn't unusual and that he created much of the conflict there.

Friday night, I talked to the spiritual support group. People were shocked, of course, and Charlotte definitely empathized with me and later confirmed her opinion of the minister's behavior was similar to mine. Everybody had something to say, without judging, except Don, ironically. He was one of the last to comment and was very uncomfortable with my mentioning names and drawing conclusions about people's motivations. I thought this was strange because the group knew everyone else who was involved without my mentioning names. I felt he was trying to shut me up because he was uncomfortable with unpleasant emotions being expressed.

Part of New Thought thinking suggests that, in conflicted situations, the other person is reflecting back to us some aspect of our own behavior. After the group meeting, Charlotte worked with me to discover what it was in my behavior that the minister reflected back to me. It all came back to the issue of power. I felt angry that this was another situation where a man had power and wouldn't allow me to do what I knew how to do. It was never about my competence; it was about my unwillingness to act submissive and act in a traditionally feminine way. What was revealed as Charlotte and I talked was that my masculine side projected more strongly than my feminine and that they weren't as completely integrated as I thought. Everything negative that I said the minister did was what my masculine side did to defeat me. When I stopped doing those things, the two would be integrated. Charlotte thought that since this had come to the surface, it wouldn't repeat itself again. What she said made some sense. I hoped she was right because I wanted to continue living in New Mexico, and that aspect of my behavior seemed to go against some deep-seated cultural norm about how women should behave.

A few days later, Frances and I spent a lovely vacation day immersing ourselves in the beauty and art of Santa Fe. That usually uplifted me, but that evening I felt so sad. I often felt so lonely I didn't think I could go on, and I had recently had a particularly bad night when all my fears surfaced. I never knew when this depression would hit—it invariably came up with no warning.

Then my mother had a stroke and relapsed; she wasn't well enough to communicate with me, and talking was the core of our relationship. It felt as if she were already gone, and I was deeply thankful for my dear friend Frances for her nurture and support.

Frances was also disillusioned with our church, the minister in particular, but we needed a place to explore our spirituality and were excited to find a women's group on the feminine divine. The women were from fifty to eighty years old, and the energy of the group was powerful. I connected with several in the group and liked the leader, who was a therapist with some Jungian background. The spiritual support group was stimulating, but this dynamic was more intimate and different because of the lack of men. Being with these women was very healing.

After a few weeks, I regained my balance and felt that I did have a community of friends at church. I saw a psychic and her reading clarified several issues. She pointed out that I was stubborn and needed to release that so I could see all my options. She confirmed that writing the book was healing, but that it would also sell and that I would use it as a manual to teach others. She confirmed that a man who was traveling now would come into my life and that things would be clearer by March or June. The big message was to release all regrets of the past. I had everything I needed to succeed. I just needed to do the work.

The End Is the Beginning

I dreamed I was on a journey. I got out of my car and was walking ahead along a dirt road to see whether I was on the right road. A tanker truck came barreling down on me and almost didn't make the corner. I felt it was trying to hit me, and it was wild, mean energy. I awoke feeling anxious and hoped the dream was not a premonition.

Immediately after I was fired, I began to work with a therapist using EMDR techniques to release the pain and anger I felt, especially toward the minister. The treatment was simple. I identified a vivid image related to the traumatic event and focused on it, moving my eyes back and forth as I followed the therapist's fingers moving across my field of vision. When the level of distress around this issue subsided, the therapist asked me to find a positive belief related to the issue. Then she continued to stimulate my eye movement. This continued until I felt confident in this new belief. I was amazed by how much my anger was reduced by this technique. Everything I needed showed up.

I made a gratitude journal. Remembering all the things for which I was thankful was always uplifting. I was grateful that my mother's health had improved and the good communication between my brother and me during this difficult time was harmonious. I was excited about the feminine divine group, and I felt more connected to those women than I did to the women in the other spiritual support group. I had begun to lose what would be twenty pounds. My sinus allergies went away. Pondy's health and eating habits improved. All was well.

Despite the fact that I didn't have a job, I loved my life. I was often filled with joy. The Chicano art I saw at the National Hispanic Cultural Center was an incredibly inspiring treat. It was colorful, bold, passionate, and rebellious. I loved the domestic scenes with tiny details, such as a rosary on a dresser, or a favorite saint on a table beneath the window, making each room seem to belong to a real family. It was very spiritual like the magical realism writers were creating with such brilliance in Hispanic or African American literature. I, too, lived on that border between reality and the spirit.

In March, I knew that I had to visit my mother. When I arrived in Houston, I thought I was prepared for the experience, but it was more painful than I could have imagined. She was back in a critical care facility where the physical therapists and doctors visited her each day. On the first night, she could hardly stay awake, and it was very difficult to understand or hear her. She often fell asleep in the middle of a sentence. The next morning, she spoke more clearly, almost like our old conversations.

After the occupational therapist's session with her, Mother was inspired and wanted me to move her arms and help her exercise the side that was paralyzed. She was awake and motivated, and for the first time, I thought she might recover. She was able to lift her right arm and open and close her fingers. I prayed she would get functional use of that hand again, and I was thankful we could always depend on her to try her very best, for the last thing she wanted was to be a burden.

Strangely, I began grieving long before my mother passed away. I felt the loss of long telephone conversations keenly and realized that those times were certainly over. I wanted to live closer so I could see her more often but knew that somehow everything was in divine order. Because my brother worked from home, he was in a position to care for Mother, and from what my sister-in-law said, he had mellowed and was showing her great kindness. It had changed him, and I knew that he was giving back to her all the love and care she'd given him through the years. No matter what her weaknesses were, she had been nothing less than heroic in fighting for her children's lives when we were so sick. Her illness also released the tension between my brother and me as we put aside our own needs to see that she received what she needed. But I was surprised to hear him say that although he supported President Bush, the deposing of Saddam Hussein brought up serious ethical issues for him. As a result, we were able to have a political discussion without it being a debate.

In a dream, a woman and I were looking for something. She was the person who taught the Roots of Religious Science course I was taking. As we walked, many of my friends and my mother's friends joined us. Someone told a story, and my mother said, "That's what I call the light coming through." I said, "I've never heard you say that." She said, "Well, maybe I said that's life coming through."

My mother was old now—just as she knew she would be, just as she expected. She was more wrinkled than her mother had been when she died at ninety-nine. She had high blood pressure and arthritis—just as she knew she would. She'd had a heart attack and a stroke and could hardly speak. She couldn't take care of herself. Her greatest fear had come true as she knew it would because these were the things one had to endure when one grew old. She believed they were inevitable. She fought old age every inch of the way, seeing it as her enemy, not her guide into more maturity and wisdom. At eighty-four almost all her worst fears had come true. She couldn't drive any longer and was dependent on others for transportation. Before the stroke, she could move about using the walker. Now she couldn't turn over in bed by herself.

Our relationship had always depended on talking, and now her speech was so slurred that I couldn't understand her on the telephone and could understand only part of what she said in person. We talked face to face, but she fell asleep every few minutes. In my fear that she was slipping away forever, I sometimes woke her up, and my sadness over losing her almost debilitated me at times. In the end, she was the one person I could always talk to who eventually accepted me just as I was, and she no longer felt the need to make me into her image or give me advice, for my experience had moved beyond hers. She did what she could do and merely listened. When she was gone, who would be the witness to my life? Who would care enough to listen to my ramblings?

I didn't think about growing old anymore. Menopause had been hell; nothing could be worse than the mood swings, insomnia, hot flashes, and brain fog I experienced then. I now felt that I was actually growing younger. I chose not to feel driven any longer, even when I was eager to achieve a goal or finish a project. I awoke slowly checking for fragments of dreams I wanted to catch. I said no to social events when I needed solitude to be in touch with my soul. I didn't accept the idea that aging meant things became worse; they simply changed. The best was yet to be.

I now focused on how to manifest the income I needed. According to the philosophy of religious science, we could manifest what we wanted only if we were truly being ourselves; the desire had to come from a genuine place inside. I also remembered that the universal law could only manifest our thought —it couldn't make decisions for us; thus I had to be clear about what I wanted.

At the spiritual support group, one of the women said, "Things have to be congruent to manifest and I hear you saying two things."

"What do you hear me say?"

"You say you want a job, but you also say you want to receive money without a job. That isn't congruent."

"You're right. I'm tired of all the politics in the workplace. I want to win the lottery," I said, laughing, "or receive money from some source without having a job."

With a quizzical look on her face, she said, "I don't know what I would do with a lot of money."

Without saying so, I thought that might be a block to receiving it. "So my intention for the week will be 'The universe is the source of my supply, and I receive all the wealth I need and more to spare.'"

The group shook their heads in agreement that was a good choice. This affirmation felt open, expansive, and accepting. In addition, I needed to update all the image collages I created years ago to reflect my current desires in terms of a job, man, house, and travel, and they needed to reflect that I was open to new ways of generating money. After the meeting, I made a list of everything I wanted and tried to define it more clearly. Having a visual representation of what I wanted would help me accurately visualize what I wanted to manifest.

I finally called about substitute teaching. I had applied in the fall, but they had so many people to interview that they had said they'd contact me in January. I'd forgotten about this because I was preoccupied with my mother. When I called in March, no one had a record that I had applied. Fortunately, the director of substitute services pulled my file right away and the next day I was eligible to begin. This wasn't the first time the central office had misplaced paperwork. I was pleased to learn that the pay was higher than I expected, but I was hoping to hear about a transition specialist position I had applied for. At least the substituting was some income, I'd be through by mid-afternoon, and I wouldn't have papers to grade.

I dreamed that I was with a group of people and we were out on a hill, trying to dig for tiny stones. Every time I thought I'd found the right size stone, there was always more of it hidden under the ground, and I couldn't see the size of the rock accurately from the surface. In my life, there was often much hidden beneath the surface of situations that eluded my awareness, but I continued digging for what I wanted, trying to find the understanding that would help me succeed.

I became aware of a deep change growing in me, and by the end of the week, it became clear. I saw divine order in my situation. Maybe the money I was borrowing from my mother was the perfect source for which I'd been affirming and was part of the divine plan that supported me in writing the book. All I knew was that I had to write and I felt at peace.

Don, who so much wanted to be supportive of me when I was fired, soon retreated into the safety that his position on the church board offered him. He became so loyal to the board that he refused to tell me what people were saying about my being fired. I didn't follow this thinking because the meetings were public, but I felt wary of him.

After watching a Brian Swimme tape on loss and destruction in the universe with my spiritual group, Kathy's husband Mark commented that Swimme must have been preaching to a group of people who were unaware because he came on so strong. A couple of us commented that was unlikely because the audience was a class at Pacifica Institute where depth psychology was taught. I thought Swimme was dynamic and expressed effectively the awe and passion he felt about his subject. During our conversation, it occurred to me that people who had been taught not to express their emotions felt uncomfortable when others showed their passion, and that was part of the reason I'd been accused of being loud and aggressive. People mistook my passion for anger.

Charlotte was being friendlier and even asked me to have lunch with her, but although I admired her, I found it impossible to connect to her emotionally. That seemed strange because usually it was easy for me to bond emotionally with people.

During the next week, I was restless at the spiritual support group, not really wanting to be there. Half of the meeting was a discussion between Mary Beth and Mark on how to restore a piece of furniture. When it was finally my time to speak, I was still struggling to identify my lack of focus. As I began to speak, Mary Beth reminded me that time was almost up and two others still had to speak.

After the meeting, I told Mary Beth that I was upset that she had interrupted me. "It felt," I said, "as if you weren't interested in what I was saying."

"Well, you didn't have a point. You were just swimming around in your stuff."

"Just swimming around? Has it ever occurred to you that that's my process? It's a lot like the creative process. It's not neat and logical, but that's what I need to do to solve problems."

"Okay, well, I didn't get that."

"Look, you've made comments before that you don't think art has much value and you imply you think artists are pretty flaky. But we made a commitment in this group to treat each other respectfully. I'm an artistic person and I don't appreciate being treated as if I'm a flake."

"Georganne," Charlotte interrupted, sounding angry, but controlled, "what do you want from Mary Beth?"

"Like I just said, I want respect even if the way I do things is different from others."

"What do you really want?"

"I just said it. I want Mary Beth to be aware her comments are sometimes hurtful."

"I really am sorry, Georganne," Mary Beth said gently.

I could feel her sincerity, so I accepted her apology and thought that was the last of it. Charlotte, however, had another agenda. "It was not inappropriate for Mary Beth to call time on you. We've agreed on keeping the time people speak as equal as possible."

"Theoretically," I responded, "but we haven't been calling time on each other, and sometimes some people have even taken most of the evening when they needed that."

"No, we do keep time."

"Well, you've been out of town a lot, so maybe it seems that way to you, but it hasn't been happening."

"I'm feeling that you aren't being open with me about what you want."

"Why are you grilling me?" I asked.

Kathy finally spoke up. "I don't think it's right of you to attack Mary Beth."

I turned to Mary Beth. "Do you feel that I attacked you?"

"No, I was surprised by what you said, but I see your point. It's okay." She smiled and patted me on the shoulder.

Charlotte wouldn't leave it alone. "I think you have a lot of unresolved anger and none of us want that expressed toward us."

"You're off the wall, Charlotte. Mary Beth and I have made our peace. Leave it alone."

Kathy jumped in again. "We can't just ignore it. You shouldn't have done that."

By this time, I was beginning to feel angry. The men hadn't said much, but looked disturbed by the whole thing.

"You're the last person who should talk to me about

appropriate behavior." As soon as I said it, I regretted it. I knew I had only created more hostility between us. I turned to Charlotte, who was still trying to force the conversation where she wanted it to go.

"Charlotte, I don't know what you're trying to do, but I don't like it. I've always thought you were my friend, but frankly, right now, I don't feel very trusting. It feels like you're really angry at me about something else and you're not being open about it."

"Obviously you never have trusted us."

"Really, how do you figure that?"

"If you don't trust us now, you obviously never have trusted us."

"No, I've trusted this group for two years, but at this moment based on your reactions, I don't feel trusting. Charlotte, you've tried to twist every word I've said. Mary Beth and I are okay. Leave this alone."

With that, everyone jumped into the fray. Charlotte's voice was louder than the rest. "You're not being honest with us about what you want from this group."

"What I want right now," I said standing up, "is to leave. This is insane. I'm leaving." With that I walked out.

I was very hurt, but the next day I called Mary Beth to see if we really were okay with each other. We were. If she and I were at peace, why couldn't the others drop it? I was amazed by Charlotte's behavior and the hostility I felt from her. I thought that, at first, she was just defending Mary Beth, but it became obvious that she had some idea about me that she was trying to prove.

Perhaps I needed to move on. The group had helped me through rough times, but I felt increasingly estranged from them. The women were all quite different from me, and being around the couples was a constant reminder that I was alone. Mary Beth was practical and didn't understand creativity. Kathy and I had to work hard just to be polite when we were in the group, but she put up her loving side and no one had any idea she was capable of being inconsiderate. Charlotte was cerebral, and even when she was being loving, it didn't feel that way. I began to wonder about other incidents. Had Charlotte asked me to lunch just to convince me to take the youth education job so she would be free of those responsibilities? I remembered that the lunch had taken place just before she had asked me to grade some papers for her when she and Don wanted to go out of town for the weekend. She wasn't happy when I refused.

"Well, I just thought I'd give you an opportunity to make some money," she'd said. "I thought you needed work." She was so insistent, it made me uncomfortable.

"I'm sorry, but I'd do almost anything but grade papers. That's the part of teaching that I'm totally burned out on."

I turned to the healing runes once more for guidance and healing. The wisdom I received was that I had to turn the situation over to God and accept what happened. It couldn't be changed, but I needed to do whatever I could to restore harmony. I needed to trust my own feelings, too. What would result from following this wisdom was serenity.

The situation brought many concerns about the group to the surface. People sent emails about their different perceptions of the group and how they thought it should work. Certainly, one of the issues was how to continue. I was pleased that Charlotte rose to the highest level saying that we needed to just move on. Others felt we needed to discuss the matter.

In the middle of this chaos, on May 11, 2003, my mother made her transition. The night before, my sister-in-law heard her repeating the Lord's Prayer; then, the morning before she died, a friend of my brother came to see her and read a passage from the Bible that was one of her favorites. Around the middle of the day, her body shut down. Thankfully my brother was with her. He tried to revive her, but by the time the paramedics arrived, she was in the last stages of dying. It happened quickly, and they said without pain. I was thankful she was finally at peace.

I wasn't surprised by her passing. A few weeks earlier, she had had another stroke that made it impossible for her to swallow food, so a tube by which she would be fed a liquid diet was inserted in her stomach. She'd always said, "When they have to start feeding me through a tube, just shoot me." That was the last straw for her.

Although I knew that what I saw in the funeral home was only the shell she'd inhabited, I needed to see it in order to say goodbye one last time. She had always worn little make-up and didn't look quite real fully made up. My brother and sister-in-law had to make some decisions before I arrived and their choices were good, even perfect. Blue was her color, and so the casket they chose was a radiant, metallic blue, and the dress she wore was a blue print I had given her that she wore often.

And I wept, not just for my loss, but with relief that she was through with the pain and suffering of her life. I knew she would now have the love that eluded her in this world, and I wept for relief too, knowing I was free of the burden of being unable to make her happy.

We met her in New Orleans and buried her beside my father under the old oaks hung with Spanish moss, under a cloudy sky threatening rain that never materialized. Her best friend and another woman from her former church were there telling us that others would have been there, but they were cooking for an event and knew she would understand because she'd helped them with those tasks many times. Her grandchildren, for whom she had been like a second mother, couldn't bear to see her buried and had chosen not to come. They honored her at the memorial service later in the week. The burial ceremony was short and quiet, and I sadly realized it would be a long time before I returned to New Orleans.

I was grateful that wasn't the end of it. I needed the process to stretch over days in order to fully accept her passing, to honor her with memories of good times, and to give serious thought to my part of the eulogy. As it turned out, I offered a poem about our connection as women and the mysteries several generations had shared. On the day between the burial and the memorial service at her church, my brother and I went through her papers and photographs reliving family history, laughing at ourselves, and trying to remember all the people we saw in the photographs. I was happy to find a few pieces of her clothing that I could wear, knowing they would be a warm reminder of her just as my father's flannel shirt was a comfort. Throughout the process of saying goodbye to our mother, the peace between my brother and me was sincere and precious. Not once did we disagree about what should be done.

I was concerned the memorial service would be so traditionally Christian that it would upset me, but I was fine with it because it was appropriate for Mother. She didn't believe what I believed, but the kindness and sincerity of the people who attended were what mattered to me. The assistant minister who presided over the service read the poem I had written far better than I could have. I met many of the people who had meant so much to her, especially those in her Bible study class.

When I thought of my mother, I thought of her at the sewing machine gathering seventy yards of white net for my prom dress, slathering on the concoction of iodine and oil we used to get a good tan in the summer, or playing the piano while my brother played the violin and I sang, my mezzo voice blending with her soprano. She taught me so many things, and I, in turn, taught her.

Returning from Houston, I had a phone message from Mary Beth acknowledging my mother's passing and telling me I was in her thoughts and prayers. I also had a kind message from Charlotte, but there was nothing from Don, Kathy, or Mark. They all had extremely difficult mothers, so perhaps they didn't understand what I was feeling.

When the feminine divine class had ended, several of us formed a new women's spirituality group. While I was away, they performed a ritual for me, and one woman lit a vigil candle. When I returned, they treated me to dinner at the Artichoke Cafe. One had a lovely card and note, and another gave me a geode she had broken open and said, "Sometimes things look bad on the outside, but inside there is something beautiful." That was certainly true in this situation. I was deeply touched by the effort and emotional support these women I'd known only a few months offered.

This response seriously contrasted the behavior of my other spiritual support group. Perhaps we were simply becoming disconnected because a couple of people in that group had frequently been absent over the previous year. But something even more important happened the night I confronted Mary Beth. The incident seemed to stir up many of the group's repressed feelings and resentments. Those negativities surfaced because the incident was perceived as something that threatened the group and revealed that we weren't one in our vision of what the group was. I had destroyed the group illusion that we were in perfect harmony. It was an opportunity to examine that and perhaps to re-evaluate the group's needs; instead, the energy of the group, except for Mary Beth, constellated into a new form of energy, separating me from the group. For the group to be saved, the scapegoat is usually sacrificed.

Before the next group meeting, I had lunch with Charlotte in an effort to understand what she was thinking and feeling. She seemed distant. When we sat down to eat, I began.

"Charlotte, it really upset me the other night when you said you didn't believe I trusted the group. I really have trusted all of you for the last two years. It's just that what happened that night made me reconsider if you all actually care about my feelings or understand who I really am."

"You either trust us or you don't. If you don't trust us now, why should I believe you ever did?"

"Because things change. People do things that hurt each other and that hurt me."

"Georganne, you need to stop and listen to yourself. If someone hurts you, it's because you let them hurt you."

"Yes, to some extent that's true, except in order to not be hurt, I'd have to shut down my feelings. I did that one time. It isn't healthy."

"It's not surprising that you're unhappy. Everything you say is negative. Listen to yourself."

"Right now, Charlotte, I'm saying what I need to say and I'd appreciate your listening to me."

"Go ahead."

"Since January I've been feeling that you're all more distant.

I'm not as comfortable as I used to be. Then when I was fired, Don could have spoken up for me, but he didn't."

"I think he did all he could do. He cares very much about your well-being."

"I think Don cares most of all about his position with those in power."

"Negative again."

I ignored her and went on. "The two of you, especially you, have created this life where you're withdrawn…"

"Negative. What did you just say?"

"You choose to withdraw from society by never watching the news or reading newspapers or…"

"What did you just say? You're going to ruin your life with this negative thinking."

"Stop interrupting me."

"You're going to ruin your life with this thinking."

"Well, I'm not in denial and I'm not going to be a hermit. I want to be in touch with my feelings and know what I'm feeling. I want to live *in* the world. I want to care what others do."

"You are going to have a very unhappy life."

"Charlotte, stop it. I feel like I'm being harassed. Why are you so angry at me?"

She looked up with a cold stare that cut through me, "I'm afraid you may confront me the way you did Mary Beth."

"Why does that scare you?"

"It's upsetting. It would be embarrassing."

"But we can't be honest with each other if we always hide our feelings."

"Negative again."

"This is abusive. You don't care about my feelings. I just lost my Mother and you haven't said one comforting word to me."

"You're ruining your life."

She continued eating her pie. I sat for a moment staring at her cold, unemotional face. There was no flicker of warmth there. I couldn't believe that the woman I knew who was so innovative and open-minded in her work was taking no responsibility for the pain she helped cause; instead she blamed it all on my thinking.

"I don't think this is proving to be helpful. I'm going to leave unless you have something new to say to me."

"Suit yourself."

I left the restaurant still stunned by her bizarre behavior, unable to reconcile the person I thought she was with the person I had just seen. There was much hidden beneath the surface.

I still wanted to create some peace in this situation, but I was afraid that if I just showed up at the next meeting, they would gang up on me. I decided the best thing to do was to talk with each person separately and address individual concerns first to discover if everyone shared Charlotte's fears. What I knew about the group now was that each of them had serious issues around expressing themselves authentically and issues around being in touch with their feelings. Before the next meeting, Mark and Kathy each called separately to encourage me to attend. Mark even went so far as to say that he felt attending the group to work it out was the honorable thing. I got the impression that he thought it was gossip for me to talk to people individually. I never thought about this being a set up, but later I wondered how I could have been so naïve.

Ignoring my intuition not to go, I went to the meeting. It began innocently enough although Mary Beth and Charlotte weren't there. According to Don, Charlotte refused to be in my presence. We expressed our expectations of what each of us wanted from the group. I apologized for having created a situation, but pointed out that Mary Beth, the person to whom my comments were directed, was at peace with me, and that I didn't understand why everyone else was upset. They were only too happy to tell me. One of the things that upset them most was that I used people's names to talk about the people who had encouraged my firing although this wasn't confidential information. They felt I was just gossiping when I told them about the firing. I repeatedly asked how that was different from the stories they brought to the group about other people who had hurt them when the people were recognizable to us all. They did not answer.

As the evening went on, I discovered that the group, in fact, did not care about my feelings. They insisted that I always blamed other people for my problems and never took responsibility for them. Kathy was particularly angry, admitting she'd let her anger toward me build up, and that she should have talked to me sooner. It was then I realized why she and Mark had been so adamant about my coming to the meeting. He wanted her to have an opportunity to vent so she would feel better despite her never having had the time when I had previously asked her to talk.

The other accusation was that the night I had talked about being fired, I had overstepped the boundaries of the group into therapy. Despite our original agreement that we didn't want to do therapy, but only give spiritual support, there had been several occasions when others had been so upset that we had listened to them cry all evening. I asked how this was different from what I did. No one answered.

Throughout, Don had remained quiet, smiling slightly in the way my ex-husband had always done just before he revealed something that would hurt me. He seemed to particularly enjoy Mark's comparison of me with one of his *crazy* ex-wives. He finally spoke.

"I don't want to hear anything else from you. You're a very evil person and I don't want you in my house again. I'll continue to host the group if they want, but you aren't welcome. I want you to leave."

"Now," I asked, "or when we finish the meeting?"

"Now," he said with an even larger smirk, reminding me of a small boy who had just played a successful trick on his arch enemy.

I looked around at all of them, knowing they would never contradict Don. For a moment, I considered what I needed to do to take back my own power in this situation. In turn, I faced each one, making direct eye contact and said, "I am not your scapegoat."

When I finished, I glanced at all of them. "Whatever I've done that displeased you, I know one thing for sure. I've never deliberately hurt anyone in my life. I don't live that way. Like everyone, I've hurt people accidently, and I'm sorry, and I've apologized. But what you've done here, this evening, is to try to turn me into a scapegoat. That is something I've never done, nor would I participate in anything so low. Your actions are mean spirited. I feel sorry for you that you each feel you have so little personal power that you can't express what you feel without a group behind you. Everything you've accused me of this evening is exactly what you're guilty of. I'm the mirror in which you see yourself. Take a good look." With that, I picked up my purse and walked out.

Embracing the Light

The women in my divine feminine group were an amazing gift from the universe. One was an artist who had moved into the apartment behind her studio. It was a mess but a unique space that she turned into something quite interesting. Because I loved making spaces into homes, just looking at it made my creative juices flow. With two other artists, she shared a courtyard full of trees, and a little fountain backed with a tiled picture of Mary that she had turned into a goddess altar. It reminded me of the dream I had to live in an artist's loft.

The last time we had a meeting there, we drew medicine cards. My life path card was the storyteller, which was about how we learn and expand from hearing each other's stories. My animal card was the mouse. The mouse was good with details and organization, but needed to remember to look at the big picture. On the other hand, things that appeared insignificant to others were important to the mouse. The mouse always wanted to go deeper, always thought there was more to learn. It was clear that this mouse and I had plenty in common. The challenge, however, was to scrutinize people and situations to know the truth. Spirit was making sure I remembered what I was supposed to have learned from my experience with the spiritual support group: ignoring my intuition because I didn't want to think badly of a person was a recipe for disaster.

In January of 2001, I had had an astrocartography map done by an astrologer, Julie Bresciani, who was also a Jungian analyst. I wanted more guidance about where to live although I was still strongly rooted in the idea that I could create a good life in New Mexico. The map did indicate I'd do better in the East and that the influences in North Carolina were positive in all aspects of my life, but she thought I would feel too confined there. This was what I also felt when I had visited Asheville.

On the map, the most negative astrological energies lay near

Albuquerque, Denver, and Nebraska. Looking back at this map now, in 2003, after all the negative experiences I had had in the West convinced me it would be wise to pay attention to this information. Neptune was a double influence near Albuquerque, creating a fantasy that was greater than the reality of my experience. Its influence also caused me to feel like a martyr—vulnerable, drained, and betrayed. Mars was also a negative energy, making everything a challenge and reinforcing the martyr aspect. Nevertheless, I still felt uncertain about a move during the rest of 2003, in part, because I hoped to teach a couple more years and be eligible for retirement benefits. I was still attached to practical solutions.

I listened again to the tape of my conversation with the last psychic with whom I had talked. She reminded me to ask my spirit guides which material from my journals to use in the book and which to delete. Knowing that I had this spiritual connection gave me confidence that I could write a book that would inspire and help others. When I asked for guidance and had trouble understanding the message, the guides reminded me, "Be quiet and listen." I had to take the time to find the stillness in myself.

Along with writing and substitute teaching, I continued to clean out my extensive files containing personal and teaching materials. It simplified my life and was also essential preparation for a move if I decided to leave Albuquerque. Decisions were always difficult for me and the process of deciding what to eliminate was torture. I was always afraid I'd need something again, and in typical Libran fashion, I could see equally good reasons for keeping the item or throwing it away. This was especially difficult with the materials I used to teach in high school because I didn't know whether I would ever teach teenagers again. Often, I asked for guidance, and if the answer was that it was no longer useful for me to keep, I released the paper into the wastebasket, in most instances. As I released more of this clutter, the energy in my writing space became peaceful and orderly.

Kathy wrote while she and Mark were traveling in Arkansas. They expressed condolences for my mother's passing, and Kathy said that she was sorry about what happened with the spiritual support group. I had no sense, though, that she felt she could have changed the outcome. She said she thought about her and me. And that was the problem—she only thought of those things and did nothing. I didn't respond to the letter. I had moved on. The EMDR treatment had helped reduce the emotional charge attached to these issues. The lesson I learned from Kathy was that loving a person didn't mean I had to allow them to harm me; it meant that if their behavior harmed me, I needed to bless, forgive and release them from my life.

Frances continued to be friends with Kathy. This lack of loyalty hurt, but Frances was my only close friend in Albuquerque other than Ron, who was so busy, so I tried to believe I could get past it. Eventually, though, just before I left Albuquerque, the tension severed our relationship.

When I felt sorry for myself, the world seemed to be a place where nothing I valued was valued by others, where being responsible was not an asset, and only silence was rewarded. A dream embodied these frustrations as well as the disappointment that, after my mother's death, I'd been unable to maintain the depth of relationship with my brother that I desired. In the dream, I visited my family, and on the first day my mom and I went out and had a nice day together. After that, I waited to get dressed each day or waited to eat breakfast, hoping my brother and I could spend some time together, but it never happened. When I mentioned this to him, he made excuses. Later, as I waited in the front room, which had a large pond where there were two ducks, I found an insect and put it in the water as food for the ducks until someone said, "Uh, oh—it probably got the ducks." Was I putting something emotionally unhealthy into the situation with my brother when I thought I was being positive? After years of communicating through our mother rather than directly, we had to get to know each other again. Who he really was puzzled me.

I had several dreams in which people, often men, were kind to me, and I wondered if these were a sign my inner masculine was more in balance. In one, a man, who was my partner, and I fed an abandoned cat. In another scene, we were on a beach talking about what we wanted to do. He pointed at some caves on the opposite shore, and I told him I'd really like to see the caves, so he went to check and see whether this was possible. He came back and said, "Yes, we can go." On our way to the boat, we passed four or five people we knew. He winked at one of them, and I asked him why he did that. He said it was a signal, but he didn't explain.

In this dream, the part about the caves was powerful because caves were where pre-Christian Europeans worshipped the goddess, the place that was her womb, and among the Greeks, the entrance to underworld. I shuddered to think that I needed to descend still deeper into the darkness to find the answers for my own rebirth. Perhaps the dream was pointing out that my masculine was now integrated and I needed to give more attention to the feminine.

When I discovered that Natalie Goldberg was teaching a summer nonfiction workshop in Taos, it seemed like perfect timing. The workshop was full, but I was put on the waiting list and read the two books she required so that I'd be prepared if I did get in. Even though a wildfire threatened Taos on the weekend of the workshop, no one cancelled. Still, the books I read were most valuable and a reminder that the universe always filled our needs although its method might not be what we expected.

I was impressed with Laura Hillenbrand's *Seabiscuit*. I had dreaded reading it because I had no interest in horses or horse races, but by the middle of the first page, I was hooked. What touched me deeply was how she wove together the stories of the horse, the jockey, the trainer, and the nation and how they helped heal each other. Her book was a wonderful teacher of how to make a story come alive through relationships.

The other book was *Mitchell and Ruff: An American Profile in Jazz* by William Zinsser. This was the story of a trip to China to introduce jazz. Zinsser made it interesting by interweaving personal stories and historical information with the events of the trip and by using skillful flashbacks. Hillenbrand's book read like a novel, but this one, although not in novel form, took the reader on a journey that was interesting every step of the way. These books lit the fire in me to create something profound and beautiful.

    I often thought about my mother, and after recovering from the initial feelings of loss and the shock that there was no longer anyone between me and mortality, I was surprised at how empowered I felt. I was proud of finally having the courage to do what I'd wanted to do my whole life—to write. The irony was that my mother would never have thought it was acceptable for me not to be employed to do that, yet it was her inheritance that now made it possible, and this fact healed much of my resentment toward her for not being supportive earlier in my life. Although I periodically experienced some fear about the writing, most of the time I knew I would complete and sell the book and become a successful writer, teacher, and speaker. I refused to consider any other possibility.

    I also continued reading memoirs and biographies. Jean Houston's autobiography *A Mythic Life* touched me deeply. Because her interests in psychology, spirituality, and myth paralleled my own, she was inspiring. It was a glimpse into the life of a woman who was totally herself, treated as an equal by men, and who truly followed her bliss—the kind of woman I wanted to be.

    My anxiety about working in education did not diminish as I continued to substitute teach, but I was successful in releasing the anger and hurt I felt toward the spiritual support group. Periodically, I would think these feelings were healed, but then a heavy emotional charge returned, and I obsessed about it and released it again. Finally, one day in meditation, the events came to consciousness but felt very distant. With this detachment, I felt the events causing the turmoil were of no consequence. There was no emotional charge and I was at peace. This detachment allowed me to see the lessons I had learned from this experience. One was that if I didn't want to be a victim, I needed to make myself unavailable for that role. Another was to never assume that anyone was more or less spiritual or talented than I was, for we were all one. God's power was in all of us. With this healing, I had the clarity to make wiser choices.

On some days, writing was difficult, and I started to question whether I could write well enough to complete the book I had begun. Organizing the material was a challenge because there was so much more of it than I could possibly use, and it wasn't clear whether I should write in the past or the present tense. I asked for guidance and was told to plot out the chapters, which I did for the first four. If I didn't let fear deter me and was willing to make mistakes in order to learn, I knew I would eventually find the right solutions to the problems that arose.

Always hungry for a deeper understanding of life, I began reading Eckhart Tolle's *The Power of Now*, underlining almost every line. His perspective and philosophy answered many of the questions I had grappled with for the previous year. Tolle wrote that the ego and negative emotions could create the pain-body which became like an entity, an energetic constellation capable of taking over one's life. That explained why it was so difficult to let go of old emotional pain. When he described how love could be an addiction, I thought of my relationship with Neal, but I was making progress. It was good to feel the past pain dropping away. Now if I started down the path of thinking that led to that pain, I was able to stop those thoughts, turn away, and release them.

As we neared the end of another year, 2003, I was actually living and writing in a serious way. I didn't have a partner, but I lived peacefully, knowing that he would come in divine order. I knew that the priority in my life was to finish this book and that writing it was changing my life, facilitating new insights, opening my consciousness to more positive ways of thinking, and empowering me to believe in my divine self. I lived in one of the earth's most beautiful and spiritually powerful places. I had peace in my heart. I had the spiritual tools I needed to continue my beautiful spiritual journey and to manifest whatever I needed. I had a new circle of women friends, as well as some old ones, who loved the arts and literature as much as I did. They shared my values and a respect for the sacred in whatever form it appeared. I could not have found a better way to celebrate the winter solstice than with them, and I used this reflection as part of our ritual:

"To begin my day today, I look out on the silhouette of mountains sharp against the beginning of blue sky. Above the peaks, pink magical clouds with dark interiors float, and hanging from them is the slightest sliver of a silver moon. I love this moment when the day is suspended between darkness and light, when one can anticipate all possibilities, when we know all good things are possible because the day is moving toward light. And so we remember, whatever darkness challenges us in our lives, whatever darkness smothers the world in ignorance, whatever shadows flicker in the twilight of a day, a season, or a life, we are moving toward light and the light that shines eternally on our journey. All is well. Father, Mother, God bless us. And so it is.

Epilogue

In January 2004, my astrologer, Julie Bresciani, drew a chart and wrote an analysis on North Carolina indicating multiple, positive influences from the Sun, Mercury, and Venus. These suggested that money, relationships, community, and work should all be very successful there. There were positive influences for a second marriage and finding a soul mate. I would meet people in my career with whom I had *positive* karma from past lives. In fact, in some areas, this chart was stronger than my natal chart, and the wounding influence that revealed my deepest wounds in the Southwest was hidden in the East.

Julie explained the archetypes in my natal chart and how the powerful and negative role of my mother's refusal to support who I really was had affected me. She explained that my chart showed that my lack of support from family and others was because I didn't conform to their vision. I was creative and unconventional, but in former lives I had sacrificed who I was for relationships. In this life, my life purpose was to liberate myself, find my voice, communicate my vision, and most of all, show up as the heroine in my own life.

In the end, my enchantment with New Mexico and the peace I found there was not enough to keep me in the desert. My time there was the Jungian Nigrado, the place where I was forced to face the shadow, to confront everything that was not working in my life. It was the stage in my spiritual journey that brought my ego in contact with its greatest fears. The desert had purified me, stripped me of everything I held dear, leaving only the skeleton of my soul on which to build a new life.

That summer I headed for western North Carolina, longing for a place that felt like my roots. The lush green summer welcomed me with a symphony of birdsong and crisp, fresh morning air. The mountains embraced me, and the afternoon thunderstorms quenched my deep thirst and gave life to the soil from which I have grown a new and joyful life. Here, in this beautiful place, I dance the dance of life and continue to awaken to who I truly am.

Acknowledgments

I want to thank all the people who have encouraged and helped me to complete and publish this book. First, I thank Southwest Writers in Albuquerque for the opportunity to meet successful writers and learn from them how to be a writer. I thank Karen Jones Meadows, the first writer I met who was making a living from writing, for her friendship and inspiration. I am also grateful for the Smokey Mountain Writer's Workshop and the Candy Maier Scholarship Fund which made it possible for me to study with Davis Miller, Neal Thompson, and Steven Samuels, all wonderful teachers who each in his own way empowered me to keep writing.

I greatly appreciate those friends who read my manuscript and offered constructive criticism: Kendall Hale, Eleanore Buchanan, Allan Buchanan, and Eddie Twigg, and the members of Robert Kelley's critique group. In addition, I am grateful for the expert editing of Shelley Lieber and H. Glenn Court, Sarah Benoit's technical and marketing support, Joseph D'Agnese's and Brad Swift's guidance and formatting, and the advice of Dan Lazar, Theresa Swann, and Jack Boyd, and members of *Freelance Fridays*. Without them, I would have been lost in the complexities of new technology. Most importantly, I thank Bob and Dottie Spruce for their encouragement and support. I am truly blessed.

About the Author

Georganne Spruce has a master of fine arts degree in dance and a bachelor of arts in theater. She taught English, drama, and dance at the high school level in public and private schools and modern dance at The Naropa Institute, Colorado State Ballet Studio, and the University of Nebraska at Kearney where she created a dance minor program. She was dance director for the Mount Airy Fine Arts Project and studied at the American University-Wolf Trap Performing Arts Program with Erick Hawkins, Viola Farber, Anna Sokolow, Bill Evans, and Twyla Thorpe and in New York at the Alwin Nikolais-Murray Louis Lab. In Washington, DC, she danced with the Choreo 18 Dance Company. In 1994 she studied literature in West Africa on a Fulbright-Hays Travel Abroad Grant. She has published essays and poetry in *Western North Carolina Woman*, *Asheville-Citizen Times*, *Pure Inspiration Magazine*, *Spirit of the Smokies*, and at www.irascibleprofessor.com. She currently teaches workshops on how to release your fear and writes a blog of inspirational essays at www.awakeningtothedance.com.